Field Methods Casebook
for Software Design

Field Methods Casebook for Software Design

Edited by:

Dennis Wixon
Judith Ramey

WILEY COMPUTER PUBLISHING

John Wiley & Sons, Inc.
• New York • Chichester • Brisbane
• Toronto • Singapore • Weinheim

Publisher: Katherine Schowalter
Senior Editor: Marjorie Spencer
Managing Editor: Micheline Frederick
Text Design & Composition: Publishers' Design and Production Services, Inc.

Designations used by companies to distinguish their products are often claimed as trademarks. In all instances where John Wiley & Sons, Inc., is aware of a claim, the product names appear in initial capital or all capital letters. Readers, however, should contact the appropriate companies for more complete information regarding trademarks and registration.

This publication is designed to provide accurate and authoritative information in regard to the subject matter covered. It is sold with the understanding that the publisher is not engaged in rendering legal, accounting, or other professional service. If legal advice or other expert assistance is required, the services of a competent professional person should be sought.

Library of Congress Cataloging-in-Publication Data:

Field methods casebook for software design / edited by Dennis Wixon,
    Judith Ramey.
        p.   cm.
    Includes bibliographical references (p.).
    ISBN 0-471-14967-5 (cloth : alk. paper)
    1. Computer software—Development. 2. System design. I. Wixon,
Dennis. II. Ramey, Judith.
QA76.76.D47F54   1996
004.2'1'019—dc20   96-13746
                                                                 CIP

Printed in the United States of America
10 9 8 7 6 5 4 3 2 1

Dennis Wixon dedicates this book to JoAnne, Michael, Amy, and Ella.

Judy Ramey dedicates this book to Lindell and Frances Ramey, and the rest of my family in Texas.

Dennis would like to thank John Whiteside for introducing me to usability and teaching me to look beyond the surface of things. I would also like to thank Sandy Jones, Karen Holtzblatt, and Minette Beabes for expanding my horizons on how to understand peoples' work. Finally, I would like to acknowledge my current supervisor Pat Baker for her support and guidance. I have learned much from her.

Judy would like to thank Ernest Kaulbach and other medievalists at the University of Texas who first taught me how to study a culture, and Wayne Verona and the other technical communicators at Texas Instruments Incorporated who taught me that a culture didn't have to be dead to be worth studying. I would also like to thank my colleagues in the Department of Technical Communication at the University of Washington for putting up with me and my lab with such good humor.

We also thank our Marjorie Spencer, our editor at John Wiley, and Margaret Hendrey, our editorial assistant.

Wixon (Ramey) attributes all errors and omissions to Ramey (Wixon).

Preface

It's not what you know that's dangerous.
It's what you know that just ain't so.
—Will Rogers

ASSUMPTIONS AS THE ORIGIN OF DESIGN

Design begins with assumptions about users and their work. These assumptions are either explicit or implicit; they are either well-founded or not well-founded. But, they always exist, and they always guide development. Those assumptions we make about the users and their work can take many forms and exist at many levels. At the lowest level, assumptions can be very explicit: "No one needs more than a VGA screen." At the highest level, they can compress many assumptions into a single assertion: "Our users are knowledge workers." Regardless of the type of assumption, they all share one characteristic: They can be wrong.

How Do We Know?

How can we be sure that our assumptions are well-founded? Because assumptions can be implicit, an even more basic question is "How do we know what we are assuming?" One way to test assumptions is to build something (a product, a tool, an artifact) and then test it. While that approach is guaranteed to work, it can be expensive. An analogous situation existed when the first iron bridges were built for railroads. The only way to be sure they would work was to drive trains over them and see if they collapsed.

One answer is to reduce the cost of "learning by testing" (through, say, the use of paper prototypes). Another is to look for processes that test our assumptions earlier in the process. Or we can go back even further and look for processes that will help shape the assumptions we make. Field research methods are aimed at generating this kind of up-front understanding. Thus they function best at the early stages of design, where leverage is high. They also function best where we know the least; that is, where we are designing for new markets or for users who are unlike us.

Why This Book?

This book is intended for the practitioner, and in it we seek to answer three questions:

1. What is field research?
2. Why (when) should I use it?
3. How do I do it?

The form of our answer is a set of case studies. We choose this approach to provide the maximum amount of detail and the greatest range of variety. In our view, detail is important because it gives the practitioner a deeper understanding of the methods in action. Maximum variety means that the cases are more likely to match real situations that you confront. The variety is also reflected in the way the cases are described. Some cases concentrate the nuts and bolts of actually doing field research. Others concentrate on how the data is shared so that it impacts design. Still other cases look at the organizational context in which such work takes place. Others place the kind of applied field research we do in a broader context, such as Ethnography, Participatory Design, or Contextual Design.

Is This Book For You?

If you've read this far, then the answer probably is yes, but you can get a better sense of what's really in the book by leafing through the chapters and skimming the executive summary included at the beginning of each chapter.

We hope that this book will promote the use of applied field research for product design and the evolution of field research methodology. We believe that these methods represent some of the most effective ways to design from a user's point of view.

Dennis Wixon and Judy Ramey, August 1996

Contents

About the Authors

Note: The Authors' biographies are listed in order of the appearance of the author's work within the text.

Judith Ramey joined the faculty of the Department of Technical Communication, College of Engineering, University of Washington, in 1983. In 1989 she founded the UW Laboratory for Usability Testing and Evaluation (LUTE), and since then has served as its director. Through LUTE, she has conducted a number of corporate-sponsored research projects, including the medical imaging study described here.

Dr. Alan H. Rowberg, MD is an associate professor and Director of the Picture Archiving and Communication System (PACS) Section, Department of Radiology, University of Washington Health Sciences Center.

Carol Robinson has a M.S. in Technical Communication and has done usability work for a number of software companies. Currently Carol is a Usability Analyst for Health Systems Technologies, a company that makes software for managed care organizations.

Michael J. Muller is a Work and Usability Analyst in the Collaborative Systems group within the Applied Research organization of U S WEST Advanced Technologies.

Rebecca Carr is a Methods/Training Developer in the Operator and Information Services organization of U S WEST Communications.

Larry E. Wood has a Ph.D. in Cognitive Psychology and is currently a Professor of Psychology at Brigham Young University. For several years he has taught a graduate course in User-Centered Design. His research interests include all aspects of User-Centered Design of software applications.

Dennis R. Wixon is Usability Program Manager for Digital Equipment Corporation. Over the past 20 years, Dennis has worked on interface design and evaluation methodology. He holds an M.A. and Ph.D. from Clark University, and has published numerous papers on interface design.

Christine M. Pietras is a human factors consultant specializing in user interface design and usability evaluation. She is currently developing an interface style guide with a major transportation company. Previously Chris worked at Digital Equipment, where she collaborated in designing business solutions. Chris holds an A.B. in mathematics from Smith College and an M.S. in Industrial Engineering and Operations Research from the University of Massachusetts at Amherst.

Paul K. Huntwork is a consulting engineer at Digital Equipment Corporation. Paul has lead efforts at Digital to adapt and invent world class methods for use in development of products and systems. Previously Paul worked at Computervision, Control Data Corporation, and the IBM Federal Systems Division where he led prototype-SEI process assessment and maturation drives.

Doug Muzzey is currently MIS Manager for Thermal Dynamics Incorporated, located in West Lebanon, NH. At the time this work was done, Doug was the development manager for the TeamLinks for Macintosh and Team Route workflow products, and sponsored the usability and customer partnering for the TeamLinks product family. He holds a B.S.C.S. (1978) from Florida Technological University and an M.B.A. (1991) from Rivier College.

Martin Rantzer is a system developer at Ericsson Radio Systems in Linköping, Sweden. Before joining Ericsson Radio, he worked at Ericsson Infocom as project manager for the development and integration of the Delta Method. Currently his work includes assessing new concepts and techniques for user-centered system development, and studying how they can be integrated into existing development models.

Robert C. Graf is a usability specialist at Microsoft Corporation. He conducted the current study at Dun & Bradstreet Software Services, Inc., where he managed the Usability Lab. Robert led software design projects and supervised the quality assurance group at Minitab, Inc., a developer of statistical analysis software. He holds a Ph.D. from the Pennsylvania State University in Cognitive-Motor Behavior.

David E. Rowley manages the development of data handling products at Varian Chromatography Systems. He is active in the San Francisco Bay Area chapter of the ACM special interest group on computer-human interaction, serving as chair in 1995-96. He continues to pursue usability engineering techniques that fit into the ever-changing management and quality paradigms facing research and development organizations.

Susan M. Dray, President of Dray & Associates, is a consultant with over 17 years experience, who pioneered in the development of usability methods and user-centered design. She has done both ethnographic and traditional usability studies in the US, Europe and Asia, and consults to clients worldwide.

Dr. Dray received her Doctorate in Psychology from UCLA and is a Certified Human Factors Professional. She held various positions in Human Factors research and consulting at Honeywell and American Express Financial Advisors in Minneapolis, Minnesota, prior to establishing her consultancy in 1993. She is a Fellow of the Human Factors and Ergonomics Society. She edits the Business column of the magazine, *Interactions* and is also on the editorial board of the international journal *Behavior and Information Technology*.

Deborah Mrazek is a Certified Human Factors Professional who has been in the field for 13 years. She has performed all aspects of Human Factors Engineering at Rancho Seco Nuclear Generating Station for five years. She was involved in implementing Human Factors programs for HP Computing Systems for four years. She then performed Human Factors Consulting internally for a variety of HP divisions. For the past two years she has been leading the Software Human Factors Team at the HP Vancouver (InkJet Printer) divisions. Currently, she is with the HP Corporate Customer-Centered Quality team, consulting in the area of customer-centered design methods and practices.

She became involved in international usability testing several years ago. She has performed a variety of usability studies in Europe and regularly consults with HP design teams around the world.

Diane S. Brown is a Principal Human Factors Engineer at ATL Inc., where she established the human factors program. She has been working in human factors and user interface design for software and hardware systems for nine years. In addition to human factors training, she received a B.S. in Mathematics and a Master's degree in Biophysics from the University of Utah.

Kristin Bauersfeld recently left Claris to join the Interface Design Group at Netscape Communications Corp. While at Claris, Kristin was responsible for interaction and user centered design on a number of Claris' future technologies and products. Before joining Claris, Kristin worked as a member of the

OpenDoc and PowerTalk Human Interface teams at Apple and at NASA Ames Research Center. She received her M.A. in Experimental and Human Factors Psychology from San Jose State University.

Shannon Halgren joined the Interface Design Group at Claris in 1993 to manage the new Claris Usability Studio. In her position, Halgren is responsible for conducting all facets of usability and user centered design research. Before joining Claris, Halgren worked as a member of the Human Factors Group at GO Corporation, Compaq Computer Corporation, IBM, and Lockheed. She received her Ph.D. in Experimental Psychology-Human Computer Interaction from Rice University in Houston, Texas.

Stanley R. Page is a Manager of Human Factors at Corel Corporation. He has over 11 years of experience in human factors research and user interface design, including five years at WordPerfect and Novell. His degrees include a Ph.D. in Instuctional Technology from Indiana University and a Bachelor of Fine Arts degree from Utah State University.

Dianne Juhl has been with the Microsoft Usability Group since 1992 and with Microsoft Corporation since 1987. Since joining the Usability group, she has worked with various Microsoft product teams to conduct user-centered design projects. Prior to joining the Usability Group, Dianne was the program manager for a client-server project that put the Microsoft Library's catalog on the corporate network and on desktops of Microsoft employees worldwide. Dianne holds a Master of Science degree in Library and Information Science from the University of Washington. She holds a Contextual Design Coach certificate from InContext Enterprises.

Janette Coble is a research associate in the Section of Medical Informatics at Washington University School of Medicine, in St. Louis, Missouri. She holds an M.S. in Computer Science from Washington University and has had training in Cognitive and Experimental Psychology. Her current work includes performing Contextual Inquiry, usability testing of clinical software, and the design of user interfaces. Before joining Washington University in 1993, she worked at McDonnell Douglas Corporation, where she researched and applied object-oriented and user-interface technologies.

Judy Maffitt is a Senior Analyst in Information Systems at BJC Health System in St. Louis, Missouri. She holds a B.S. in Mathematics from the University of Illinois at Urbana-Champaign. Her current work includes the development of procedures, standards, and interfaces for normalizing and transmitting clinical data to a Clinical Information System. Before joining Barnes Hospital in 1987, she worked for Continental Telephone Company (CONTEL) in Wentzville, Missouri, and Hewitt Associates in Lincolnshire, Illinois, where she developed mainframe business applications.

Matthew J. Orland is an Associate Professor of Clinical Medicine at Washington University School of Medicine, and is in practice with specialties in internal medicine and endocrinology. He obtained a B.S. degree in Engineering and Applied Science at Yale University prior to his M.D. degree from the University of Miami School of Medicine. He is currently a consultant to Information Systems activities within the BJC Health System, and is an active participant in the design and development of the clinical workstation for Project Spectrum.

Michael Kahn is the head of the Section of Medical Informatics at Washington University, St. Louis and is Director of Advanced Clinical Information Systems at BJC Health System. Dr. Kahn received his M.D. degree from the University of California, San Diego, did his Internal Medicine internship and residency at St. Mary's (a UCLA affiliate program), and received his Ph.D. degree from the University of California, San Francisco. Most recently, as head of the Section on Medical Informatics, Dr. Kahn's group has developed a number of expert systems for Quality Assessment. In addition, Dr. Kahn leads the Clinical Information Systems group within Project Spectrum.

Mary Beth Butler is Group Manager of Desktop Usability Testing at Lotus Development, where she established the first usability lab. Ms. Butler has a B.A. in Psychology from Brown University, and an M.B.A. from Northeastern University. Ms. Butler serves on the Board of Directors of the Usability Professionals Association.

Marie Tahir is a usability specialist at Lotus Development. She has worked in the software industry for six years. Prior to that, she was an editor at the University of California at Berkeley. Ms. Tahir has a double B.A. in English and Dramatic Arts from the University of California at Berkeley.

John M. Ford received his Ph.D. in Psychology from Brigham Young University in 1993. John is employed by Alpine Media in Orem, Utah, where he works as a project manager and instructional psychologist. His professional interests include interviewing tools and techniques, certification test development, and performance support.

Aki Helen Namioka was first introduced to Participatory Design not through her work as a computational linguist for Boeing Computer Services, but rather through her involvement with Computer Professionals for Social Responsibility (CPSR). In 1993 Aki and Douglas Schuler co-edited the book *Participatory Design: Principles and Practices* published by Lawrence Erlbaum Associates. The book grew out of the first Participatory Design conference (PDC'90) and featured several conference speakers.

Christopher Rao is a Harvard law graduate, who was a teaching fellow at the Harvard Negotiation Project. He later chose the frontier of the Internet over the divisiveness of law. Currently president of the web publishing firm AD1440, he also teaches business negotiation at University of Washington Extension, focusing on how improved process can reduce inefficiency and stress in negotiating.

Karen Holtzblatt and ***Hugh Beyer*** are the developers of Contextual Design, a customer-centered design process extending the Contextual Inquiry data-gathering technique.

Dr. Holtzblatt originated the Contextual Inquiry approach to field data collection and has pioneered the introduction of this technique into working engineering teams. She has used customer-centered processes for the past nine years to design and evaluate software, hardware, and business processes.

Hugh Beyer has worked in the industry as a programmer, architect, and consultant for twelve years. He has designed and developed object-oriented repositories and integrated CASE systems, and has developed processes for using customer data to drive object-oriented design.

Holtzblatt and Beyer are co-founders of InContext Enterprises Inc., a firm that works with companies such as Microsoft and WordPerfect, coaching teams to design products, product strategies, and information systems from customer data.

Introduction

This collection of essays grows out of a workshop on field-oriented design techniques offered by the editors at CHI `95. The workshop, originally scheduled to take place over one and a half days, grew to two full days, and in fact we even ended up having lunch brought in on both days so that we could continue our discussions uninterrupted. The interest of the participants was sturdy enough to carry them through the preparation of their case studies as chapters in this volume. We also include three chapters that are invited contributions discussing the three most widely recognized forms of field research currently in use in product design: Ethnography, Participatory Design, and Contextual Design.

Design is ultimately tool-making—putting an "enabler" between the worker and the work. Moving from the simplest physical tool to the most complex cognitive tool does not change the basic process: fashioning the idea of the tool out of the "empty space" between the workers and the work, and then refining the idea into the best possible actuality. This process is one of discovery, of filling in the details of the situated workers and work until the ideal shape of the tool is revealed.

We had two main goals in this work:

- To provide numerous case studies—actual examples of field research that explore and demonstrate the two aspects of discovering design: doing research in the field and systematically incorporating the findings into the development process.
- To look at the research disciplines and perspectives that are the foundations for these case studies—to present in more detail the theoretical frameworks, assumptions, values, and perspectives of the three main schools of thought in field research motivated by product development.

The volume opens with the case studies and reserves the three "framework" chapters until the end. The chapters themselves cluster around seven broad themes: focus on roots in Ethnography and Participatory Design; focus on the development process; two organizational case studies; focus on details of method; examples of Contextual Design; an example of bringing the field into the lab; and finally, frameworks: Ethnography, Participatory Design, and Contextual Design.

FOCUS ON ROOTS IN ETHNOGRAPHY AND PARTICIPATORY DESIGN

In the first three studies in this collection, the authors describe projects in which they borrowed methods and techniques of field research from established practice in Ethnography and Participatory Design and then modified the methods so as to accommodate the specific demands and constraints of their product-design contexts.

As part of a larger effort to define the requirements for a proposed imaging workstation for diagnostic radiologists, Judith Ramey and her research team at the University of Washington conducted the study reported here ("Adaptation of an Ethnographic Method for Investigation of the Task Domain in Diagnostic Radiology"), in which they combined the ethnographic "stream of behavior chronicle" and the retrospective verbal protocol (also known as "stimulated recall") to capture both radiologists' task performance and their own expert commentary on it.

The method has four phases: first, the team gathered the stream of behavior by videotaping radiologists as they worked in their normal work setting. Then, a member of the team viewed the tape and formulated questions and hypotheses about the work. Next, in a second videotaped session, the team member showed the radiologist the original tape and asked for a running commentary on the work (the "stimulated recall"), into which, at the appropriate points, she interjected questions for clarification. Finally, the team categorized and indexed the behavior on the original tapes for various kinds of follow-on analysis.

The method proved especially useful in uncovering detailed behaviors (marking on films and reports, pointing at and touching films, using the fingers as "calipers," etc.) that the subjects were no longer aware of or were only marginally aware of. These behaviors, which for the subjects had slipped beneath their conscious attention or interest, turned out during the stimulated-recall sessions to be important features of practice and generated numerous specific requirements for the user interface of the proposed system.

The authors describe this method in detail, explain how they analyzed the original videotapes and the commentary tapes, and discuss how the method can be integrated into an overall user-centered design process based on standard human-factors techniques.

The second case in this first group, "Using the CARD and PICTIVE Participatory Design Methods for Collaborative Analysis," by Michael J. Muller and Rebecca Carr of U S West Technologies, describes a project in which the authors were forced to take a longer step from their methodological foundations.

The authors describe a new use for two methods that originally were created to support the classic Participatory Design goal of direct end-user participation in design. Both CARD and PICTIVE rely basically on paper representations of system states that analysts and users can discuss and modify. The investigative team uses the system images provided by CARD and PICTIVE to iteratively exercise, discuss, and critique detailed work scenarios.

However, in the case reported here (in which the goal was to develop a model of the work of directory-assistance telephone operators) the investigators were unable to work directly with the operators. Instead, trainers had to serve as subject-matter experts and spokespeople for the operators. Offsetting this disadvantage, the investigators were able to hold two-thirds of the sessions in or near the operators' work area, so that they could easily role-play the work, observe actual work, or even take live calls themselves.

Thus, what was already known of the users' work was present (in the form of the initial CARD representation), and most of the time the users' work setting was at hand, but the users themselves were not. So, even though the team used tools created within the Participatory Design tradition, the work itself (as the authors explain) was not truly "participatory."

The authors also found that the nature of the operators' work required that they modify their methods. The work under study had a significant noncomputer component: it required social interaction with the customer and significant mental work on the part of the operator. CARD and PICTIVE, however, were tied specifically to representations of system activity. Thus the investigators had to devise new "cards" for these new categories of user activity.

But in spite of the many constraints, this exercise led the team to a much richer understanding—and thus representation—of the mental work of the operators. In turn, this led to a richer understanding that to some extent all workers are knowledge workers, even though their job may be classified in some other way (such as "clerical"). And finally, this effort underlined the power of qualitative, collaborative analysis to illuminate dimensions of work that can be missed by more reductive quantitative analytical methods. The authors close with a discussion of the cost-effectiveness of the effort and consideration of several issues about the robustness and replicability of the study.

In "The Ethnographic Interview in User-Centered Work/Task Analysis," Larry Wood of Brigham Young University describes an approach to interviewing that he developed during a software development project by synthesizing insights from the two fields of cognitive science and ethnography. (The project in question was developing a software application to support ordering telecommunications services on the campus of Brigham Young University. The goal of the interviews was to produce a description of current work practice, derived from practitioners themselves, for use in later stages of the user-centered design effort.)

A key assumption in the development of Wood's method was that the people currently doing the work should be respected as experts at it. Thus, Wood used the insights of cognitive science into the nature of expertise and the organization of expert knowledge, namely: expert knowledge is generally organized hierarchically; it is stored as "chunks" of patterns with associated procedures, and thus can be viewed as "object" knowledge and "process" knowledge; and, to a large extent, it is automatic (or tacit) and thus may be difficult for the expert to articulate.

Armed with this model of expert knowledge from cognitive science, Wood was able to draw from Ethnography interviewing techniques that responded to both the features of expert knowledge and the difficulties of eliciting that knowledge from the interviewee. The method first uses semistructured interviews to elicit object identification (concepts and relationships as expressed in expert terminology). Once interviewers have a reasonable grasp of the experts' object knowledge through interviews, they can go on to develop a more detailed work model (combining and extending object knowledge with experts' process knowledge) by augmenting interviewing with systematic observations of work. The emerging work model is then documented and returned to the practitioners for validation or correction.

In presenting his case study, Wood provides numerous examples of actual questions to ask during the interviews, discusses the role of the interview in the larger design process, and provides extended examples of techniques for documenting the resulting model so that the interviewees can most easily judge its accuracy.

FOCUS ON THE DEVELOPMENT PROCESS

In the three articles previously mentioned, the authors focused a great part of their attention on describing the methods used and their strengths and weaknesses. In the following two articles, the authors shift the emphasis from methods *per se* to the design process itself, how it can accommodate or respond to field usability data, and how field research fits into the overall flow of activities.

FOCUS ON THE DESIGN PROCESS

Working from within a user-centered design process, Wixon, Pietras, Huntwork, and Muzzey were able to use a variety of field research methods, integrated into an overall design process that also featured innovative total quality approaches and prototype testing and evaluation ("Changing the Rules: A Pragmatic Approach to Product Development"). Some of the field research activities were planned in advance, and others were selected to meet needs as they were encountered during the phases of the design process.

In planning the design process for the product (a workgroup application for the Macintosh), the team identified the user interface design as critical to the product's success; therefore, they decided early on that they needed to establish "design partnerships" with a set of customers for iterative feedback. In the first phase of development (definition of the product concept), they conducted Contextual Inquiry and work-based interviews. In the second phase, in which they made decisions about the product's capabilities, they used surveys of customers and Vector Comparative Analysis, a computer-based tool for analyzing the scores customers have given various possible product features. In the third phase of development (design of the user interface), the team returned to field research methods, using Contextual Inquiry and artifact walkthroughs. During the implementation phase, they did user-interface prototype tests and evaluations. Finally, during the formal product test, they conducted tests in which customers used the product for production work. Thus field methods were integrated with a suite of other methods, each used at the point in the process where it would be most effective.

The authors provide extensive reflections on their experience during this design effort. In general, they learned that when they listened closely to what their customers said, they discovered that many of the assumptions that had driven their early thinking were completely wrong; but also by listening carefully, they were able to identify the product functions and characteristics that were "delighters" to their customers.

In "The Delta Method: A Way to Introduce Usability," Martin Rantzer describes a method meant to serve as a framework to link together existing usability tools and practices systematically in order to supplement the early phases of traditional software development. Called the Delta Method, the approach focuses on design of software interfaces (here understood—quite rightly, we might add—to include user documentation), with the goal of supporting the system designers and technical communicators (neither of whom could be assumed to have formal education in human factors or usability) as they carry out the customer and user analysis and the design of a prototype.

Intended both for internal use at Ericsson Infocom Consultants AB of Sweden and for sale to customers, the Delta Method was developed as a joint effort by Ericsson Infocom and Linkoping University. The development process had three phases: method inception, field studies, and analysis. In the first phase, usability activities were identified from the perspective of the academic partners (including such activities as user and task analysis), then adapted to the requirements of industry. This first formulation of the method was then tried out in a pilot project in the field (a commercial project within Infocom). Based on an analysis of the field studies, the method was revised.

Rantzer then describes the features and processes incorporated into the final form of the the Delta Method. The approach is unusual in its emphasis on the importance of user information and hence on the necessity of having technical communicators as part of the team; the other two team groups are the system designers and the customer representatives. The first task is to capture the customer's vision of what the system should be; this vision will then be supplemented and validated iteratively in user and task analysis . Then the group proceeds to conceptual design, formulation of usability goals, prototype design, and usability tests.

Finally, Rantzer describes the process of generalizing the Delta Method so as to make it flexible enough to be useful in a range of different organizations. For example, one finding was the need to tightly integrate the Delta Method activities into the process documents already in use; the familiarity of the larger document aided the acceptance of the new usability activities.

TWO ORGANIZATIONAL CASE STUDIES

The next two articles in the collection are especially useful in understanding the "politics" of field research in product design—that is, the influences of differing goals in doing the research, the varying needs and goals of the partners in the research, and the susceptibility of the research to larger business decisions.

In "Field Research of Sales Personnel and Processes for the Design of a Sales Automation Workstation," Robert Graf working at Dun and Bradstreet Software, Inc. (DBS) describes field research he did for a new release of an existing system intended to support the internal sales staff. The system, which consisted of a notebook PC, applications, local and central databases, and the hardware and software needed to communicate with the central databases, was intended to increase sales, reduce the cost of sales, and provide better competitive information.

Graf describes the process he went through to clarify the business situation and usability issues to be investigated. When it became clear that user acceptance was a major issue, Graf proposed a field study so that he could get a realistic picture of the realities of the sales process and understand the role of mobile computing in it.

Once in the field visiting satisfied and unsatisfied users of the current release, Graf discovered the need for flexibility; although he had planned to videotape the sessions, the interviewees objected, and thus he and his team found themselves gathering data only through handwritten and typed notes. When he began the data analysis, he encountered difficulty arriving at the best organization of the mass of narrative data; finally, he decided to provide a summary report, three detailed task analyses (one for each of the critical audiences, with a "day in the life" approach), and two business models (a model of the idealized sales process and a model of all the information the sales person needs to do his or her job).

Following on the distribution of the report, the team did a usability inspection of the product that yielded a prioritized list of usability issues to be addressed in the next release. Also, a new organizing concept—the "deal"—was developed to integrate all the various parts of the product. Unfortunately, however, the system did not receive funding for a major redesign. Nevertheless, Graf concludes that this field research did much to provide his organization with a vision of the power of field research.

David Rowley of Varian Chromatography Systems, in "Organizational Considerations in Field-Oriented Product Development: Experiences of a Cross-Functional Team," also provides an organizational perspective on field research, but focuses specifically on issues related to field research done by a cross-functional design team—a team composed of people from different areas within the company (engineers, technical writers, marketing personnel) and tasked with the design of a specific product.

The team whose field research is reported here was responsible for the development of the data-handling product line. The team was made up of applications experts, engineers, marketing personnel, technical writers, technical support staff, and manufacturing staff. Whereas before the adoption of such cross-functional teams only marketing might have visited customer sites, now all of the members of the team have the opportunity direct contact with end users.

This team had had some earlier experience with usability investigations in the form of mobile lab tests, but had not had a systematic way to capture the bigger picture of users in their setting and communicate it back to the rest of the team. In addition to this general goal, the team wanted to investigate the requirements for specific new products. To accomplish these goals, the team decided to use Contextual Inquiry and to capture data on videotape as much as they could. Also, based on their market, they decided to conduct the study in Europe.

Rowley describes in detail how the team arrived at their focus statements for the study, approached the logistics of visiting foreign pharmaceutical labs, conducted the actual visits and interviews, and worked to create a balanced and unbiased picture of the work being supported. He points out that the recommendations for change were documented in the team's change control system, and thus were fed into the standard company mechanisms with no need for special procedural accommodations.

Rowley finds that removing the barriers often found between functional departments results in improved communication and coordination within the team, but the lack of centralization may reduce the scope of the impact of field study findings. That is, while it may be easier to impact the design of a product developed by the team conducting the study, it is harder to effect change in the design of products developed by other teams. Also, the amount of data generated was overwhelming; Rowley recommends a number of changes to their process so as to make the research findings more accessible and manageable.

FOCUS ON SPECIFICS OF METHOD

The authors of the next three articles give us a detailed view of the nuts and bolts of field research that can often determine its success or failure.

In "A Day in the Life of a Family: An International Ethnographic Study," Susan Dray and Deborah Mrazek report on the field research they did for Hewlett-Packard in response to the challenge presented by having to design for a very different audience from the standard business market: the global home and family market.

In addition to standard marketing information, the design team needed information about how and by whom the product would be used, so that they could optimize its ease of use. To gather this information, the researchers used a number of methods: naturalistic observation, Contextual Inquiry, ethnographic interviews, and artifact walkthroughs. The unifying idea was that, to gain insights into how families use computer technology, they would go to the homes of representative familes in the US and in Europe to see firsthand.

Dray and Mrazek provide substantial detail about the logistics of arranging the family visits and the actual visits themselves. Especially concerning the visits to European homes, they emphasize the importance of the "social" dimensions of the visit, as well as describing the formal data collection activities. They believe that their focus on the social dimensions—providing food, focusing early on the family's children, taking snapshots, etc.—provided the essential credibility and rapport that they needed to gain the committed participation of the families. For their core data collection activities, they asked each family member for a demonstration of typical activities on the computer, they reviewed sample outputs, and they documented the setting (location of supplies, documentation, other equipment, etc.), after which they continued with a less formal discussion and closing. The team then conducted a separate structured debriefing to capture the critical insights of each visit.

The special challenges of doing field research in the medical equipment industry is the focus of Diane Brown's article "The Challenges of User Based Design in a Medical Equipment Market." Brown's employer (ATL, Inc.) builds medical ultrasound imaging systems. Historically, ATL's engineers designed in response to requirements statements and evaluations provided by former users now employed in ATL's marketing department; but, in response to customer complaints, management agreed to create a group focused on usability. After several somewhat unsatisfactory attempts to get information from end users about how to improve usability, the group determined that in order to better support their users' work, they needed to pursue new ways of understanding the context in which the problems were encountered, as well as gain a detailed understanding of what the users were trying to accomplish.

Thus they began to conduct field studies. These studies fell into three different categories: efforts to answer very specific questions about processes, efforts to understand surrounding work tasks so as to incorporate them into the system functionality, and finally efforts to make fundamental changes by rethinking the human-system interaction from first principles. Their chapter focuses on this last effort.

Brown describes in detail the evolution of their approach from the first, unfocused site visits through the process of redefining and sharpening their focus, and choosing new sites to visit based on more specific criteria. At the sites, the team videotaped the work performance. Brown describes in detail the follow-up interviews they conducted with the workers they observed and the transcription and segmentation they performed on the videotapes of the work so as to extract a hypothetical model of the work and terminology. They then correlated the two: after they organized the observations, they reviewed the interview transcript and extracted the goals (what the worker was actually trying to accomplish). To help in the data analysis, the team developed several tools. One, resembling musical notation, allows them to graphically show patterns of work over time. They also began to use Contextual Design methods (see Holtzblatt and Beyer, this volume) to organize and graphically describe their findings.

The author closes with a description of the process of generating design requirements from the data and impacts that the data may have on the design. In reflecting on her experience in doing this field research, she identifies a number of areas where they might improve their processes and tools.

In "'You've got three days!' Case Studies in Field Techniques for the Time Challenged," Kristin Bauersfeld and Shannon Halgren then at Claris Corporation describe three field study techniques, adopted from traditional methods, that they designed to work with very short time frames for conducting research, interpret the findings, and apply the results. This effort to do field research was motivated by an opportunity for the Interface Design Group to get involved at the conceptualization phase of design of several new products, a departure from the more typical pattern of coming in at the end to do lab-based usability tests.

The first of these methods is the "Condensed Ethnographic Interview." In this short interview conducted in the user's environment, the users are asked to begin discussing their daily activities; for each regular task of interest to the researchers, the researchers might ask more questions or request a demonstration. The session is videotaped for followup analysis.

In the second technique, "Passive Video Observation," two cameras are placed in the user's setting—one to capture the area view and one (or a scan converter) to capture the user's computer screen. The two images are mixed onto one screen using a video mixer. The taping takes place for about two to three hours, with the user having the ability to turn it off (or off and then back on) if they need or want to. The researchers then collect the equipment and view the session videotape for analysis.

The third technique, "Interactive Feature Conceptualization," is basically a technique that enables users to organize and rate the importance of their own processes and terminology. Based on the condensed ethnographic interview contents, the researchers record all of the mentions of tools, forms, processes, and software features on sticky notes. The user then goes through an exercise of sorting and rating them. The session is videotaped.

The authors provide detailed descriptions of two case studies in which they used these methods and discuss the lessons they learned from the experience.

EXAMPLES OF CONTEXTUAL INQUIRY AND CONTEXTUAL DESIGN

Based on several years of use and iterative improvement by Karen Holtzblatt and Hugh Beyer, Contextual Design offers an integrated, systematic whole-process method for getting from the research idea to the design response. A number of corporate design teams have adopted the method; the next two articles report case studies of its use.

Building on a tradition of seeking feedback from users begun in the early years at WordPerfect, Stan Page and his cross-disciplinary team at Novell Inc. undertook to do field research as input for the next generation word processing application ("Contextual Design in a Large Commercial Software Company"). Their focus was purposefully broad: the work practice surrounding the making of documents.

The team, composed of members from development, human factors, documentation, marketing, and usability testing, used the Contextual Design process as taught by Holtzblatt and Beyer. This method was chosen for its special strength in structuring the process of converting research findings into design. (For details of the method, see Holtzblatt and Beyer, this volume.)

When the research effort showed promise, management decided to basically double the effort; the original team was divided in half and new people added to each new team. One team continued the research into the making of documents; the other expanded its scope to include all business work practice. Page describes the way the new participants were trained and the way the two teams organized themselves to conduct their work. He also describes the methods used by the teams to communicate with each other and with the company at large. He underlines the importance of getting the results of the research into new design, and offers examples of features derived from the work (which include Make-It-Fit and QuickTasks).

Microsoft has long been known as both an innovator and early adopter of usability methods; Diane Juhl describes the systematic use of Contextual Design along with a number of field-oriented design methods. Because the team was approaching a relatively new market (the home market) and one of the aims of the products was to develop new software opportunities, the team decided to choose a set of structured field research methods.

The team included members from the sponsoring organizations and the usability team. While the focus of the work was quite specific, it was also broad. As a result, the team generated a large data pool, over 2000 data points, 300 design ideas, and 200 work models. They also developed a list of over 20 typical tasks. This work (combined with the reporting of the results) was completed in 60 days, contradicting the common belief that field research takes a long time.

Reporting such large set of data was a challenge. In addition to traditional approaches of reports and presentations, the team developed a data base of affinity diagram, and have put the work models on line. The data have been extensively re-used in developing business cases, evaluating designs, and creating focus statements for future studies. In reporting their results, the team faced management questions about sample size, succinctness, and quantification of the results. The team is currently working to address these questions in future projects, and will be continuing to refine and develop these methods.

The third case in this section reports on the use of the method (in the form of Contextual Inquiry) in a medical products development effort (Janette Coble, Judy Maffitt, Matthew Orland, and Michael Kahn, "Using Contextual Inquiry to Discover Physicians' True Needs"). This effort was undertaken as the requirements generation task for a clinical workstation intended to support clinicians in viewing test results for their patients from office, home, or hospital. The team chose Contextual Inquiry (CI) because they felt that going to the users' actual environment would be the only way to ascertain the actual needs of the physicians, especially those needs buried in the physicians' tacit knowledge (see Wood, this volume).

After describing in detail the selection of sites to be visited and the conduct of the typical session, the authors describe their process of analyzing and interpreting the data. Following each session, the researchers walked back through their notes of the session and created several different products from the information that they had obtained: a sequence model, a flow model, a context model, detailed observations, a user profile, and an issues list. The authors describe each of these products in detail.

At the halfway point of the research and at the end, the researchers consolidated their findings from all of the sessions by building an affinity diagram. Next, the researchers derived requirements from their observations. After they had formulated the requirements, they returned them to the physicians so that the physicians could rate their importance, and finally they produced a requirements document enriched with insights from the research.

AN EXAMPLE OF BRINGING THE FIELD INTO THE LAB

The last of the case studies in this volume presents an alternative to going out to the users' environment to gather data; instead, it brings the field into the lab. Mary Beth Butler and Marie Tahir, in "Bringing the Users' Work to Us: Usability Roundtables at Lotus Development," describes a method in which they and their co-workers at Lotus Development Corp. attempt to recreate a portion of the user's environment by having the users bring samples of their work to the Lotus offices. Users sit with product team members around a conference table and use these samples (data files, sample applications, or hard copy printouts) to explain their work.

Seeing the work that users do is considered invaluable to ensuring that product designs meet users' needs. Initial attempts at Lotus to visit users in their workplaces were time-consuming, and were not as productive as the researchers had hoped; usability roundtables have provided them with an effective alternative for learning more about their users' work.

In this case study, the authors describe in detail how the usability specialists in Lotus work with the product developers to plan and arrange the roundtable sessions. The sessions, a form of artifact analysis (a technique used in Ethnography), are focused on uses of specific product features or work patterns. Participants are encouraged to bring along a co-worker, from whom the team might get additional information. As the name implies, the discussion between the user/

participant and the development team members is informal; however, the team does have an agenda of questions that they hope to cover during the course of the roundtable. The moderator (almost always the usability specialist) takes notes during the session and prepares a brief report.

The authors close with an assessment of the benefits and drawbacks of the method, and discuss ways that it might be used in the future.

FRAMEWORKS: ETHNOGRAPHY, PARTICIPATORY DESIGN, AND CONTEXTUAL DESIGN

Behind these field-research case studies is a background of methodological thought that can be divided roughly into three main schools: Ethnography, Participatory Design, and Contextual Design. The final three articles in this collection explain the evolution of these perspectives and the ways in which they have inspired research methods for use in the process of system design.

Ethnography is the foundation discipline upon which the other field research approaches build. Ethnography is the description of cultures; it emerged as a discipline from social and cultural anthropology. In "An Overview of Ethnography and System Design," John Ford and Larry Wood first describe Ethnography's defining motive—description without bias—and explain its impact on the methods of ethnographers. They then draw out the similarities between the research of an ethnographer and the requirements definition of a system designer, and trace the evolution of the methods that system designers have historically used to try to understand their users' requirements, arriving finally at the current interest in using ethnographic methods.

The great advantage of ethnographic methods is in the insistence on maintaining the perspective of those inside the culture being described. Thus these methods are particularly effective in helping system designers accurately understand audiences about whom they have little or no prior knowledge. Ford and Wood briefly describe several research approaches that are basically specialized types of ethnography intended to support system design: Participatory Design, Contextual Inquiry, Joint Application Design, and PICTIVE (see Muller and Carr, this volume).

Finally, the authors identify several trends to watch for in the evolution of interest in and use of ethnographic methods in system design. The first one is especially intriguing: the development of sophistication about field research goals and methods among the users whose culture is being studied and the reflexive effects it might have on method.

In "Introduction to Participatory Design," Aki Namioka and Christopher Rao describe the evolution of Participatory Design from its Scandinavian roots and provide an overview of its main tenets and practices.

The essential characteristic of Participatory Design is commitment to the primacy of the worker. It believes that the goal of technological development is to build better tools to support workers, and that the workers themselves are the only ones with the expertise to judge how best to improve their work and work setting. Thus the technology designer becomes primarily the implementer of the workers' vision. Participatory Design uses techniques from several closely related approaches to put theory into practice. Ethnography, with its focus on highly contextualized understanding, has contributed a number of perspectives and field-research techniques (see Ford and Wood, this volume). Cooperative design techniques such as role-playing games have been pressed into service. Reciprocal evolution has contributed a focus on the study of work practices with technologies. And Contextual Inquiry (see Holtzblatt and Beyer, this volume) has contributed not only field-research techniques, but also business processes for evolving a design out of the field research findings.

In closing, the authors argue that even though the United States does not have the same strong trade-union tradition as Scandinavia, nevertheless our pragmatism and our long tradition of democracy provide a congenial atmosphere in which to practice Participatory Design.

In "Contextual Design: Principles and Practice," Karen Holtzblatt and Hugh Beyer open with a brief overview of the origins of their method as a response to a challenge to come up with a way to effect fundamental change in products. The core idea that animated the method was that to build radically better products it was necessary to have a thorough understanding of how customers work. This insight led to the first formulation of Contextual Inquiry, built on roots in ethnography, psychology, and systems engineering.

As Contextual Inquiry was exercised in projects over time, its practitioners encountered problems and limitations with its original formulation that led Holtzblatt and Beyer to make a series of modifications and extensions to it, resulting finally in the system of Contextual Design as it is now practiced: "a structured, step-by-step roadmap to guide a team from initial project set-up and field interviews through design and the transition to implementation."

Contextual Design provides a very fully specified step-by-step process for doing field research and converting the results into design. It pays attention to the workgroup dynamics of design teams and to the business realities that constrain design, as well as teaching good practice in doing field research. In the remainder of the article, the authors describe in detail the phases in the process of Contextual Design and the types of outputs developed during each phase (work models, affinity diagrams, consolidated work models, scripts, user environment models, and iterative prototypes, leading to the final design). They close with a brief consideration of the need for continued evolution of the method to respond to new needs and issues as they arise in practice.

WHERE TO GO FROM HERE

This volume of essays can only open the door on the complex subject of the use of field research in product design, but several points seem especially important to make.

First, and most importantly, being successful in field research can require a fundamental change of perspective. The field researcher must be deeply humble and respectful in the face of the work practice and culture under study. The researcher must also be exhaustive in uncovering, scrutinizing, and containing the effect of his or her own assumptions, biases, and preconceptions about the worker, work practice, and culture. And, when the researcher turns to design, he or she must be careful not to lapse into the kind of "technological colonialism" that leads to improving workers' practice "for their own good." That is, the researcher must first commit to the philosophical position that justifies and animates field research: the culture and the people in it are worthy of respect.

Secondly, the use of field research in product design is very young. A researcher embarking on an effort to incorporate field research methods into his or her toolkit needs to do the homework required—which is to learn as much as possible about method. This means going to the foundation texts in Ethnography and related disciplines; it means following up the excellent references in the essays in this collection; it means going to workshops and conferences that address the topic. Armed with this background in the literature and current practice, one can develop good judgment about appropriate ways to scale and modify techniques to fit the constraints of a given situation.

Finally, as researchers and practitioners we need to develop a sense of community as we take part in the evolution of design practice.

Each of us who has used field research in product design should consider presenting a description of the project at a conference or in an article. Those who have modified an existing method or developed a new one to fit the demands of their design situation should document the new method for others. At conferences, those who are further along can offer workshops and presentations for people just beginning to use these methods.

We hear a lot these days about the need to succeed in an increasingly competitive global market, and the need to enhance the productivity of our workers. We might add to these concerns a desire to empower workers and to create pleasure in work. To help us achieve these goals in system design, we need to know as much as possible about the people and the contexts for which we are designing. We need to ground our designs in workplace realities, and discover better design in the limitations or unmet needs experienced by the user in the user's world. Product development processes built on field research can help us achieve these goals. We offer this collection in the hope that it will stimulate the use of field research and lead to further published discussion.

Adaptation of an Ethnographic Method for Investigation of the Task Domain in Diagnostic Radiology

Judith Ramey
Alan H. Rowberg
Carol Robinson
University of Washington

EXECUTIVE SUMMARY

A number of user-centered methods for designing radiology workstations have been described by researchers at Carleton University
(Ottawa), Georgetown University, George Washington University, and
University of Arizona, among others. The approach described here differs in that it enriches standard human-factors practices with methods
adapted from *Ethnography* to study users (in this case, diagnostic
radiologists) as members of a distinct culture. The overall approach
combines several methods; the core method, based on ethnographic
"stream of behavior chronicles" and their analysis, has four phases: (1)
first, we gather the stream of behavior by videotaping a radiologist as
he or she works; (2) we view the tape ourselves and formulate questions and hypotheses about the work; and then (3) in a second videotaped session, we show the radiologist the original tape and ask for a
running commentary on the work, into which (at the appropriate
points) we interject our questions for clarification. We then (4) categorize and index the behavior on the "raw data" tapes for various kinds

of follow-on analysis. We describe and illustrate this method in detail, describe how we analyze the "raw data" videotapes and the commentary tapes, and explain how the method can be integrated into an overall user-centered design process based on standard human-factors techniques.

INTRODUCTION

User-Centered Design, the processes that incorporate user input from the requirements phase forward, has become increasingly prevalent in the design of imaging workstations; such processes have been reported on by researchers at Carleton University (Ottawa), Georgetown University, George Washington University, and University of Arizona, among others.[1] Most of these practices, however, are built on the hypothesis-testing model of traditional empirical research. As we approached the problems of designing a workstation for diagnostic radiology, we felt that our first step must be to back up and look at the hypotheses about radiologic practice themselves; thus we looked for a more exploratory model for our research. We wanted to explore the whole context in which diagnostic radiology is practiced, in order to confirm that we had adequately accounted for all the significant dimensions of actual practice. To meet this goal, we hit upon the methods of Ethnography, a type of anthropology, as a working point of departure.

Ethnography is the systematic, inductive study of a culture. "Systematic" is intended to mean that there is a well-formulated set of rules and protocols that constitute a defined standard of practice. "Inductive" is intended to mean that the research starts without hypotheses or controls.[2] One studies an unfiltered record of behavior, and hopes to extract from this "stream of behavior" the actions, the goals of the actions, and the values that animate them. By iteratively sampling behavior and confirming its interpretation with the members of the culture, one builds (or validates) a model of the world from within the viewpoint of the culture under study.

Why draw on Ethnography? Generally, the activity of any group of people is embedded in a social context, which implies shared history, habits, goals, and values; the specific social context of a given group of people amounts to a culture. Typically, the most fundamental qualities of this set of history, habits, goals, and values are so deeply embedded as to be unexamined by the members of the culture. (This phenomenon is expressed in popular terms in aphorisms such as "if you want to know about water, don't ask a fish.") Furthermore, the members of a culture—any culture—are poor at self-description. They fail to report the mundane, the subliminal, and the subattentional—the details of behavior that, routine and "boring" as they are, constitute a substantial portion of actual behavior.

Formal research hypotheses, on the other hand, tend to focus on only those issues that are assumed *a priori* to be substantive. That is, hypotheses select certain variables and posit certain relationships of dependence among them; as far as possible, intervening circumstances and behaviors are explicitly filtered out. Even in formal descriptive studies, which can be more exploratory in nature, the research focuses on a subset of behaviors by virtue of having controlled the scope of the behavior under study.

We chose Ethnography because we wanted to validate the commonly held understanding of the practice of diagnostic radiology that we had acquired from the literature in the field, interviews with practitioners, the experience of team members, etc. We felt that there was at least a possibility that opinion or "conventional wisdom," the shorthand description of their practice used by diagnostic radiologists, might be masking behaviors we needed to know about to design a fully functional workstation. We also wanted to assign goals and values to the work, the workplace organization, etc. Understanding the larger goals of specific patterns of behavior is particularly important when one expects to redesign the behaviors (as is the case with the design of a computer workstation), so that even with a redesign of behavior the goal is still met or better met. Further, understanding the values that animate the work can help the designer to prioritize the functions that are essential and must appear in the core system, as opposed to those that are desirable but that can be implemented in later improvements of the system. Also, we wanted to elicit the expression of these goals and values from the radiologists themselves as they actually looked at a detailed record of their own work.

Before going further, it is important to underline that the ethnographic approach described here is intended to provide an earlier supplement to other more commonly used methods by explicitly grounding the generation of hypotheses in a description of practice; it is not intended to replace other methods.

The culture we studied was the practice of diagnostic radiology. We used a variety of ethnographic methods; our core method, based on "stream-of-behavior chronicles" and their analysis, had four phases: (1) first, we gathered the stream-of-behavior by videotaping a radiologist as he or she works; (2) we viewed the tape ourselves and formulated questions and hypotheses about the work; and then (3) in a second videotaped session, we showed the radiologist the original tape and asked for a running commentary on the work, into which (at the appropriate points) we interjected our questions for clarification. We then (4) categorized and indexed the behavior on the "raw data" tapes for various kinds of follow-on analysis. This discussion briefly describes our objectives and provides an overview of the full set of methods we used, and then focuses on our use of stream-of-behavior chronicles and commentary tapes.

OBJECTIVES

We had four main objectives in this study:

- To work in the context of system development; that is, our goal was not to build theory, but to make a timely contribution to a design process.
- To validate, enrich, and correct previous opinions; that is, we wanted to produce findings that would lead to *data-driven* decision-making about the design.
- To escape possible observational biases; that is, we wanted to gather *all* the data we could about the practice of diagnostic radiology, without intentional or unintentional selection biases.
- To present findings in the most useful, durable format; that is, we wanted to devise a means to move our insights downstream in the development process (to those who would write the requirements document, the specification, the design, and even the code) without loss of the richness of the data.

This study represents an effort to validate the method; it was not intended as a full-blown application of ethnography to this problem domain. In the following discussion, we note the additional steps that a full-scale application would have included.

OVERVIEW OF METHODS: "GROUNDED" INVESTIGATION

To put the study of the interpretive activities of diagnostic radiologists in context, it is useful to provide an overview of the whole study, which examined both diagnostic radiology and its support environment—the radiology records fileroom organization and activities, its relationship to the hospital information system, the information flow between entities, etc. All of our methods were "grounded"—that is, they proceeded inductively, looking at actual practice and asking for interpretation from the people who actually conducted each activity.

In looking at *diagnostic activities*, we used two main methods: (1) investigative interviews and observation, and (2) ethnographic "stream-of-behavior chronicles" of the radiologists' work with the data captured on video[3], followed by interpretation of the chronicles by the radiologists themselves (data also captured on video). In this category, our study was limited largely to the University of Washington Medical Center. We found that our data fell into the following three categories (to be explored in more detail later in this paper):

■ Administrative/database/workplace issues.
■ Interpretive activities.
■ Other uses of images (conferences, teaching files, etc.).

We also studied the *department of radiology as a domain* —how it gathered and managed information, how it interacted with the hospital information system in general, etc. In studying the domain, we used two main methods: investigative interviews and participant observation. We used standard techniques for the investigative interviews; we pursued participant observation by acting as apprentices, for instance, to fileroom personnel. The goal of the participant observation was to become more intimately acquainted with actual practice—division of work, rules of thumb for getting work done, rule-breaking (for instance, the removal of films from the fileroom system by radiologists who chose to build personal files of films) and how it was handled, etc. In this category, we supplemented our study of the University of Washington Medical Center with less detailed studies of three other hospitals: one other urban teaching hospital, one urban nonteaching hospital, and one rural nonteaching hospital, regionally dispersed in the U.S.

We found that our data fell into the following categories:

■ Information organization and flow (formal, informal, and rule-breaking).
■ Variability among hospitals.

Although this paper focuses on interpretive diagnostic activities and not on the domain in general, it is useful in illustrating the output of the method to mention some of our findings in this category. Regarding information flow, for instance, we found that a significant portion of fileroom activity was devoted to the management of films from outside institutions (for instance, one of five "stations" in the UW Medical Center Radiology Records is devoted entirely to this function). To further complicate the function, there is variability among hospitals in the coding scheme of films, studies, and patients; and also, once the outside films are included with the local patient records, the outside films are very frequently jumbled with local films, shoved into incorrect subfolders in the patient film jacket, etc. Thus both work and stress are generated by lack of adequate translating and tracking systems for outside films.

DETAILS OF THE KEY METHOD: STREAM-OF-BEHAVIOR CHRONICLES AND THEIR ANALYSIS

To study the activities of diagnostic radiologists as they actually read films, we began by simply observing in the reading rooms (two different people served as observers, but with one early exception, only one observer was present at a time). This activity had two goals: we wanted to learn as much as we could about the environment and activities, and we wanted the radiologists to get used to our presence so that we could reduce the likelihood that they were changing their behavior (behaving more formally, for instance) because we were present.

We then began the process of gathering the stream-of-behavior by videotaping. We filmed one session of on average an hour in length with each of four radiologists: one chest radiologist reading alone; one chest radiologist working with a resident; one orthopedic radiologist working with a resident; and one neuroradiologist working with a resident.

After each session, we viewed the videotape ourselves and formulated questions and hypotheses about the activities. Then we held a second videotaped session, as close as possible to the original "raw data" filming as the radiologists' schedule would allow, which proved in this study to be within about three days. In the second session, we showed the radiologist the original tape and asked for a running commentary on the work as he watched it (this method is known in the literature as a "retrospective thinking-aloud protocol" or "stimulated recall"). At the appropriate points, we interjected our questions for clarification. We had four goals in this phase of the process: first, we simply wanted to be sure that we understood the activities; second, we wanted to elicit the radiologist's terminology and segmentation of the actions into separate tasks; third, we wanted to provoke a discussion of the goals and values of the components of the work; and fourth, we wanted to note any cases where the radiologist commented on behaviors that he had not been aware of.

Because of schedule constraints, we went through the process of taping work sessions and getting the commentary on them only once; ideally, this process would be iterative, to protect against possible idiosyncratic or anomalous characteristics or events in the sessions. Also, it would be very desirable to go through the process at different institutions, to account for local differences in practice.

Finally, we categorized and indexed the behaviors on the tapes that we had identified through our observations and the radiologists' commentaries. For this detailed analysis, we arbitrarily chose a "slice" of each of the four "raw data" tapes (about 22 minutes, or one-third of the length of the whole tape); the four segments varied slightly in length because we did not cut into the reading of a study (that is, each began at a point where the radiologist turned to a new study and ended after the radiologist had finished with a study). In the future, we hope to gather and analyze data in automated ways (for instance, by using event-logging software for our post-hoc analysis); for this study, however, we relied on manual methods. We used two independent raters of the video data, with resolution of conflict by rule-making. The results of this analysis are presented in more detail below under "Summary of Selected Results."

To report our results, we prepared a "highlights" videotape consisting of segments illustrating each behavior of interest, paired with segments from the commentary tapes in which the radiologist explains the behavior and/or assigns goals and values to it.

In the future, we hope to build a database, with access through hypermedia, that allows the designer to view a wide variety of information at several levels of detail: the requirement statements themselves, tables that document the frequency of the behavior that led to each requirement, state transition diagrams that show the interrelationships among activities, video segments illustrating the behavior (with commentary on the goals and values of the behavior), and even the full "raw data" and commentary tapes. The designer can then look at the information at the level of detail necessary to resolve design issues, peeling back layers if necessary to get at an increasingly detailed account.

SUMMARY OF SELECTED RESULTS: INTERPRETIVE DIAGNOSTIC ACTIVITIES

The following discussion focuses on topics supported by the data analysis of the tapes discussed above. The tables in the discussion present data gathered from four sessions arbitrarily selected from the "raw data" tapes. These sessions have an average length of 21:40 minutes (about a third of the length of each "raw data" videotape). The data in these tables must be viewed with care; they are included to indicate that hard descriptive data can be extracted from stream-of-behavior chronicles, but because of the restricted size of the sample, they must be further supported by more extensive analysis before they can be taken as a completely reliable description of practice.

It is useful to know how many images typically make up a study, and how long the diagnostic radiologist devotes to the interpretation of a single study. Table 1.1 presents the average number of images per study in the studies that were read during our time sample, while Table 1.2 presents the average length of time that the radiologist devoted to a single study.

The data from the sessions we analyzed fell into the following categories: administrative/database/workplace issues, interpretive activities, and other uses of images (conferences, teaching files, etc.). A discussion of each follows. (The tables draw on the analysis of the "raw data" tapes; the rest of the discussion includes insights drawn from the commentary tapes as well.)

Administrative/Database/Workplace issues

In the area of administrative/database/workplace issues, we found that the following activities were significant: seeking supplementary information, suffering interruptions (including consultations with clinicians and others), sequencing and overlapping of activities, and using built-in quality-control functions that the radiologists themselves had developed. (We do not include in this discussion some well-understood activities documented on our tapes, including initial consultation of

TABLE 1.1 Average Number of Images per Study.

Chest and Ortho Plain Film	Neuro CT
5.25	74.5

TABLE 1.2 Average Time per Study.

Chest and Ortho Plain Film	Neuro Ct
2:35 minutes	8:32 minutes

the requisition for patient demographics and activities involved in dictating reports.)

Table 1.3 presents the average number of times the radiologists sought supplementary information while reading films in our sample session. The radiologists looked at old reports and old films by digging them out of the patient's film jacket; they also read the outside of the film jacket (both as an index to the studies to be found in the jacket and as a source of useful information in itself) and looked at the requisition again (for instance, to reread the clinical indications). In neuroradiology at UW, there is a log book kept on the counter of the Alternator in which the radiologists write their findings, preliminary to or in parallel with preparing their report; in our sample session, it was also consulted. (The log book amounts to a "workaround" for the delays in accessing reports after dictation and before transcription.) The frequency of these activities underlines the need for easy access to and viewing of supplementary data, and suggests that even more supplementary data might be useful.

The radiologists we filmed also suffered a number of interruptions. Most of these interruptions were due to traffic through the reading room, noise from phones and paging, etc. We also captured one

TABLE 1.3 Average Number of Times Subjects Sought Supplementary Information per Session.*

Reference	Chest and Ortho Plain Film	Neuro CT
Old Reports	.66	0
Old Films	.66	0
Film Jackets	1	0
Requisition	1.66	0
Log.Book (Neuro CT only)	n/a	3

*Average Session = 21:40 minutes

interruption due to a request from a clinician for a consultation with the radiologist on a different study; on the commentary tape, the radiologist commented that such consultations might be requested five or more times during a typical day. This information suggests that the user interface of the system needs to have clear orientation information, so that the radiologist can keep track of his or her place even when interrupted, and also points to the need to be able to suspend a session (one or more) in order to activate another session, and then return easily to the original study.

We noticed on the tapes that many of the routine activities involved in starting a study (looking at the requisition for patient demographics, beginning the transcription, positioning the Alternator panels, etc.) were done more or less in parallel; that is, they were not sequenced in any particular order even within the performance of a specific radiologist, but were overlapped and intertwined. We note this because it suggests that a workstation design that presents these functions in a fixed linear order may be perceived as clumsy or obstructive.

We also discovered that the orthopedic radiology group had extended the radiology information system's bar-coding function to include built-in quality-control functions; at the end of a study, for instance, they can bar code the study's accession number and a code from a list of descriptors such as "film underexposed," which allows them to build a historical record to be consulted periodically (say, at the end of each month). The fact that these users had gone to the trouble to build this function indicates that it is important enough to be offered in a workstation design.

Interpretive activities

The interpretive activities of the radiologists included pointing at, marking on, and annotating films; manipulating films; and scanning image sets.

Table 1.4 summarizes the number of behaviors per session that can be classified as *pointing at images* (including touching them), *marking on images* (for instance, numbering vertebrae), and *annotating* (either on the film, on the requisition, or on a separate notepad).

Pointing behaviors are very frequent. The radiologists themselves were surprised at the frequency with which they point at and/or touch images; they commonly offered the explanation that since the images contained rich graphical information that was hard to verbalize, pointing was a very efficient way to communicate to another person what feature was of interest. However, interpersonal communication was

TABLE 1.4 Average Number of Pointing, Marking, and Annotating Behaviors per Session.*

Chest and Ortho Plain Film	Neuro CT
27	29

*Average Session = 21:40 minutes

not the only motivation for pointing; we saw several instances of a single person reading alone who pointed at, touched, or rested his fingers on one image while looking back and forth between it and another image. (We also saw instances of one person pointing simultaneously at two images in the cases where we studied a radiologist with a resident.) Motivations for these behaviors included setting up a point of reference on one film to be compared to a point on the second film. This pointing behavior suggests a need for a complex, multicursor pointing function, not only for consultation but for the single user as well.

The prevalence of marking on films points to the need for overlays (for both textual and graphical information). In the commentary sessions, it was noted that some marks are meant for the radiologist's own use, some for colleagues, and some for the technologist, clinician, etc. This suggests that a system might usefully offer overlays with several different levels of access.

Concerning annotation (usually writing on the requisition or on a separate notepad), a further design implication is the potential usefulness of a preliminary "notetaking" mode. For instance, when a resident views a study prior to going over it with the radiologist, the resident notes down preliminary conclusions, questions, etc.; then these issues are resolved in the joint session with the radiologist and the final dictation done.

Table 1.5 summarizes the number of *image manipulations* per session.

One of the instances of removing and returning an image occurred because the radiologist wanted to revise the standard presentation order of the study that the fileroom personnel had used; this suggests that, in addition to site-level rules of thumb for ordering films, individual user preferences should be supported. The use of the hotlight and the changes in Alternator lighting underscore the problems with luminance and glare reduction, and the need for easy lighting control/change.

Table 1.6 summarizes other viewing behaviors used in *scanning sets of images* in the sessions we analyzed: moving the alternator pan-

TABLE 1.5 Average Number of Image Manipulations per Session.*

Manipulation	Chest and Ortho Plain Film	Neuro Ct
Takes image off alternator (& returns)	3	0
Uses hotlight	1.33	0
Changes alternator lighting	8.66	1

*Average Session = 21:40 minutes

els that contain the films, changing the physical viewing position relative to the image set (what we came to call "manual zoom/roam"), and looking at an image while the image is moving (for instance, after pressing the button to lower or raise an alternator panel, following the image with the eyes as the panel moves).

These behaviors raise several difficult questions when one looks at system design. First, there is fairly constant, seamless movement of the radiologist's attention across the flat display of the images on the alternator; this movement includes a significant number of movements that appear to be "context-setting" sweeps of the whole image set, intermingled with a number of rapid advances on and retreats from small areas of specific images. Also, in one of the commentary sessions, one radiologist noted that he preferred to have images arrayed horizontally on the lower panel of the Alternator, because he was conscious of a break in his visual sweep when his eyes had to jump

TABLE 1.6 Averages of Viewing Behaviors Per Session.*

Viewing Behavior	Chest and Ortho Plain Film	Neuro CT
Moves panels	19	4
Changes physical viewing position ("manual zoom/roam")	77.33	35
Looks at image while image is moving	16.66	9

*Average session = 21:40 minutes

the gap created by the meeting of the edges of the lower and upper panels. There is some suggestion here that the human peripheral and transient-response visual systems are contributing to the understanding of the image set. In addition, the direct access simultaneously to a large number of images at full resolution cannot currently be implemented given technology constraints. Here there is a need to redesign behavior in scanning image sets so as to meet diagnostic goals; it is not clear to what extent the redesign will need to have an impact on the training and routine habits of the practice of radiologists. In this area more formal studies are clearly necessary.

Other Uses of images

Our data also provided evidence in support of uses of images outside of direct diagnostic interpretation; radiologists also need to build files of images for patient-care conferences, for teaching files, and for personal files of classic examples or comparison films.

CONCLUSIONS

At this stage in our use of the ethnographic methods described in this paper, we feel confident that the method has proved useful.

The data we have collected, although limited by the range of our subjects and the size of our time sample, is not impressionistic or anecdotal—it can be analyzed using a variety of post-hoc techniques to yield a detailed manipulable description of practice. Further, the method provides a compressed view of a complicated process; it has bandwidth—that is, it provides a rich view of the actual environment that we propose to automate. This data can be used throughout the design process; when issues arise or clarification is needed, more detailed layers of information are always accessible by recourse to the actual "raw data" record of activities.

However, two points are worth emphasizing: first, this instance of the use of ethnographic methods to study the task domain in diagnostic radiology was quite limited, and must be validated by similar studies that are more comprehensive in scope; and second, the results that we obtained (or that might be obtained in larger studies using the same or similar approaches) generate hypotheses that need to be confirmed through iterative usability studies across the entire design process, concluding in formal clinical evaluations.

ACKNOWLEDGEMENTS

This research was funded by IBM Corp. and the Keck Foundation through the University of Washington Center for Imaging Systems Optimization (CISO). Equipment and facilities were provided by the University of Washington Laboratory for Usability Testing and Evaluation (LUTE) (Judith Ramey, Director). The authors wish to thank the radiologists and Radiology Records personnel of the UW Medical Center who generously donated their time to our study. The authors also wish to acknowledge the work of Susan Hawkins, graduate student in Technical Communication, who was responsible for a large part of the numerical data analysis of the videotapes in this study. We further wish to acknowledge the cooperation of the following: Hospital of the University of Pennsylvania, Philadelphia, PA; Overlake Hospital, Bellevue, WA; and Spahn-Kenedy Memorial Hospital, Kingsville, TX.

NOTES

1. I offer only a selection of the relevant articles from recent SPIE Proceedings:

    Braudes, M. et al. 1989. "A software development and user interface rapid prototyping environment for picture archiving and communication systems (PACS)." SPIE 1093 *Medical Imaging III: PACS System Design and Evaluation* (1989): pp. 220–229.

    Braudes, M. et al. 1984. "Workstation modeling and development: clinical definition of a PACS user interface." SPIE 1093 *Medical Imaging III: PACS System Design and Evaluation* (1989): pp. 376–386.

    Coristine, Tombaugh, and Dillon. 1989. "Observational assessment of field trial site for the implementation of a PACS network." SPIE 1093 *Medical Imaging III: PACS System Design and Evaluation* (1989): pp. 392–398.

    Dillon, G. et al. 1989. "User testing of the image navigation system for a radiological workstation." SPIE 1093 *Medical Imaging III: PACS System Design and Evaluation* (1989): pp. 143–153.

    McNeill, S. 1988. "Comparison of digital workstations and conventional reading for evaluation of user interfaces in digital radiology." SPIE 914 *Medical Imaging II* (1988): pp. 872–876.

O'Malley. 1989. "An iterative approach to development of a PACS display workstation." SPIE 1093 *Medical Imaging III: PACS System Design and Evaluation* (1989): pp. 293–300.

Tombaugh, Dillon, and Coristine. 1989. "Goal setting and user testing to ensure a PACS interface satisfactory to radiologists," SPIE 1093 *Medical Imaging III: PACS System Design and Evaluation* (1989): pp. 345–351.

2. Fetterman, David. 1989. "Ethnography Step by Step," *Applied Social Research Methods* vol. 17. pp. 11–12. Sage Publications, 1989.

3. For an excellent collection of nineteen articles about the value and use of video data, see the special issue of *SIGCHI Bulletin*, vol. 21 no. 2, October 1989, edited by Wendy E. Mackay and Deborah G. Tatar.

Using the CARD and PICTIVE Participatory Design Methods for Collaborative Analysis

Michael J. Muller

U S WEST Advanced Technologies

Rebecca Carr

U S WEST Communications

EXECUTIVE SUMMARY

We describe the adaptation of the CARD and PICTIVE participatory design methods to a situation calling for collaborative analysis. Our discussion considers the strengths and weaknesses of these techniques for analysis, and the relationship of these techniques to other analytical approaches.

INTRODUCTION

At the invitation of the editors, we use this chapter to explore the field-work aspects of a previously published experience with collaborative analysis. We wish to state clearly what is and is not new in this chapter. Muller et al. (1995c) presented an analysis of a portion of this work in terms of scenarios and representations; Muller et al. (1995a) described the contents of the analysis, the relation of the collaborative analysis to convergent quantitative analyses, and some of the organizational implications of the conjoint analyses. The methods used in the analysis have been described in earlier publications (Muller 1991, 1992; Tudor et al. 1993).

In this chapter we focus on how we have used the methods in the context of field-oriented practices, with an emphasis on realistic advice to practitioners like ourselves.

BACKGROUND

We were asked to perform a task analysis of the work of Directory Assistance (DA) telephone operators at U S WEST Communications. The initial goals of our study were to develop a mathematical model of the operators' work, with the intention of using the model to develop quantitative assessments of vendors' technology initiatives toward automating the DA operators' jobs. The sponsoring organization requested the analysis in general form; based on earlier analyses of the work of Toll and Assistance operators (Gray et al 1993; John 1990), our organization proposed to use GOMS/CPM modeling as the analytical method.

Our collaborative analyses were the result of a happy accident. Because there were many factors affecting the work of the DA operators, the formal modeling portion of our analysis (with its heavy reliance on intensive measurement of work performance) was postponed. We had the opportunity to do qualitative work in advance of the planned quantitative work. This, as it turned out, changed everything.

PLANNING THE STUDY

We selected two participatory methodologies for our qualitative analyses, for the most part because they were convenient and appeared likely to produce the information needed at this stage of the analysis.

The CARD (Collaborative Analysis of Requirements and Design) and PICTIVE (Plastic Interface for Collaborative Technology Initiatives through Video Exploration) methods have been used extensively for participatory design. The CARD technique uses physical playing cards with representations of computers systems and/or the users' work domain printed on them for high-level task critique and redesign (Tudor et al. 1993). The PICTIVE technique uses common office materials for low-level, detailed design of the appearance and dynamics of screens, windows, and similar interface components (Muller 1991, 1992). Our use of these techniques was different from our conventional participatory design practice in two major ways:

- At this phase of the analysis, we were not able to work directly with the telephone operators. Instead, we worked with subject matter experts (SMEs) from the training organization within the Operator and Information Services organization. Thus, this was not a participatory activity, because the users did not participate. It was, to a significant extent, interdisciplinary and collaborative.
- We were analyzing work practices, rather than designing systems or work that might be done (in part or in whole) using systems. Thus, we were attempting to document current practices, not invent new ones. Had operators been involved in the team, we might have used the language of Mogensen and Trigg (1992), and called our approach another example of participatory analysis. Without operator participation, it is safest to call it collaborative analysis.

Thus, this work is based on techniques from the broader domain of participatory practices throughout the software lifecycle, a domain that one of us has termed PANDA (for Participatory ANalysis, Design, and Assessment) (Muller 1995). This is to say, there are numerous opportunities to bring users and other stakeholders into software analysis, design, development, and evaluation work at various points in the lifecycle. In one sense, there are individual techniques and practices that can be used within the lifecycle (for surveys, see Kensing and Munk-Madsen 1993; Muller et al. 1995b). There is also a growing number of lifecycle approaches that integrate participatory activities within a lifecycle model (for a survey, see Hallewell Haslwanter 1995). In principle, we might have adapted any of perhaps ten different participatory techniques for our collaborative analysis. We chose CARD and PICTIVE for convenience and familiarity.

Refining the Methods for Work Analysis

In this section we discuss the alterations we made to the CARD and PICTIVE methods.

CARD

Tudor's initial work with CARD had involved literal screen dumps printed onto cardstock. The analyst and the users manipulated these materials to sketch out a system-oriented workflow, and to critique that workflow. Users found it straightforward to express their views of the current work and of the system that supported it, by laying out cards, discarding cards, clipping cards together, and writing on the cards.

However, our analysis was different, for several reasons. First, we were not pursuing Tudor's goal of system assessment. Instead, we were working at a much earlier point in the lifecycle, involving work analysis. Second, we were not attempting to innovate either work methods or systems, and we were not particularly intent upon performing evaluation of work or of technology.

The most important difference was that the DA operators' job involves many non-computer-related work components. One way to describe this work is that it is intensively human-to-human, with computer systems as tools to support human communication and service, or as aids to the operators' skilled performance before the customer as audience. Yet another way to describe the job is that operators and customers engage in collaborative query clarification, with the computer as the last stage in resolving a socially constructed query.

We therefore modified Tudor's initial CARD model in two important ways:

■ In addition to CARD-based representations of conventional computer-oriented functionality (Figure 2.1), we provided explicit CARD-based representations of the noncomputer-based aspects of the operators' work; for example, different types of operator conversational turns, customer conversational turns, and so on. Examples are shown in Figure 2.2.

■ We provided explicit CARD-based representations of operators' mental work; for example, developing a search strategy, planning a search input, using the operators' expert knowledge, performing a mental transformation, and so on. Examples are shown in Figure 2.3.

The representation of non-computer-based work components turned out to be crucial for understanding the operators' work as an integrated human service. The representation of operators' mental work turned out to be crucial for understanding the richness and complexity of real DA work, and for developing a new approach to the support technologies for the job. An example of the results of a CARD session using these materials is shown in Figure 2.4.

PICTIVE

The PICTIVE approach required much less modification than the CARD approach. PICTIVE is, by its nature, very much focused on the computer artifact. We developed large screen images and keyboard images, using removable notes for all of the labeled or shaped compo-

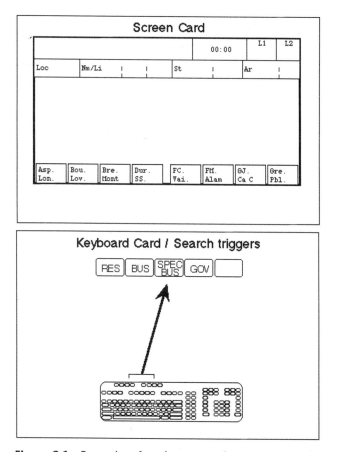

Figure 2.1 Examples of cards representing computer-oriented functionality.

nents. As our work progressed, we used these paper artifacts to be able to point to critical computer components, to annotate them, and to propose replacements or refinements of them to one another. An example is shown in Figure 2.5.

CONDUCTING THE STUDY

With the exception of two sessions, the six analysis sessions took place at or near the operators' work area. This allowed us to work with paper and pencil for the critical analysis portions of the sessions, with the opportunity to turn immediately from the paper to the actual opera-

Figure 2.2 Examples of cards representing events in the operators' work that are not computer-oriented.

tors' workstations, and (when needed) to take live calls and understand certain aspects of the work through direct observation.

On a global level, the project involved two types of analysis that went on simultaneously. First, the team constructed a series of work-oriented representations of operators' work (e.g., Figure 2.4). Second, the team critiqued and refined the provisional class hierarchy of work components that the CARD practitioner provided as a starting point (Figure 2.6).

Our process model was roughly the same as that described for CARD and PICTIVE as participatory design methods (e.g., Muller et al. 1994) see Figure 2.7. We began by making sure that each participant knew the personal and organizational stakes of the other participants. We then engaged in mutual education regarding specific expertise

Figure 2.3 Examples of cards representing operators' mental work.

domains that certain participants believed that the other participants needed to know. These included:

■ Formal requirements for operators' work
■ CARD and PICTIVE as methods

We then explored a series of work scenarios. While each of these might, in practice, take less than a half a minute, discussions of each could go on for over an hour. The methodology, then, stressed the microstructure of operators' work, but allowed us to distort the time dimension of that work in order to meet our analytical needs. Because we were working with paper materials, our time distortions did not impose a burden on any human processes.

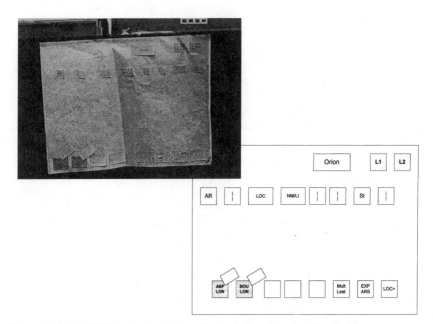

Figure 2.4 A CARD representation of a task flow involved in looking up a number of a residence.

Each session was recorded on videotape. However, the most important "products" of each session turned out to be the CARD materials arrayed against background sheets of papers (e.g., Figure 2.4). We used these later for analysis, and also for presentations to labor and management stakeholders.

Because our work involved the same team over multiple sessions, we were able to introduce one more innovation to the CARD method. In the course of our discussions, we found that it was necessary to develop, refine, and extend the category of operator mental work. We agreed that the original set of cards to represent this area of our analysis was insufficient, and we innovated new cards as we identified new aspects of operator mental work. The CARD practitioner in the group revised and reprinted the CARD materials from one session to another, adding the new types of mental work to the materials. This approach reflected one measure of the group's achievements. Moreover, the reflection of these achievements (and of the growth of our shared knowledge) in the physical form of the cards meant that we could see our achievements easily, and that we could depend upon those achievements in our subsequent work. This approach was also a

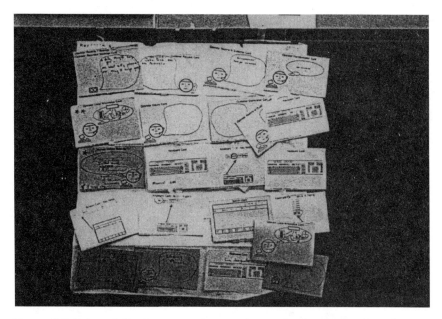

Figure 2.5 Using pictive to represent screen images in the operator's work.

means of "keeping faith" with the group—taking the group's work seriously as an extension of the CARD practitioner's initial, incomplete analysis.

ANALYSING AND INTERPRETING THE DATA

We interpreted the outcomes of the collaborative sessions as evidence that operators perform a portion of their jobs as knowledge workers, exercising sophisticated analysis, judgment, and decision-making as experts in their domain (see also Clement 1994). These interpretations were highly persuasive within multiple organizations, as described below.

Different types of analysis were conducted at different points within the work. Each session was, of course, a form of collaborative analysis, mutual education, and shared innovation. In a second sense, the CARD practitioner had to analyze each session immediately afterwards in order to prepare for the next session (see the previous paragraph's note about refining materials between sessions).

Class Hierarchy of Cards for Directory Assistance CARD Game

Items in **bold** are actual cards. Items that are <u>underscored</u> are classes of cards. Colors of cards within each class are given in [brackets].

- <u>Customer conversation [green]</u>
  Customer request
  Customer clarification
  Customer conversation (other)
- <u>Operator conversation [grey]</u>
  Operator inquiry
  Operator conversation (other)
- <u>Operator mental work [blue]</u>
  Information translation
  Use of local knowledge
  Choose and plan type of search ("strategy")
    - **Named search strategy**
    - **Unnamed search strategy**
    - **Strategy (other)**
- <u>Keyboard activities [yellow]</u>
  Softkey
  Key field
  File trigger key
  ExpLoc and Page keys
  Audio key
  Toll key
  Keyboard (generic)
- <u>Screen activities [orange]</u>
  Personal response system
  Audio response system
  Operator recorded message
  Voice recognition
  Automated voice event (other)
  Automated system action
- <u>Miscellaneous cards [white]</u>
  Title card—("The Directory Assistance CARD Game")
  New ideas card

Figure 2.6 Class hierarchy of work components represented by cards.

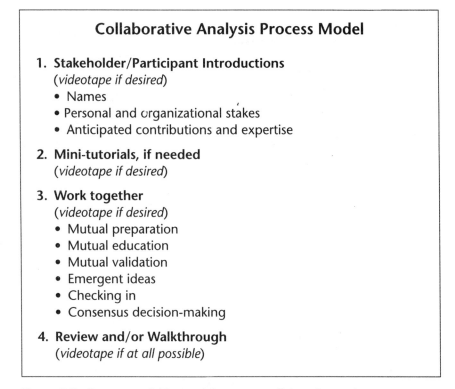

Collaborative Analysis Process Model

1. **Stakeholder/Participant Introductions**
   (*videotape if desired*)
   • Names
   • Personal and organizational stakes
   • Anticipated contributions and expertise

2. **Mini-tutorials, if needed**
   (*videotape if desired*)

3. **Work together**
   (*videotape if desired*)
   • Mutual preparation
   • Mutual education
   • Mutual validation
   • Emergent ideas
   • Checking in
   • Consensus decision-making

4. **Review and/or Walkthrough**
   (*videotape if at all possible*)

Figure 2.7   Process model for participatory or collaborative work.

In a third sense, a different type of analysis took place after all of the sessions were completed. In this third, integrative form of analysis, the CARD practitioner worked alone to translate the work-oriented CARD representations into a systems-oriented engineering vocabulary. This proved remarkably effortless, much to everyone's surprise. Figure 2.8 provides an example of a GOMS/CPM-style timeline analysis that was based on the work-oriented analysis previously shown in Figure 2.4.

In reporting, we provided a series of analyses in the formats of both Figure 2.4 (work-oriented) and Figure 2.8 (systems-oriented). In the language of an influential analysis (Floyd 1987), the work-oriented representation of Figure 2.4 is part of a process-oriented paradigm, and the systems-oriented representation of Figure 2.8 is part of a product-oriented paradigm. The success of the project appears to have derived in part from making a series of convincing translations between these two paradigms.

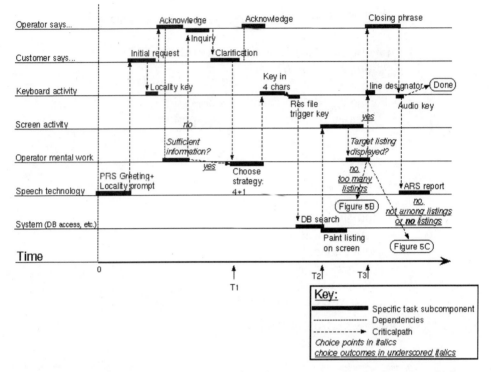

Figure 2.8 A timeline representation of the task flow involved in looking up the telephone number of a residence.

We provided work-oriented and systems-oriented representations in various reports to technical management, business management, and labor. Different constituencies made different usages of the two types of representations. Interestingly, all constituencies appeared to gravitate toward the work-oriented representations.

Subsequent Quantitative Analyses

As we mentioned in the "Background" section of this chapter, our original instructions were to conduct a quantitative analysis of the work of DA operators. We were eventually allowed to bring recording equipment into DA offices, and we conducted the planned analyses—but not for the original purposes.

Informed by our qualitative analyses, we refocused the quantitative analyses on critical attributes of expert performance. We used the quantitative analyses (a) to confirm what we had found qualitatively, and (b) to develop numerical estimates of the importance of the qualitative findings. This story is told in detail in Muller et al. (1995a). In brief, the quantitative analyses strengthened our claims that operators perform a large proportion of their jobs as knowledge workers. The combination of the qualitative and quantitative results appeared to be quite convincing. The qualitative results gave concrete, contextualized examples of knowledge work, and the quantitative results showed that the knowledge work was a major attribute of the job.

IMPACTING THE DESIGN

There were three major impacts of this work. First, the work-oriented representations proved valuable for convincing both technical management and business management that operators perform important parts of their jobs as knowledge workers (subsequent quantitative analyses provided additional support for this claim; see Muller et al. 1995). This, in turn, caused the company to think differently about the job and about various technology programs that were intended to automate portions of the job (e.g., Lennig 1990; McEwan and Bergman 1993). This new thinking led to new analyses during vendor technology trials, and to important new understandings about why the vendor technologies did not initially perform as expected, thus revealing how to improve them (MacRae, Muller, and Springer 1994).

The second was on the field of HCI. Previous reports had characterized operators' work as entirely routine (Gray et al. 1993; John 1990), and operators themselves as "surrogates" for the customers, who were the intentional users (Lawrence et al. 1994). During the same period, Kidd (1994) developed the concept of knowledge work that is done by a class of people who are named "knowledge workers," rather than by many different people (whose work may in fact be a combination of knowledge work, clerical work, and other types of work). Our qualitative analyses, combined with subsequent quantitative analysis, made a strong case for treating operators' work as knowledge work, and operators as expert consultants who incidentally use a computer system to provide quality service to their customers. We could then turn the notion of knowledge workers around, and ask about the non-knowledge work components of the people considered to be "knowledge workers"—such as ourselves. Thus, our analyses contributed to a blurring of the conventional boundaries between people called "knowledge workers" and other people whose work is traditionally held in less esteem.

The third impact was based on our narrow escape. As noted earlier, the original plan was to perform GOMS/CPM modeling on the DA operators' job, based in part on the spectacular success of similar modeling on the work of Toll and Assistance operators (John, 1990). Because of the effects of other workplace factors, we were temporarily prevented from collecting the data that would have formed the basis of the GOMS/CPM analyses. During the interim period, we conducted the qualitative analysis described here. The qualitative analysis convinced us that the original GOMS/CPM analysis would have failed to capture the most important components of operators' work—that is, the knowledge-based, skills-based components that are the foundation of quality customer service. If we had pursued the original plan, we would have made a big mistake. We were fortunate to be forced to do qualitative, collaborative work in advance of the more formal, quantitative work. We proposed that most analytic projects include an initial qualitative component as a standard part of their structure.

ASSESSING THE COST/BENEFIT

U S WEST has a long tradition of field work, held in balance with a tradition of laboratory work. Our work was perceived within this matrix as being a good example of relatively inexpensive, highly effective field work. The total session time required from subject matter experts (SMEs) was less than forty staff hours (divided over the three operator services training staff). The total time required for materials development and production was less than twenty staff hours. The total analysis and documentation time was perhaps twice that. This work paid for itself in understanding, redirection of effort, downstream technology understanding, and improved mutual understanding and work relationships among all the stakeholders in the technology explorations regarding operators' work.

REFLECTING ON OUR EXPERIENCE

In this section we review the insights we developed as a result of this work.

Questioning Assumptions

One of the strengths of our approach was that our methods were sensitive to breakdowns and other disconfirmations of assumptions (e.g., Bödker 1991). The detailed consideration of operators' practices helped us to understand, for example, that DA operators' work could not be modeled through a small set of routinized, invariant call flows (as required by most formal modeling approaches). Similarly, our exploration of the strategies, knowledges, and judgments involved in operators' work showed us that the job could not be described in terms of the "routine operations" that involved "no problem solving," as had previously been published regarding other operators' work (e.g., Gray et al. 1993; John 1990). In our analysis, the formal modeling approaches could not be applied to work that is as rich and as varied as that of DA operators.

We suspect that many other qualitative methods would have had similar virtues of requiring us to reflect on what we had taken for granted. What was crucial for our success was the postponement of focused, quantitative work until the qualitative work had given us insights into the most important work attributes to study. What was crucial for our qualitative understanding was our dialogues across our different backgrounds, knowledges, and assumptions. We were aided in our mutual understanding by the concrete, contextualized, low-tech "common languages" of the CARD and PICTIVE materials. However, we do not believe that these materials were the only way to achieve communication across differences. Indeed, other chapters in this book make powerful arguments for the use of other qualitative methods to achieve similar goals.

Collaborative—not Participatory—Analysis

The most obvious problem with our work is that it was not truly participatory. It was collaborative, in that an interdisciplinary team of SMEs and one technologist worked together. It was qualitative in that the analysis developed in this work provided no quantitative data, but it was nonetheless convincing for the analysis team, as well as their technical, managerial, and labor stakeholders. However, the work suffered actually and potentially from a lack of operator involvement. The actual problems that we encountered were these:

■ All participants were managers, although some of the SMEs had previously worked as operators. Nonetheless, we represented a management world view, and we were not compelled by the presence of labor representatives to work in a way that was informed by the daily realities of the job.
■ Initially, the operators did not know that the work was going on. When they learned of the work (from us), they were initially skepti-

cal and distrustful. Their initial buy-in would have made the work easier, and would have improved the quality of the work outcome.

■ Because the operators did not know about the qualitative work until after it was completed, they could not help us to define objectives or to develop research questions that would serve operators' and their union's needs (e.g., Communications Workers of America [CWA] and U S WEST 1994). Much of the work that could have been accomplished in this way had to be done later, at greater expense—or has never been done.

The potential problems are more worrisome:

■ The outcome of this work was considered a good description of operators' real work. However, this may have had more to do with the beliefs and practices of the particular analysis team, than it did with the structure of the study. If different people had been involved in a similarly structured study, they could easily have chosen analytical tools that were less sensitive to work conditions. They could thus have easily developed a different, more traditional reductive model. This model would have been a poor fit to actual working conditions, and would have been a major problem for operators to live within.

It is troubling that so much depended on the choice of method, and perhaps on the sympathies of the analysts. We look forward to the day when practices such as CARD and PICTIVE (and other work-oriented analyses described in this book) become more institutionalized, both within organizations and within the field of HCI. Without a firmer commitment to methods that respect work and workers, we will be in danger of reductive analyses that fail to capture the human intricacies of work, and that fail to create workplaces that we would hope to work in.

REFERENCES

Bödker, S. 1991. *"Through the interface: A human activity approach to user interface design."* Hillsdale, NJ: Erlbaum.

Clement, A. 1994. "Computing at work: Empowering action by "low-level users."" *Communications of the ACM* **37**(1), 52–63, 105.

Communications Workers of America, International Brotherhood of

Electrical Workers, and U S WEST. 1994. *"Job design team future vision."*

Floyd, C. 1987. "Outline of a paradigm change in software engineering." In Bjerknes, G., Ehn, P., and Kyng, M. (Eds.) 1987. *Computers and democracy: A Scandinavian challenge.* Brookfield, VT: Gower.

Gray, W.D., John, B.E., and Atwood, M.E. 1993. "Project Ernestine: Validating a GOMS analysis for predicting and explaining real-world task performance." *Human-Computer Interaction* **8**, 237–304.

Hallewell Haslwanter, J.D. 1995. *Participatory design methods in the context of human-computer interaction.* M. Sc. thesis. Sydney, Australia: University of Technology.

John, B.E. 1990. "Extensions of GOMS analyses to expert performance requiring perception of dynamic visual and auditory information." *Proceedings of CHI'90.* Seattle, WA: ACM, 107–115.

Kensing, F. and Munk-Madsen, A. 1993. "PD: Structure in the toolbox." *Communications of the ACM* **36**(6), 78–85.

Kidd, A. 1994. "The marks are on the knowledge worker." *Proceedings of CHI'94.* Boston, MA: ACM, 186–191.

Lawrence, D., Atwood, M.E., and Dews, S. 1994. "Surrogate users: Mediating between social and technical interaction." *Proceedings of CHI'94.* Boston, MA: ACM, 399–404.

Lennig, M. 1990. "Putting speech recognition to work in the telephone network." *IEEE Computer.* August 1990. 35–41.

MacRae, M., Muller, M.J., and Springer, C.J. 1994. "U S WEST's enhanced speech technology trial." ADAS workshop (notes). Atlanta, GA: Northern Telecom.

McEwen, S. and Bergman, H. 1993. "Automating directory assistance service: A human factors case study." *Human Factors in Telecommunications: 14th International Symposium.* Darmstadt, Germany: R.v. DeckerUs Verlag, G. Schenck, 301–309.

Mogensen, P. and Trigg, R., 1992. "Using artifacts as triggers for participatory analysis." *PDC'92: Proceedings of the Participatory Design Conference.* Cambridge, MA: Computer Professionals for Social Responsibility, 55–62.

Muller, M.J. 1995. "Diversity and depth in participatory design: Working with a mosaic of stakeholders in the software lifecycle." Tutorial at CHI'95. Denver, CO: ACM.

Muller, M.J. 1991. "PICTIVE—An exploration in participatory design." *Proceedings of CHI'91.* 225–231.

Muller, M.J. 1992. "Retrospective on a year of participatory design using the PICTIVE technique." *Proceedings of CHI'92.* Monterey, CA: ACM, 455–462.

Muller, M.J. 1995a. "Telephone operators as knowledge workers: Consultants who meet customer needs." *Mosaic of creativity: Proceedings of CHI'95*. Denver, CO: ACM, 130–137.

Muller, M.J., Hallewell Haslwanter, J.D., and Dayton, T. 1995b. "A participatory poster of participatory practices." *Proceedings of Computers in Context: Joining Forces in Design*. 10–20 (Arhus Denmark, August 1995) and *Proceedings of IRIS 18: Design in Context*, p. i (Gjern Denmark: Gothenburg Studies in Informatics, Report 7, June 1995).

Muller, M.J., 1995c. "Bifocal tools for scenarios and representations in participatory activities with users." J. Carroll (Ed.), *Scenario-based design for human-computer interaction*. New York: John Wiley & Sons, Inc.

Muller, M.J., Wildman, D.M., and White, E.A. 1994. "Participatory design through games and other group exercises." Tutorial at *CHI'94*. Boston, MA: ACM, April 1994.

Tudor, L.G. 1993. "A participatory design technique for high-level task analysis, critique, and redesign: The CARD method." *Proceedings of the Human Factors and Ergonomics Society 1993 Meeting*. Seattle, WA. October 1993, 295–299.

3

The Ethnographic Interview in User-Centered Work/Task Analysis

Larry E. Wood

Brigham Young University

EXECUTIVE SUMMARY

An interviewing strategy for work/task analysis of potential clients of software support applications is described herein. It draws on methods from the disciplines of Ethnography and Cognitive Science. The ultimate goal is to produce a descriptive model of current work practice that can be used in user-centered design of a software application. The interviewing strategy is characterized as a top-down approach where semistructured interviews are used to develop a framework for guiding direct observations of real work. Various types of questions are introduced that are designed to be used by analysts in an opportunistic fashion to suit the particular analysis goals. It is recommended that the interviews focus initially on the identification of work objects, their relationships, their categories, and their discriminating features. That information can then be used to develop task representations in which the relevant objects are used by clients to accomplish their work. Suggestions are provided for describing and documenting a work model.

BACKGROUND

In a recent article Hughs, King, Rodden, and Anderson (Hughes et al. 1995) discussed the role of Ethnography in interactive systems design.

One of the points made by those authors was that "Ethnography has a role to play in various phases of system design and makes different contributions to them." Whereas the issues addressed by the authors are of a general nature, the work reported here focuses specifically on the ethnographic interview and its potential role in the design process. The techniques described are adaptations of those developed by myself and my colleagues previously for use in knowledge elicitation for knowledge-based (expert) systems (Wood and Ford 1993; Ford and Wood 1992).

The interviewing techniques are described in the context of a software development project in which I have been involved. The purpose of the application is to expedite the ordering of telecommunication services (telephone and electronic network services) for all departments on the campus of Brigham Young University. Each academic or support unit has a designated representative to coordinate ordering of Telecommunication services (Telecom Services) for their unit. Currently, orders were processed via memoranda, following telephone and face-to-face negotiation between the unit representative and a representative from Telecom Services.

A design team for the project was organized, consisting of the manager of the Telecom Services department, the department's chief analyst/programmer, myself (acting as a usability analyst/interaction designer), and five potential clients of the order application. The clients varied widely in their experience and scope of responsibility. Experience varied from less than a year to more than ten years, and scope of responsibility varied from a small academic department (15 faculty and staff) to the entire Law School (approximately 700 faculty and staff).

GUIDING PRINCIPLES AND WORKING ASSUMPTIONS

Although the focus of this article is on interviewing techniques, I do not mean to imply that interviews are adequate and sufficient for meeting all the needs of work/task analysis. As I will discuss, it is also vitally important to observe clients doing work in their natural settings and to gather and document examples of real work. It is my goal to place ethnographic interviewing in the broader context of interaction design and to provide guidelines for making client interviews as productive as possible while also providing some concrete examples of the application of those guidelines.

The general framework presented here, in which ethnographic interviewing is embedded, I characterize generally as a top-down approach. This is in contrast to a bottom-up approach, which would be more characteristic of various versions of Contextual Inquiry (Wixon and Holtzblatt 1990; Holtzblatt and Beyer 1993). I refer to my approach as top-down because I use semistructured interviewing with clients prior to doing systematic observations of work. Doing so provides a general framework in which to interpret and document specific observations and samples of real work. On the other hand, I refer to Contextual Inquiry as a bottom-up approach because of its usual emphasis on first observing and gathering large samples of real work (i.e., collecting data), and then inductively abstracting work flows and other more general descriptions of the work/tasks being analyzed (i.e., analyzing the data).

In performing work/task analysis, I find it particularly important to consider what is generally understood about the nature of expertise, because potential clients of an application are experts in the work which the software application is intended to support, whether or not they are considered experts in the use of computer software. Therefore, it is important to recognize and respect their point of view throughout the development cycle. As suggested by LaFrance (1989), one reason that work/task analysis can be such a difficult problem for analysts is because they continue to underestimate the complexity of expertise in a given domain of knowledge. There is also a body of literature in cognitive psychology (Reimann and Chi 1989) on the nature of expertise that has implications for how one should work with experts to gain an understanding of how they accomplish their work in a specialized domain.

Important aspects of expertise that I find particularly relevant to work/task analysis are the organization of expert knowledge, the tacit nature of expert knowledge, the problem of simplification bias on the part of interviewers, and the exercise of translation competence on the part of experts. Each of these aspects will be described, and then they will be specifically addressed relative to particular interviewing techniques discussed later.

Organization of Expert Knowledge

Because concepts in human memory are obviously associated with one another, the experience of remembering or being cued with one concept results in the recall of additional relevant concepts. It is helpful to keep in mind that studies (Mitchell and Chi 1984) have shown that expert knowledge is generally organized hierarchically, at a macro level (i.e., using various taxonomic organizations such as categories and subcategories) although many other types of relationships are also present, depending on the particular domain of expertise. At the micro level, expert knowledge is stored as organized "chunks" of frequently

occurring patterns or schemas (Chi et al. 1981), with attached procedures for appropriate responses when those patterns are recognized in
problem-solving situations.

In relation to the nature of the organization of expert knowledge, I
have found it useful to distinguish between *object* knowledge and
process knowledge. Object knowledge includes the conceptual entities
and objects (both concrete and abstract) in a particular domain and
their various relationships and categories. Taxonomic relationships
(such as types and subtypes, parts, and distinguishing features or characteristics) are particularly important. Process knowledge, on the other
hand, is comprised of the knowledge required for solving domain problems **using** relevant domain concepts and objects. Another way to characterize this distinction is a knowledge of "what" versus a knowledge of
"how." As described later, I structure interviews for work/task analysis
around this distinction.

Tacit Knowledge

It is a common observation that much of an expert's problem-solving
knowledge has become automatic or tacit through extensive use, and
there has been considerable debate about its accessibility, even to the
expert (Ericsson and Simon 1993). In early stages of skill learning, an
individual consciously considers various items of knowledge during
problem solving. In well-learned tasks, much of the relevant knowledge
is no longer consciously available during problem solving, although this
does not mean that it has been "forgotten." It does mean that it may be
difficult for an expert to articulate it, especially when asked to do so
directly, independently of, or even during task performance.

While direct access to tacit knowledge may not be feasible, it is
often possible for an analyst to use information about an expert's view
of the domain to constrain inferences about tacit knowledge. As discussed later, tacit problem-solving knowledge often manifests during
observation of actual problem-solving episodes.

Simplification Bias and Translation Competence

Because an analyst is often a relative novice in the problem domain
being analyzed, there exists a potential for errors because of a tendency for the analyst to conceptually *simplify* the descriptions of problem solving provided by the expert. In an attempt to minimize the
potential effects of this "simplification bias," the interviewing techniques described here have been adapted from the disciplines of
Ethnography (Spradley 1979; Werner and Schoepfle 1987) and Cogni-

tive Anthropology (Anderson and Alty 1995) because researchers in those disciplines face a similar problem when they are attempting to elicit cultural information from informants (or cultural "experts") in unfamiliar societies. Spradley (1979) makes a convincing case for the importance of domain-specific language in this effort. He notes that potential bias can be particularly critical when the members of a culture under investigation use terms familiar to the researcher, because important differences in the meanings of the terms are not readily apparent to the researcher.

Spradley (1979) describes another potential source of bias, which he terms the exercise of *translation competence* . In contrast to simplification bias, which occurs on the part of an interviewer, translation competence is a characteristic of the cultural informant. It is expressed when informants *translate* the reality of their culture in order to explain it to an outsider. The problem is that the more an informant translates for the convenience of an investigator, the more the cultural reality becomes oversimplified and distorted.

In an effort to avoid translation bias, Spradley (1979) advocates an approach to questioning which makes minimal assumptions (on behalf of the researcher) about informants' knowledge and uses information the informants provide as the basis for further questioning. The researcher first uses very general probing techniques to persuade informants to talk freely about their domains in a global sense. An informant's language is recorded and then examined for category labels and other linguistic cues that are domain-specific. This information is then used to probe informants for additional information. Throughout the process it is necessary to verify that the researcher's emerging understanding of the domain accurately reflects the informant's expertise. For this reason, the interviewing strategies described here are considered semistructured rather than structured. Rather than designing *a priori* a specific set of questions to be to be asked in a specific order, analysts have various types of questions at their disposal to be used in opportunistic ways, depending on the demands of the situation.

INTERVIEWING STRATEGIES

As indicated earlier, this approach draws heavily upon ethnographic methods, but also makes use of techniques from cognitive psychology (Anderson 1994). Furthermore, it is centered around the distinction between object and process knowledge (described earlier). The goals of work/task analysis to be supported by the interviewing techniques described here are similar to those of Contextual Inquiry: to develop a work model describing clients' current work practices, and then to develop an enhanced work model (proposing ways in which the clients' work can be re-designed and enhanced by introducing a software support application). The latter model then is intended to provide a basis for the design of the application (both the underlying functionality and the user interaction/interface) to provide access to that functionality.

Object Identification

Because much of the information about relevant objects and their related categories and concepts is reflected in a client's use of domain-specific terminology, a significant amount of the analyst's early efforts should be spent documenting the client's use of work-related language. It is important to remember that a word or phrase need not be obviously unfamiliar to the analyst in order to be important. For example, in the domain of Telecom Services, the term **ethernet port** might have little meaning to an analyst unfamiliar with a networking domain, and would be an obvious point of focus in an interview. What might not be obvious, however, is that the term **data connection** has special significance in this domain (i.e., a connection from a computer workstation to the campus network through a Rolm telephone set), because most analysts would be familiar with the term **data** and might mistakenly assume their understanding of the term applies in this context. Thus the analyst should attend particularly to all terms and phrases that are used frequently by the client to make certain that such assumptions are tested.

The goal in the early stages of interviewing is to direct the client's attention toward the task of describing the structure of the work domain (e.g., objects and their relationships). It is important for the analyst to arrange for the client to describe the work practice in a natural way, using domain-specific terms for important objects. However, the analyst must also be concerned about keeping the client focused on that portion of the work that has been targeted for analysis. Otherwise, the interview can meander and become inefficient. It is, therefore, important for the analyst to be guiding the general direction and flow of the interview, while letting the client freely and naturally express her/his conceptualization of it. Specific types of questions are designed to assist the analyst in meeting these goals.

One way to elicit a large sample of work-related terminology is to ask Grand Tour questions, which encourage the client to verbally "show the analyst around" the physical, temporal, and abstract space of the work domain. Table 3.1 shows specific examples of such questions.

Grand Tour questioning is of particular utility early in analysis, but can be used whenever the client identifies a new subproblem. I have found the most useful types of Grand Tour questions to be Task-Related and Guided questions (see Table 3.1). Because the analyst's ultimate goal is to understand the tasks (and task interrelationships) required to perform some set of a client's work, these types of questions help keep the client focused on relevant aspects of the work domain, without causing too narrow a focus too early. Asking about typical problem-solving episodes (using Typical questions—see Table 3.1) often elicits general categories used in frequently occurring situations.

Case-Focused questions (see Table 3.1) are also useful in eliciting domain terminology. Cases are indexed in memory by the categories of which they are members. These types of questions elicit further termi-

TABLE 3.1 Object Identification Questions.

Question Type	Example
Grand Tour:	
Task-Related	"Could you discuss the major steps you go through in filling a request for services from a member of your unit?"
Guided	"Could you show me one of the previous orders you have placed, and point out the different parts?"
Typical	"Could you tell me about a typical request from one of the members of your unit?"
Case-Focused:	
Example	"Can you show me an example of a face plate template?"
Personal Experience	"You've probably had some interesting experiences dealing with requests for face plate configurations. Tell me about some of them."
Native-Language:	
Direct Language	"What do you call the buttons that allow one to select a particular line on a set?"
Hypothetical-Interaction	"How would you describe the various types of jacks to another Telecom services liaison?"
Use	"What purpose does the auto-intercom feature serve?"

nology used to characterize work-related objects by evoking the client's description of the characteristics and details of particular problem-solving episodes. They also provide a basis for keeping an interview focused on relevant topics, especially if a client tends to get side-tracked. Obviously, Case-Focused questions require reference to specific examples of work and provide the basis for further questioning about process knowledge, as will be discussed later. Their main function in early stages of analysis is to provide cues for retrieval of information about work-related objects, abstract as well as concrete.

Example questions (see Table 3.1) help the analyst to obtain more detail about terms that are already identified. Personal Experience questions (see Table 3.1) are also useful for this purpose, but can be a source of distraction if used too early in analysis. The most useful domain abstractions for early analysis are those that are relevant to many potential situations in a domain. Hypothetical-Interaction questions provide the analyst with indirect access to a larger "community" of domain experts. Communication about domain problems and knowledge between experts within this community is one of the processes that fosters the development and use of specialized domain terminology, or jargon (Spradley 1979).

Although most of the Object Identification questions are designed to elicit natural domain descriptions in a rather indirect way, there will undoubtedly be times when this strategy will fail. As discussed earlier, Spradley (1979) warns that cultural experts tend to translate their knowledge into terms they believe the interviewer will find easier to understand. Direct Language questions (see Table 3.1) can be used when this is suspected.

One technique often used by ethnographers to elicit informants' natural descriptions of terms and concepts is to ask how terms, tools, and concepts are *used* rather than what they *are* or *mean*. Direct questions about meaning tend to encourage the expert to translate. Queries about Use (see Table 3.1) prompt the informant to describe the context in which a particular term or object plays a role. This description provides information which can be used to structure even more in-depth questioning.

Perhaps the most important technique, given our focus on language, is to phrase questions to a client in domain-specific terminology. An analyst's consistent use of terminology different from that of the client will encourage the client to translate. Using the domain-specific language, however, provides a context of familiarity and encourages a client to focus on the work domain itself rather than the analyst's methods and unfamiliarity with the domain.

Whenever possible, it is preferable to interview clients in their natural work setting, i.e., the setting in which the expert usually solves problems (Bell and Hardiman 1989; Holtzblatt and Beyer 1993). The familiar surroundings serve as further cues to the knowledge clients use in performing their work. There is evidence (Mitchell and Chi 1984; Werner and Schoepfle 1987) indicating that individuals select a limited number of all possible associations for report in any given interviewing context. It would be premature to conclude that knowledge about a given term or topic is *tacit* and completely unavailable to clients simply because they fail to respond in a particular questioning context. Rather, it is advisable to extend questioning about each term over a number of interviewing contexts in order to maximize the total amount of information retrieved.

Object Relationships

In order to identify the relationships among domain categories and objects, an analyst can use questioning techniques that explore the rich, integrated organizational structure of a client's knowledge. These techniques are based on the general principle that concepts in memory are associated with one another, and that remembering or being cued with one or more domain concepts will result in the recall of additional, related concepts.

As discussed earlier, an important strategy, given the focus on language, is to phrase questions to the client using domain-specific terminology that has already been obtained in responses to previous questions. For object relationships, an analyst needs to look for category labels. A particular category term may be associated with a number of subcategories, each of which are related to the category label by a particular functional relationship. Examples of Object Relationship questions are presented in Table 3.2.

Suppose, for example, in answer to the task-related Grand Tour question listed in Table 3.1 above, a Telecom Services coordinator replied "I ask department members if they will need any network applications, in addition to their normal types of telephone use." This statement indicates that there are at least two subcategory terms in the domain defined by the category term *use* and the semantic relationship *types*. These two entities are alike in that both are types of telecommunications use, and it is likely that the client can provide further information about other types and make meaningful distinctions among them.

The most fruitful way of eliciting such domain structure is to first identify the category label and functional relationship from a sample of a client's language elicited through Object Identification questions (see Table 3.1). Then the analyst should elicit a list of category members by asking Category Member questions (see Table 3.2). Any objects for which the analyst is uncertain regarding category membership can be clarified by asking additional Category Membership questions. Once the client indicates that there are no more members in a particular category, the analyst should elicit the relevant features and dimensions of contrast that discriminate the members of a category from one another in meaningful ways for work. This is accomplished by asking a number of Contrast questions (see Table 3.2). As before, it is important to attend to the client's terminology for these dimensions and features.

The best place to begin building domain hierarchies may be with *basic-level* domain terms (Lakoff 1987; Rosch 1973), which can be tentatively identified from their frequency of use by the client, their lexical brevity (note the prevalence of acronyms and other abbreviated forms in the jargon of many domains), and, to a lesser extent, by their unfamiliarity to the analyst. The use of Contrast questions (see Table 3.2) for more information at this level exploits the larger number of distinctions and associations to these key concepts in an expert's memory.

Limiting requests for distinctions to contrast sets of category members helps an analyst avoid the problem of eliciting artificial distinctions. Ethnographers have found that informants will give *test question responses* in an attempt to provide the *right* answer, and will sometimes identify distinctions that are real, but not actually relevant to the use of

TABLE 3.2 Object Relationship Questions.

Question Type	Example
Relationship:	
Category Label	"What are the different types of telecommunication uses?"
Category Member	"Are *network apps* and *FAX/Card Readers* both types of telecommunications use?"
Contrast:	
Directed Contrast	"Could you look through this order memo and show me what other items are considered *network apps*?"
Dyadic Contrast	"What differences are there between *intercom groups* and *pick groups*?"

the objects. A constant focus on the structure of a client's work-related knowledge is an attempt to avoid this difficulty. At this point, it should be noted here that although I have emphasized categorical relationships in this discussion, there will obviously be other important relationships that must be understood (e.g., part-whole, attributes, and cause-effect), depending on the domain under study (Reigeluth et al. 1994).

I would like to note that although Object Identification questions and Object Relationship questions have been discussed in different sections, I do no mean to imply that the information should be sought from clients in any rigid order. As suggested earlier, the advantage of semistructured interviewing is that various types of questions can be used opportunistically. I usually find it convenient to mix the two types of questions to suit a particular situation and set of goals.

Work Model Development and Documentation

I prefer to limit my interviews to approximately an hour, and I tape record each one for later analysis and interpretation. I prefer not to interrupt clients, and I find that I simply can't capture all that they are telling me without doing so. Therefore, during the interview, I take only enough notes to keep it flowing. Following each interview, I review the tapes and my notes, and analyze and document the results. I then ask the client to review the description prior to the subsequent interview. At the beginning of each subsequent interview, I invite the client to make note of my errors in interpretation, and then we continue to extend and expand the model appropriately. See the Appendix for a detailed account of the methods used in interview analysis, a description of work model development, and a description of the work model.

Process Knowledge

Once a large portion of the Object knowledge has been modeled, the analyst can proceed to an examination of how clients use the objects and their categories, distinctions, and attributes to accomplish their work. It is useful at this stage to bear in mind two of the characteristics of expertise. First, it has been shown (Chi et al. 1981) that experts represent problems at a level of underlying principles and abstractions. Second, the strategies that experts use in solving problems are sometimes common across domains, and are sometimes domain-specific (Reimann and Chi 1989). The particular representations and strategies are often elusive and must be explicitly sought by a variety of methods.

Perhaps the most widely used technique developed in cognitive science to investigate problem solving strategies is think-aloud protocol generation and analysis. The term "protocol analysis" represents a family of techniques used to examine subjects' verbalizations about their problem-solving processes. Ericsson and Simon (1993) have observed that the analysis of a verbal protocol must be preceded by a domain definition phase, during which the researchers must exhaustively catalogue the labels for objects, concepts, etc. referred to in the protocol. This is consistent with my concern regarding object knowledge.

While one obviously could begin a work/task analysis with think-aloud protocols generated in the context of work-related tasks I have found it most useful to first obtain a preliminary understanding of the relevant work objects, as described earlier. Following this, it has proven considerably easier to understand how the objects are used in work-related tasks and procedures, rather than attempting to understand the objects as well as the procedures used on/with them concurrently. As I use them, methods for protocol generation simply become additional interviewing techniques. Reasoning and problem-solving strategies emerge from a variety of think-aloud protocols generated by asking clients to describe their thought processes as they solve specific work problems or cases.

There are at least three types of protocol-generating procedures that have been used in studying problem solving. As shown in Table 3.3, Concurrent Think Aloud questions simply request an expert to report the contents of conscious awareness during the solution of a domain problem. Ericsson and Simon (1993) caution that this procedure can only yield meaningful results when the task being performed concurrently with the protocol does not require the use of verbalization or other processes that tax the resources of working memory. Even when this condition holds, a problem solver is likely to provide an incomplete account of the moment-to-moment contents of consciousness. Information that is processed automatically will often not be reported at all. However, these results will still be valuable, because they provide information about the sequence in which the expert attends to various problem features and the various subgoals for which these features are relevant.

Aided Recall questions (see Table 3.3), which are a type of retrospective (rather than concurrent) protocol generation, can be used to followup results obtained in concurrent think-aloud protocols. This technique, which has been used successfully in eliciting descriptions of expertise (Kuipers and Kassirer 1983), involves video- or audio-taping the performance of an expert engaged in problem-solving and then reviewing this record with the expert at a later time, with emphasis on her/his thoughts at a particular stage of problem solving. This procedure creates a situation in which recall of processing is cued by an unbiased record of the expert's own performance. A variation on aided-recall, called cross-examination (see Table 3.3), has been used successfully by Kuipers, Moskowitz, and Kassirer (1988) to probe the limits of knowledge directly. After completing a concurrent think-aloud protocol on a particular problem, the expert is asked specific questions about it, particularly aspects that seem vague or uncertain to an analyst.

In developing work/task models of clients' work, the *problems* clients attempt to solve are obviously those that define the designated work. Therefore, any use of protocol generation should be done in the context of that work. It should be obvious in the context of any client-centered design approach that observations would be of real work episodes (specific examples of work tasks) from which more general descriptions can be derived.

Process knowledge, like object knowledge, must be represented in some manner in a work model description for future reference by the analyst and other members of the development team, especially clients. Particularly for review purposes, I have found it helpful to represent work/task descriptions both at an abstract/summary level and at a more detailed level. For the abstract level, I currently use structured outlines, an example of which is found in Figure 3.4 of the Appendix (see the Appendix for additional information regarding the analysis

TABLE 3.3 Think Aloud Protocol Generation Questions.

Question Type	Example
Concurrent Think Aloud	"Think out loud while you generate an order for adding an ethernet connection to a faculty member's office as described in this request. Do not worry about talking in complete sentences or *making sense.*"
Aided Recall (retrospective protocol)	"As we review this tape of the order you just generated, say whatever you remember about what you were thinking. Stop the tape or rewind whenever you want."
Cross-Examination	"How did you decide which type of *jack splitter* to request for the installation of this new ethernet connection?"

and documentation of process knowledge). For more detailed descriptions, some form of scenario development is very important (Carroll 1995). I find it particularly important to have representations that are understandable to the clients whose work is being modeled. Otherwise, it is very difficult for them to verify that the task/work models are valid and complete, from their perspective.

I document segments of task descriptions as they emerge during early phases of analysis (as might be the case when asking a task-related Grand Tour question originally intended to stimulate a client to talk about work-related objects), and then I fill out details through think-aloud protocols generated in the context of specific cases or examples. They are then validated against specific work examples, as discussed below.

WORK MODEL VALIDATION

It should be obvious that a constant concern during work/task analysis is to develop a valid model of the work performed by clients, including the ways they think about it—which a potential application will support. There are, of course, limitations to what can be obtained using the interviewing techniques discussed here and any resulting static description, with its combination of verbal and graphic representations. That is, of course, why is it important to conduct the interviews in the normal work context when possible, with a client being able to refer to work objects and artifacts during the interview. As discussed earlier, I prefer to conduct a series of interviews, approximately an hour in length, with time in between to analyze the results, update the work model description, and allow the client to review it prior to a subsequent interview.

It is imperative that the work model be based on real work episodes and products. Not only does this help ensure accuracy of the work model in early stages of development, but the examples and products (as long as they are reasonably representative) can be used to verify a final version of the work model and to develop more general scenarios. If the model can *run* with examples of real work, then the analyst can be reasonably confident about its validity at that stage of development (Johnson et al. 1995). Furthermore, those examples (and scenarios developed from them) can be used to verify decisions across further stages of development (e.g., interface prototyping and formal usability testing of a running application).

A strategic question that I have not yet addressed has to do with combining the results of interviews from various clients. In the case of the Telecom Services order application described here, I chose to work extensively with one client to develop a comprehensive model of the work involved in constructing orders. Copies of the description of that model were then circulated to the other members of the development team, and they were asked to review it. The client members of the team were asked to add their particular perspectives during individual interview sessions with each of them, in turn. Those different perspectives were then incorporated into a revised model and recirculated to all members for their further comment. A final interview was then conducted with each member of the team, and further revisions were made to the model until we collectively arrived at a composite work model with which everyone was satisfied. Appended to the final version of the model were scenarios and samples of representative orders previously requested by various clients. In addition, various suggestions from team members about how an application could enhance the ordering process were also appended.

Combining the interview results from multiple users the way I have described has, of course, both advantages and disadvantages. The biggest advantage is its efficiency, compared to the time required to develop complete work models independently with several clients and then to combine them into a representative composite model. A disadvantage is the risk of biasing the responses of all but the first interviewee, which goes against one of the basic tenets of the ethnographic approach. I have not collected formal data on this question, but I have found this to be another area in which samples of real work and their resulting products play an invaluable role. That is, an analyst must be attentive when a work sample from a client different from the one with whom the initial model was developed doesn't coincide with the initial description of the model. That is an indication of a potential bias. Further work with the new client can potentially correct the omission or error in the composite model. Most often, in my experience, the differences do not arise from bias or conflict among the various clients, but are a result of nonoverlapping areas of their work experience.

SUMMARY

I have described a methodology for structuring interviews with clients for modeling their work in early phases of application development. I have developed my approach by importing and adapting methods from disciplines that have a history of related activities. In doing so, I have been influenced by several considerations. First, I have been guided by the nature of expertise, some important aspects of which are:

1. A high degree of tightly integrated domain-specific knowledge.
2. The fact that a substantial portion of the knowledge is tacit and difficult to articulate.
3. A potential for simplification bias on the part of an analyst.
4. The tendency for an expert to exercise *translation competence.*

The nature of expertise has led me to place a heavy emphasis on the use of work-related language in the interviewing methods to reveal the organization of expert knowledge and to avoid the potential sources of bias. The interviewing strategies are composed of various types of questions that can be used in an opportunistic manner in a series of semistructured interviews. Object Identification questions and Object Relationship questions are designed to explore the organization of domain concepts, objects, and their distinctive characteristics.

Another consideration guiding the development of my approach has been the early elicitation of object knowledge, which is then used to assist the understanding of process knowledge and the development of work scenarios. This is done primarily through the use of protocol-generation activities in the context of real work examples and products.

Finally, I have found it necessary to document and describe the work model iteratively, in a way than can be reviewed for verification by clients and other members of a development team. Adequate descriptions include both abstract summary forms of task representations (such as structured outlines and flow charts), and more detailed representations (such as work scenarios that can be used in validation of work models and in later stages of interaction design).

ACKNOWLEDGMENTS

I wish to express my appreciation to other members of the development team for their cooperation in working with me in a research and development mode. Those individuals are: Ken Greer, Gary Buckway, Jennifer Chiara, Irene Fuja, Lynn Edwards, Carol Sant, and Alan Higley. The project was initiated by me as a research and development effort to allow me to apply some of my ideas on practice and process for user-centered design in the context of a serious development project, but one in which the final deadline was flexible.

I also wish to express my appreciation to Chris Pietras and Dennis Wixon for the valuable comments on earlier drafts of this chapter.

REFERENCES

Anderson, B. and Alty, J.L. 1995. "Everyday Theories, Cognitive Anthropology and User Centered System Design." *Proceedings of People and Computers X*, HCI '95, August 29th–31st.

Anderson, J.R. 1994.*Cognitive Psychology and Its Implications*. San Francisco: Freeman.

Bell, J. and Hardiman, R.J. 1989. "The third role—the naturalistic knowledge engineer." Diaper D. (Ed.) *Knowledge Elicitation: Principles, Techniques, and Applications.* (pp. 49–85). New York: John Wiley & Sons, Inc.

Carroll, J.M. (Ed.). 1995. *Scenario-based design: Envisioning Work and Technology in System Development.* New York: John Wiley & Sons, Inc.

Chi, M.T.H., Feltovich, P.J., and Glaser, R. 1981. "Categorization and representation of physics problems by experts and novices." *Cognitive Science*, **5**, 121–152.

Ericsson, K.A. and Simon, H.A. 1993. *Protocol analysis: Verbal reports as Data* (rev. ed.). Cambridge, MA.: MIT Press.

Ford J.M., and Wood, L.E. 1992. "Structuring & documenting interactions with subject-matter experts." *Performance Improvement Quarterly* **5**, 2–24.

Gordon, S.E. and Gill, R.T. 1992. "Knowledge acquisition with question probes and conceptual graph structures." T.W. Lauer, E. Peacock, and A.C. Graesser (Eds.). *Questions and Information Systems* (pp. 29–46). Hillsdale, N.J.: Lawrence Erlbaum Associates.

Holtzblatt, K., and Beyer, H. 1993. "Making customer-centered design work for teams." *Communications of the ACM* **36**(10), 93–103.

Hughes, J., King, V., Rodden, T., and Andersen, H. 1995. "The role of ethnography in interactive systems design." *Interactions,* **II**(2), 5–65.

Johnson, P., Johnson, H., and Wilson, S. 1995. "Rapid prototyping of user interfaces driven by task models." J.M. Carroll (Ed.), *Scenario-based design: Envisioning Work and Technology in System Development* (pp. 209–246). New York: John Wiley & Sons, Inc.

Kuipers, B.J. and Kassirer, J.P. 1983. "How to discover a knowledge representation for causal reasoning by studying an expert physician." *Proceedings of the American Association of Artificial Intelligence.* Los Altos, California: Morgan Kauffmann Publishers, Inc.

Kuipers, B., Moskowitz, A.J., and Kassirer, J.P. 1988. "Critical decisions under uncertainty: Representation and structure." *Cognitive Science,* **12**, 177–210.

LaFrance, M. 1989. "The quality of expertise: Implications of expert-novice differences for knowledge acquisition." *SIGART Newsletter;* *108* (April):6–14.

Lakoff, G. 1987. Women, Fire, and Dangerous Things: What Categories Reveal About the Mind. Chicago: University of Chicago Press.

Mitchell, A.A. and Chi, M.T.H. 1984. "Measuring knowledge within a domain." Nagy, P (Ed.) *The Representation of Cognitive Structures.* Toronto: Ontario Institute for Studies in Education.

Reigeluth, C.M., Merrill, M.D., and Bunderson, C.V. 1994. "The structure of subject matter content and its instructional design implications." M.D. Merrill (Ed.), *Instructional Design Theory.* Englewood Cliffs, NJ: Educational Technology Publications, Inc. pp. 59–77.

Reimann, P. and Chi, M.T.H. 1989. "Human Expertise." K.J. Gilhooly (Ed.), *Human and Machine Problem Solving* (pp. 161–191). New York: Plenum Press.

Rosch, E. 1973. "Natural categories." *Cognitive Psychology,* **4**, 328–50.

Spradley, J.P. 1979. *The Ethnographic Interview.* New York: Holt, Rinehart and Winston.

Werner, O. and Schoepfle, G.M. (Eds.). 1987. *Systematic Fieldwork: Vol. 1. Foundations of Ethnography and Interviewing.* Newbury Park, CA: Sage Publications.

Wixon, D., and Holtzblatt, K. 1990. "Contextual design: An emergent view of system design." *Proceedings of CHI '90: Empowering People.* Seattle, WA, ACM, pp. 329–336.

Wood, L.E., and Ford, J.M. 1993 "Structuring interviews with experts during knowledge elicitation." *International Journal of Intelligent Systems: Special Issue on Knowledge Acquisition,* **8**, 71–90.

Wood. L.E. et al. 1995. "Evaluation of Interviewing Methods and Mediating Representations for Knowledge Acquisition." *International Journal of Expert Systems: Research and Applications,* **8**(1), 1–23.

EXAMPLE—INTERVIEW ANALYSIS AND WORK MODEL DEVELOPMENT

Given that the goal of interviews and observations regarding clients' work is to develop a work model, an analyst must obviously decide how to describe the model. As part of the work model description, I have found it helpful to construct object hierarchies to provide an organized summary view of the growing object structure. Given that the initial interviews are centered around Object Identification (see Table 4.1) and Object Relationship (see Table 4.2) questions, much of the analysis of the interview notes and tapes focuses on the extraction of that information and the construction of object hierarchies like that shown in Figure 3.1.

The development of a work model description (and the construction of object hierarchies in particular) is supported by a tool I have developed (to which I have referred elsewhere as a knowledge editor (Ford and Wood 1992)) that allows me to enter information about objects and their relationships to other objects. For example, an Object Relationship question asked of a client in the Telecom Services domain might be "What are the features of the *fac/staff* class of service?" The answer to that question would include a list of items such as conf(erence), intercom, long-distance, etc. as shown in Figure 3.1. The

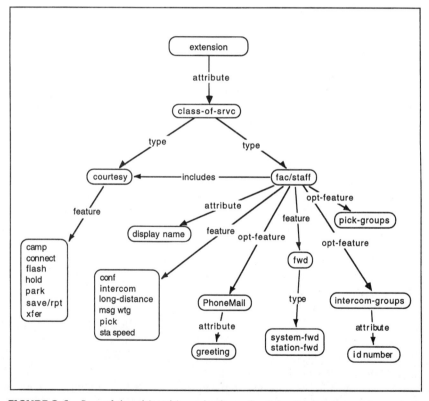

FIGURE 3.1 Part of the object hierarchy from the Telecom Services order project.

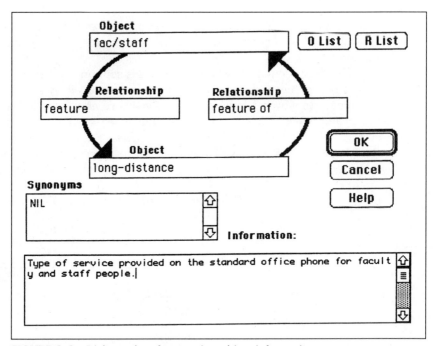

FIGURE 3.2 Dialogue box for entering object information.

knowledge editor tool allows one to enter information relevant to those objects as shown in Figure 3.2.

Information regarding objects can be viewed and browsed as shown in Figure 3.3. At any point object hierarchies can be automatically generated, manipulated, and pasted into a work model description. The knowledge editor enables one to revise the object information and re-generate the object hierarchies relatively easily, especially compared to constructing and revising them with a general, or even specialized, drawing tool.

Currently, my work model descriptions are documents consisting of some beginning narrative describing the nature of the project, followed by linked object hierarchies, structured outlines describing process knowledge, an alphabetized object glossary with definitions, and other details about objects.

While work flow diagrams are helpful in showing the exchange of information among potential users and others in their work organization, I currently use structured outlines to represent detailed process

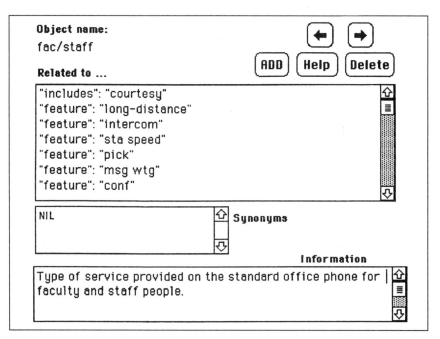

FIGURE 3.3 Display of information concerning an object and its relationships to other objects.

knowledge in the work model descriptions. Structured outlines have several advantages. First, they provide a means of representing knowledge at the global, strategic level, while at the same time representing more specific knowledge within a particular structure as needed. Second, the structure of the outline can easily be modified to reflect changes in understanding that emerge from successive sessions with an expert.

I have begun to experiment with flow charts, but they have the disadvantage of not being nearly as easy to modify and revise (i.e., I haven't devised a way to automatically generate them from a something akin to relationships among objects as with the object heirarchies). On the other hand, I have found evidence that experts using object heirarchies are faster, are more accurate, and much prefer graphical object hierarchies to outline versions (Wood et al. 1995).

I have found it convenient to document global segments of procedural information as it might emerge during object identification, and then to fill out details through analysis of later think-aloud protocols generated in the context of specific cases and examples of real work. For instance, in answer to the following Task-Related Grand Tour question (see Table 4.1) "Could you discuss the major steps you go through in filling a request for services from a member of your unit?", the following general outline of major steps in the generation of a Tele-com Services request was generated:

receive request from a client

review/negotiate details

draft a description of the request

obtain authorized signatures and account #s

In later interviews, more detailed information regarding process knowledge was obtained, such as the segment shown in Figure 3.4.

Receive request from client (usually in the form on an e-mail message)
  Choose Use type
   If telephone **Then**
    Choose Need type
    If addition **Then**
     Draw floor plan of the appropriate room
     Specify current jack locations in room
      If no jack exists at desired location
       Then specify jack installation at that location
       Otherwise Determine jack numbers for existing jacks
     Map extensions to new or existing jack (by number)
     Select set type for new telephone(s)
     Select face plate configuration from tables
      Select line appearance
      Review and select needed features
     Draft a description for request
    If change **Then** (see p. ?) for details)

FIGURE 3.4 A segment of a structured outline of Telecom Services order task.

Changing the Rules: A Pragmatic Approach to Product Development

Dennis R. Wixon
Christine M. Pietras
Paul K. Huntwork
Douglas W. Muzzey
Digital Equipment Corporation

EXECUTIVE SUMMARY

The Teamlinks for the Macintosh product was developed using a variety of field research methods, combined with innovative total-quality approaches and prototype testing and evaluation. Engineering management set the strategy and created an environment where these processes could be most effectively applied. The result was that the product concept, its functionality, and its user interface evolved in response to customer input. Usability work contributed not only to an enthusiastic customer reception, but reduced development time and risks. This work was conducted during late 1992 and early 1993.

BACKGROUND

To put this project in context, we first describe the product we were working on, our basic design process and environment, and our cross-functional team approach.

Product Overview

TeamLinks software allows Windows PCs and Macintosh computers to be integrated into enterprise-wide networks. Just as Digital's ALL-IN-1 Integrated Office System (IOS) allows organizations to rapidly develop organization-wide network applications in a time-shared environment, TeamLinks uses Digital's extensive line of network applications and services, such as electronic mail, file sharing, workflow procedures, and work group applications. TeamLinks software provides capabilities that allow the creation of company-wide client-server office applications tailored to meet the needs of any operation. TeamLinks software provides customers with a graphical user interface that integrates their personal productivity tools, such as word processing and spreadsheet applications, into local and wide area networks. This feature is independent of whether the user's desktop system is a Windows PC or a Macintosh computer.

For enterprise-wide work group computing strategies to have customer appeal, they must address both PC and Macintosh desktop computers. The introduction of TeamLinks for Windows during the spring/summer of 1992 further highlighted the need to immediately introduce similar functions on a Macintosh platform. Both the TeamLinks Program Office and customers requested a Macintosh platform that supported the core TeamLinks services of mail, ad-hoc workflow, and filing, with product availability within six to nine months.

Design Process

There were a set of high level goals for the TeamLinks project:

■ Satisfy the needs of the potential market.
■ Deliver an acceptable solution with available resources.
■ Develop a product within the opportunities and constraints of today's environment.

Based on these goals, we developed strategies to satisfy the goals. We recognized that the Macintosh users constituted a demanding market, particularly with respect to user interface design. As a result, we chose to establish design partnerships with a select set of customers to iteratively obtain comments to use as a basis for refining the project's specific deliverables.

Many design approaches (Good 1985; Ohno 1988; Sanders 1992) call for a subset or variant of the following steps in development:

1. Definition of a product conception
2. Decision about the product capabilities
3. Design of the user interface
4. Implementation of the product
5. Testing of the product

The involvement of users is seen as critical at each step in the product design process. In addition, steps are considered to be overlapping and the overall process is an iterative one. As the process proceeds, the product becomes increasingly refined and the scope of changes required is reduced. This approach means that, while customer involvement is continuous throughout the process, its form and content change as the product is refined. Table 4.1 represents the design steps and methods used for the development of Teamlinks.

We verified and refined our plans based on validated information. As product prototyping got under way, the team analyzed information from competitive products, industry consultants, and customers. A key consideration for the development team was that throughout the life cycle of the project, specific product deliverables would be changed as customer opinions became clear. As incoming data evolved into information, the cost and benefits of each change would be carefully weighed against the project's goals.

Product development thus proceeded on two fronts; one formulated in advance, the other created in response to new developments, customer comments, and experience with successes and failures of the plan.

TABLE 4.1 Design Steps and General Methods.

Step	General Method: Specific Technique
Definition of product concept	*Field research*: Contextual Inquiry/work based interview
Decision about product capabilities	*Survey of customers*: customer day, Vector Comparative Analysis (VCA)
Design of User Interface	*Field research*: Contextual Inquiry/Artifact walkthrough
Implementation of product	*Tests*: UI prototype tests and evaluations
Testing	*Tests*: Customers use product for production work

Design Environment and Cross Functional Team Approach

Use of field research methods, customer surveys, and on-site prototype testing and refinement are most effective when they are supported by the appropriate management environment and development philosophy. The problem of designing systems that meet customer needs at a reasonable cost is not new. However, customer needs, hardware platforms, and software technology have changed. As a result, the specific techniques of customer involvement and the overall development environment and philosophy have struggled to keep pace.

Since the emergence of the software industry, the ability of software groups to produce high-quality software has fallen far short of customer needs and demands. In response to this condition, government and academic specialists proclaimed a "software crisis" in 1969 and endorsed a concept of software engineering based on authoritative, hierarchical organizations and sequential application of specialized functions (Naur and Randall 1969). This model of software engineering is still prevalent in textbooks. Ironically, the model was created at a time when the competitive advantage of total worker participation in cross-functional teams, an outgrowth of Deming's approach to management, was being demonstrated in other industries (Womack and Roos 1990). The cross-functional approach is now widely recognized as a superior method of new product development. The cross-functional approach draws on the specialized expertise of each team member; it is cross-functional in terms of the communication model that is used within the team. Figure 4.1 shows how cross-functional teams speed up work.

The software crisis in 1969 was different from the current software crisis. Customer needs could be expressed as specific organizational operations, which often involved computerizing an existing business function, e.g., the payroll system. Systems addressing such organizational goals could be engineered from the top down using a hierarchical, authoritative approach. In contrast, modern systems must meet individual needs in addition to organizational goals. Also, modern systems transform work rather than subsuming existing functions (Ehn 1988). Stated simply, building a payroll system for the batch processing of checks is different from building a modern tool for financial analysis, such as a spreadsheet.

Within the cross-functional team environment, we followed a very simple approach:

- Find out what the customer needs.
- Design the product based on what you learn.
- Refine your product with your customers.

In conventional workgroups, different steps are done by different people. Communication between steps is done through documents.

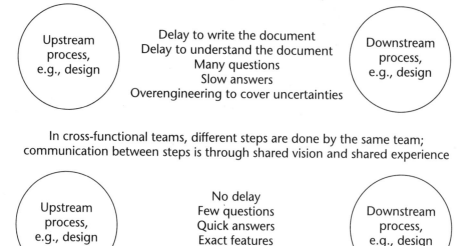

In cross-functional teams, different steps are done by the same team; communication between steps is through shared vision and shared experience

FIGURE 4.1 How cross-functional teams speed up work.

Find Out What Your Customer Needs

Determining the needs of our customers involved field research, quantitative research, and design justification through grounding.

Field Research. One of the most powerful rationales for field research is the realization that effective design begins with the discovery of exactly what users and customers want and do. Field research methods are designed to provide such in-depth understanding. These methods emphasize openness to user experience and create a dialog with users about that experience. Direct contact with users at early stages of design is viewed as an essential step, and the barriers between users and designers has been cited as a significant cause of suboptimal design (Gould et al. 1991; Grudin 1991).

Quantitative Research. Given that discovery is the first stage of effective design, the next stage is decision (Gilb 1988). Most likely, a team will not be able to respond to all user needs. Thus, it needs a systematic and objective way to make decisions. Quantitative methods provide a basis for decisions because they establish a dimension along which features can be compared.

Grounded Design. Unfortunately, many designs have an insufficient basis. Third-hand information, brainstorming, anecdotes from trade shows, and speculative talk about "what the customer really wants" within an isolated team all contribute to designs that do not meet customer needs and designs that do not reflect customer work. To ground a design means that all aspects of the design are rooted in customer data rather than in speculation. Providing mechanisms for this grounding is critical to producing an effective design.

Design Your Product Based on What You Learn

Demand pull, customer involvement, and design metaphors all contribute to a customer-focused product design.

Demand Pull. Using customer interaction to pull design features out of the development team greatly reduces the number of design decisions and the time required to make these decisions. In addition, a small subset of the functionality provided by complex systems is actually used (Good 1985). A customer focus on work essentials and not on "bells and whistles" provides unambiguous feedback that supports direct decisions (Ohno 1988).

Customer-Driven Design. Design is a process of refinement and elaboration embedded in a cycle of creation and evaluation. Customer-driven design involves the evaluation of a tentative design (the creation) with the customer's evolving understanding of their work vis-à-vis the product.

Design Metaphors. Metaphors are an effective way to generate a design from customer work and technical capabilities. Examples include the "desktop" metaphor that drives much user interface design today. Although often criticized, metaphors have been shown to be very powerful and fundamental to human thought (Halasz and Moran 1982; Lakoff and Johnson 1980; Pepper 1966).

Refine Your Product with Customers

Using an iterative approach to product design combined with prototyping helps refine the product design.

Iterative Requirements. The need to break the development of complex software into manageable pieces has led to schemes such as "separation of concerns," "top-down development," and "step-wise re-finement." Iterative design addresses this problem with a "basics first" approach. A basic idea is embodied in a prototype implementation and reviewed with customers. The iterative approach allows solutions to come into being and quickly converge to finished products under the influence of user interaction, even while users are discovering what they need. Detailed requirement specifications are not necessary to begin implementation, so there is no time lag between gathering requirements and providing solutions. This approach minimizes miscommunication and eliminates obsolete requirements (GPO 1989).

Prototyping. Prototyping supports a customer-driven design process, providing customers with an effective medium to respond to current system thinking (Wilson and Rosenberg 1988). For instance, user interface designs embody a theory about the way users work (Carroll and Campbell 1989). The most straightforward way to get feedback on the theory is to express it in a prototype. A prototype allows users to try the system directly instead of translating their work into an unfamiliar symbolic language (Ehn 1988).

WHAT WE DID

The project team developed customer partnerships early in the project life cycle. Through Contextual Inquiries, focus groups, and artifact walk-throughs, the team internalized customer needs and requirements. The new data helped establish a shared understanding among team members and manifested itself in a new product design. Vector Comparative Analysis (VCA) data summarized team learnings and provided the foundation for new designs. Figure 4.2 diagrams this process.

Find Out What Your Customer Needs

Cross-Functional Teams. The team comprised product managers, engineering managers, engineers (including some from companion products), account managers, support people, customer personnel, and specialists in marketing, human factors, graphic design, user publications, and competitive analysis. This cross-functional team took training, visited customers, analyzed data, and made decisions as a whole or in cross-functional subgroups. The mutual understanding that grew out of the shared experience and the shared data enabled faster, more stable decisions and shorter schedules.

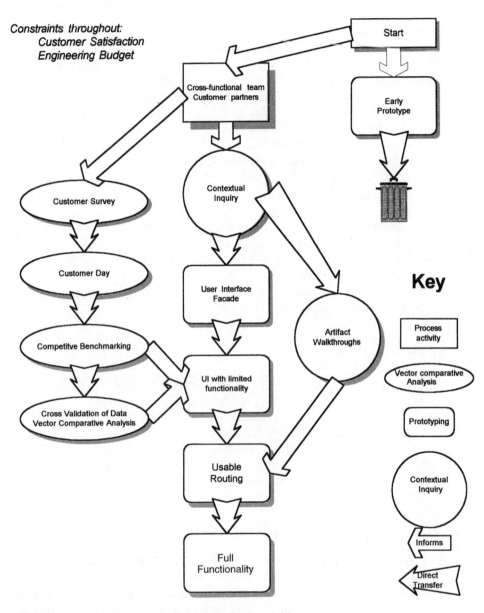

FIGURE 4.2 Overall "Find Out" and "Refine" activities.

Customer Partners. We formed product life-cycle partnerships at the start of the project with customers who represented the four industries that most heavily use PCs on the desktop: U.S. government contractors, manufacturing, pharmaceuticals, and banking. Within these industries, we identified Digital customers who used Macintosh PCs. Working with the account teams and the customers themselves, we selected partners who represented their industries. Each partner designated a specific person to coordinate their participation.

These partnerships allowed more interaction, better follow-up, clearer communication, and more consistent direction. For example, we could model their work in detail in later versions of the prototypes, and the partners could perform complex evaluations. Because we were familiar with their work and they were familiar with our product, no one experienced a high cost of learning at any stage of the project.

Contextual Inquiry. We decided to train the team in Contextual Inquiry methods so that they could interact more effectively with customers. Contextual Inquiry techniques are adaptations of the methods used by anthropologists and sociologists to understand other cultures. The Contextual Inquiry framework emphasizes three principles: (1) *context*, i.e., study user work in its natural environment; (2) *partnership*, i.e., engage customers as co-investigators to help develop your understanding; and (3) *focus*, i.e., clarify your interests and assumptions and be willing to change them based on what customers tell you (Holtzblatt and Jones 1990). Contextual Inquiry techniques have been used widely at Digital, and have shown a positive impact on market penetration and revenue (Wixon and Jones 1996).

Customer Survey. Information from customer visits was organized into a single hierarchy with benefits and needs at the top and desired capabilities and features at the bottom. A questionnaire was created to obtain quantitative customer importance weights for each node and leaf of the hierarchy. The questionnaire was sent to the customer partners. We encouraged our customers to have both IS and end users meet together as a group to score the questionnaire. We wanted them to express their varying viewpoints and reach a consensus, if possible. However, if a consensus could not be reached, we encouraged the customers to note the varying ratings and identify who gave each score. This approach allowed us to study differences between user groups and to understand where differences might occur. We also collected importance weights from an industry consultant, and additional customers beyond the partners. Figure 4.3 shows a typical question from the questionnaire:

Allocate 100 points among the following characteristics to indicate their relative importance to you as components of "support your personal diary."

_____ provide time, task management
_____ support searching calendar forward and backward in time
_____ provide quick, simple navigation to any date
_____ provide varied calendar views

FIGURE 4.3　Sample questionnaire questions.

Customer Day. Representatives from the four customer partners brought completed questionnaires to a customer day. We inquired about their experience with the questions, looking for omissions and refinements. We asked them to describe their top 10 issues and explain why they are important in their environment. The customer day information provided additional insight into user needs as well as a sanity check of the quantitative survey data.

Competitive Benchmarking. We created a score sheet from the features at the lowest level of the hierarchy used in the customer survey of importance. Engineers on the TeamLinks project and an industry consulting firm scored our existing products, alternative versions of our planned product, and competing offerings. The scoring by engineers directly contributed to their understanding of customer requirements. The information also fed the VCA process. Figure 4.4 shows a typical question from the score sheet. The raters are asked to consider two factors regarding the implementation of a particular capability. The first is the "completeness" of the capability (e.g., how completely does product X support offline work?) and the "goodness" of the capability (e.g., how well are the offline features implemented?).

Cross Validation. To minimize investment risks and to maximize the return on the wealth of information obtained from the data-gathering exercises, we revalidated the information to determine its applicability to the project. The information was cross-validated by comparing multiple sources, including the competition, industry consultants, and customers. We verified that we could understand different responses as true expressions of different needs before we used the data.

Vector Comparative Analysis. We input the customer importance weights from the questionnaire and the feature scores from the score sheet into the computer-based VCA tool (Gilmore 1991). This tool rolls the feature scores up through the hierarchy by a method of weighted

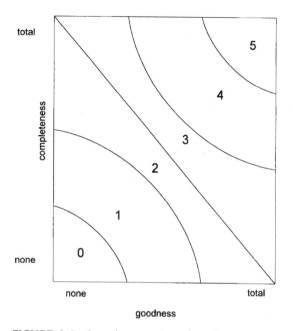

FIGURE 4.4 Sample score sheet question.

averages, to provide a score at each node. VCA can create a vector diagram for each node, showing graphically how well each product satisfies the user needs represented by the node. Figure 4.5 shows the top few branches in the TeamLinks VCA hierarchy. Digital developed VCA for use with or as an alternative to Quality Function Deployment (QFD). For the TeamLinks project, no QFD was conducted.

Design Your Product Based on What You Learn

Team Discussions. The Contextual Inquiry results contained surprises. Even though the inquiry focus was on office products, customers expressed more requirements about cost containment than about product features. The messages, discussed in detail in the section What We Learned, were clear in the raw data and became the basis for revised plans even as the rigorous VCA was being completed. At this time, an early prototype, seen only by the development team, was redirected. Real customer data enabled rapid consensus within the team on changes to the project's direction.

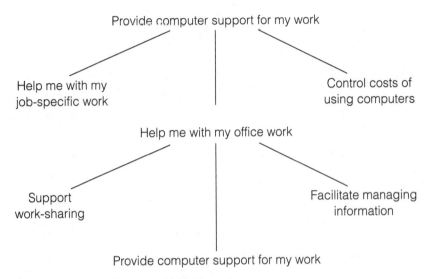

FIGURE 4.5 Simplified TeamLinks hierarchy.

Competitive Positioning. The survey and benchmark data, which was processed by VCA, allowed us to track our competitive position at all times. We could say, for instance, "If we build this alternative, we will satisfy more customers than competitor A, but will need more mail features to compete with B." In addition, when the engineers performed the benchmarking in person, they learned more than just scores. One engineer decided to keep the competitive product he benchmarked as a working tool until our own replacement product was ready, because the competitor's product was better than the tools he had been using. Such experiences challenge the engineers to build better products.

Trade-off Analysis. The computer-based VCA tool allowed precise numerical comparisons to be made on demand. Many alternatives, ranging from the most probable plan, through minor variations, to wild "what-if" scenarios, could be analyzed. The graphical displays allowed the trade-offs between alternatives to be understood at a glance. Low-customer-impact branches of the hierarchy could be identified and ignored during the period when basic directions were being established, thus simplifying the design process. Figure 4.6 shows a VCA display, annotated to clarify how the charts are to be read. In particular, the importance of an item is indicated by the angle of the vector representing it—the more important the item, the nearer the angle is to ver-

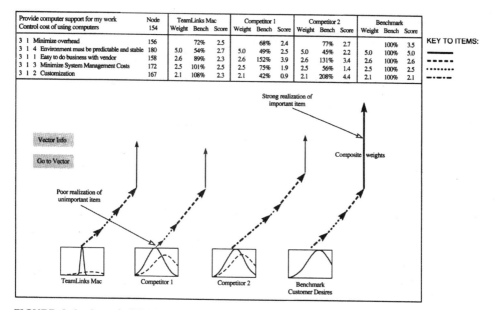

Provide computer support for my work Control cost of using computers	Node 154	TeamLinks Mac			Competitor 1			Competitor 2			Benchmark			
		Weight	Bench	Score	Weight	Bench	Score	Weight	Bench	Score	Weight	Bench	Score	KEY TO ITEMS:
3 1 Minimize overhead	156		72%	2.5		68%	2.4		77%	2.7		100%	3.5	
3 1 4 Environment must be predictable and stable	180	5.0	54%	2.7	5.0	49%	2.5	5.0	45%	2.2		100%	5.0	
3 1 1 Easy to do business with vendor	158	2.6	89%	2.3	2.6	152%	3.9	2.6	131%	3.4	2.6	100%	2.6	
3 1 3 Minimize System Management Costs	172	2.5	101%	2.5	2.5	75%	1.9	2.5	56%	1.4	2.5	100%	2.5	
3 1 2 Customization	167	2.1	108%	2.3	2.1	42%	0.9	2.1	208%	4.4	2.1	100%	2.1	

FIGURE 4.6   Sample VCA Vector Display.

tical. The length of a vector shows how well the item is realized in a given plan—the better the realization, the longer the vector. Therefore, long vertical vectors represent important items that are implemented well, and short horizontal vectors represent unimportant items that are not implemented well. For example, if we compare TeamLinks to Competitor 1, we find the following:

- The capability of Customization (3 1 2) is not very important (weight of 2.1; shallow angle of bottom vector), and TeamLinks has a moderate score (2.3; long vector) compared to Competitor (.9; short vector).
- The capability Minimize System Management Costs (3 1 3) is also not very important (weight of 2.5; shallow angle of vector immediately above Customization), and Teamlinks and Competitor 1 have similar scores (2.5 and 1.9 respectively) and arrows of similar length.
- The capability of Environment Must Be Stable and Predictable (3 1 4) is very important to customers (weight of 5 with a vertical vector at top), and Teamlinks has a moderate score (2.7 the a relatively long vector); so does Competitor 1 (2.5, relatively long vector).

Refine Your Product with Customers

In addition to the techniques already described to bring customer input into the design of TeamLinks for Macintosh, we also used four cycles of prototyping to confirm and refine our designs. In preparation for the third cycle, we spent a day with each of the customer partners collecting information (including actual forms and documents) on one of their key business processes. This information enabled us to simulate real processes during the final cycle, thus putting our products to an ultimate test. The four cycles are shown in Table 4.2.

Based on Contextual Inquiry principles, artifact walk-throughs allow a design team to look at processes that take place over time and that occur among groups of people. The name is derived from the approach of asking customers to bring the actual artifacts of a process (e.g., notes, memos, forms, and documents) into the walkthrough as a reminder of the full complexity of the process. In the presence of the artifacts, we ask for the overall process goals, any known issues and problems, and a list of process steps. For each step of the process, we ask "Who makes requests?" "Who does work?" "Who approves?" "What is the cost in person effort, materials, and equipment?" "What is the normal cycle time?" and "What problems and issues exist with this step?" Each type of information is recorded on a colored Post-it note and assembled into an annotated flow diagram of the process. Thus, these walk-throughs emphasize articulating a process in detail, grounding it in a specific customer example. We chose artifact walk-throughs as the natural approach to gathering data in order to customize our prototypes to each customer situation. At the same time, the walk-throughs uncovered additional general requirements.

TABLE 4.2 The TeamLinks Prototyping Cycles.

Cycle	Content	Presentation	Data Collection
1	User Interface Facade	Macintosh Powerbook	One-on-one contextual interviews
2	User Interface and limited functionality	Client software only	Sample tasks (scenarios), user diaries, and phone calls
3	Usable workflow filing and basic mail	Client and server software	Customer forms and work tasks user diaries and phone calls
4	Full functionality	Client and server phone software	Daily use visits by team and calls

WHAT WE LEARNED

Significant changes in functionality and the user interface were made based on user reaction to the prototypes. The following section discusses these changes.

Unlearning Things We Thought We Knew

The previous section of the paper discussed tools and techniques that we used to achieve our goals (i.e., satisfy the needs of the potential market, deliver an acceptable solution with available resources, and develop a product within the opportunities and constraints of today's environment). Before actively gathering data, we developed a set of assumptions about our customer's needs and preferences for working. On subsequent visits we discovered that some of our assumptions were flawed and that we needed to change our original plans to better satisfy customer demand. In this section we describe our initial assumptions, discoveries made throughout the data-gathering process, and new designs derived from our discoveries. Table 4.3 lists a comparison of our original and revised designs.

TABLE 4.3 Comparison of Original and Revised Designs.

Original Design	Discovery	Revised Design
Mail		
Develop new X.400 TeamLinks mail client for Macintosh	"Build one mail client and do it right"	Leverage existing X.400 mail client and focus on developing mail-enabled workflow applications
Workflow		
Develop information manager application that contains routing services	"Help us utilize our available desktop resources." "Build a 'real' Mac Product"	Develop independent components that work well with existing Macintosh applications
Filing		
Develop information manager application, in addition to Mac file system	"Document manager should look and work like a Mac"	Provide access to ALL-IN-1 IOS file cabinet as an extension of the Macintosh file system

Lesson One

Our initial assumption was that customers need an information manager to navigate and to view file cabinets. TeamLinks for Windows provided an information manager to assist Windows users in viewing, naming, and navigating the ALL-IN-1 IOS and DEC MAILworks file cabinets. The file cabinet is a logical container based on the physical metaphor of a filing cabinet. It enforces a hierarchical relationship, providing drawers that contain only folders and folders that contain only documents. The file cabinets represent the central storage areas for all objects within the TeamLinks environment.

To parallel the TeamLinks for Windows environment, the team proposed an information manager for the Macintosh product. Figure 4.7 shows the proposed information manager window. Users would be presented with a single, global view of the file cabinets through the information manager. This proposal adds an additional document management layer on top of the native document management. The team planned to display the information in a manner as similar as possible to the Macintosh desktop display.

However, our customers stressed: "Document management should look and work like the Mac." The Macintosh desktop presents a single, global view to the users. They do not want a replacement. Our part-

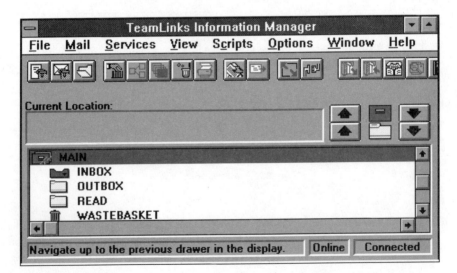

FIGURE 4.7 Teamlinks for Windows Information Manager.

ners urged us to support document views and navigation that are native. After attending the Apple Developers Conference, the project leader also concluded that we would build a noncompetitive application if we followed our proposed plans.

The team decided *not* to build an integrated information manager. The revised design in Figure 4.8 shows how users can access the remote ALL-IN-1 IOS file cabinet as they do remote network volumes. In this approach, the ALL-IN-1 IOS file cabinet becomes an extension to the file system. This paradigm builds on the Macintosh user's prior knowledge, making the interface comfortable and familiar.

Lesson Two

Our initial assumption was that we should follow the TeamLinks for Windows lead and create one tightly integrated application. Given the TeamLinks for Windows working model, the team proposed to develop a similar application for the Macintosh platform. Original plans detailed

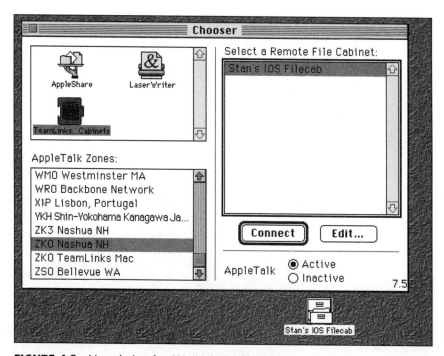

FIGURE 4.8 New design for ALL-IN-1-IOS file cabinet access.

a large, integrated application. The Information Manager window would provide the central world view of documents stored in file-cabinet folders. Users would display these objects by double-clicking to invoke the appropriate editor or viewer. We also envisioned the Information Manager window to have its own set of menus and a toolbar. When accessed, each service would be represented by its own window with unique menus and toolbar.

Additionally, rather than enhancing the existing X.400 mail client (DEC MAILworks for Macintosh), the team planned to create a new mail client for the TeamLinks product. This decision would have resulted in two competing mail clients.

We quickly changed our plans after listening to our customers. During our early visits, our customers stressed: "Help us utilize our available desktop resources." Digital's office products need to work with existing Macintosh applications. Customers want to use their existing word processing, graphics, and other business applications while working with our office applications. The customers emphasized that TeamLinks components must work well together.

Throughout our interviews, we heard: "Build a real Mac product." Our customers stressed that our Macintosh office products must look and feel like Macintosh applications as well as adhere to the Apple Human Interface Guidelines. They encouraged us to take advantage of color, direct manipulation, and point-and-click paradigms. In following these standards, we enable users to transfer their skills from one application to another, thus reducing training costs.

We also heard: "Build one mail client and do it well." Customers want consistency across our applications. If two Digital office products provide X.400 mail support on the Macintosh platform, each should present the same user interface. This practice will help reduce customer costs by eliminating additional user training. From Digital's perspective, it makes good business sense to take advantage of existing products and resources where appropriate. Our customers cautioned against developing a new X.400 mail client for the TeamLinks product when DEC MAILworks for Macintosh already exists. They encouraged us to direct resources toward developing a single, strategic mail application that is simple to use, X.400-compliant, reliable, and available for popular desktop computers. They mentioned mail-enabled applications, such as workflow, conferencing, and time management.

The team decided to take advantage of existing components. Rather than build a new mail client, the TeamLinks and DEC MAILworks for Macintosh project teams collaborated to enhance the existing DEC MAILworks client and provide workflow support.

The TeamLinks team focused on developing the workflow component that would assist users with routing forms and documents for review and approval. As a result, the TeamLinks design migrated from a large, integrated application to components that work well together and allow users to exchange information that they have created with other popular Macintosh applications. Depending upon specific needs, customers can purchase a mail-only package, a workflow package, or a comprehensive package with mail, workflow, remote ALL-IN-1 IOS file cabinet access, and conferencing applications. Throughout development, the team refined designs, adhered to Macintosh guidelines where possible, used color to add value, and implemented point-and-click paradigms.

Lesson Three

Our initial assumption was that: "Time management is important, but we still have time before missing the opportunity to implement this feature." Time management was viewed as an important product requirement, but the team did not fully appreciate the consequences of not implementing a time-management solution. Due to limited resources, the team relied on another internal group to deliver these services. If a time-management product were to become available before the TeamLinks release date, it might be integrated into the package.

However, our customers stressed: "Help me manage my time." Customers often described their struggle in trying to schedule a meeting with a group of people, and quickly followed this description with a request for time-management support. People spend a great deal of time trying to manage their calendars. Two of our four partners rated time-management support as their top priority. People want to browse one another's calendars, get assistance in finding common meeting times, and schedule resources and events across their organization or company.

One partner stated that they would not be able to migrate their ALL-IN-1 IOS users to TeamLinks for Macintosh until a time-management solution was in place. VCA data indicated that if TeamLinks for Macintosh had an integrated time-management model, the product would be in better competitive standing.

An office industry consultant told us that we only had six months to release an integrated time-management module. If we delayed any longer, we would miss the opportunity. The team had been considering third-party time-management providers, but negotiations had stalled. The team decided to reemphasize negotiations, and a contract was signed within a short time.

Lesson Four

Our initial assumption was that we would port TeamLinks for Windows to the Macintosh platform and that Mac users would like the results. We originally planned to port the TeamLinks for Windows application first, and then retrofit a Macintosh user interface. The team proposed an initial design that contained a rich set of functions identical to those in TeamLinks for Windows, but gave little thought to what Macintosh users really wanted from a groupware office application. The importance of simplicity and ease of use was not clear to all team members.

However, our customers stressed: "I don't learn new functions unless I see clear value to my work." "The most valuable tool is the one you already know how to use." "Less is better." "All I wanted to do is create mail and read it." and "Build a real Mac product."

People use tools and applications to simplify work tasks. Tools should support existing work rather than create new work. People use tools if they add value; otherwise, they quickly abandon them. Customers want simple, elegant solutions.

Porting TeamLinks for Windows to the Macintosh platform would not succeed, even if a user interface that resembled an actual Macintosh user interface were provided. Macintosh users easily spot and freely reject a ported Windows application. Vendors who have ported Windows applications to the Macintosh platform have failed to gain product acceptance.

The team decided to adopt simplicity as a theme. Although mail and workflow add value, they must be simple to use. We decided to take advantage of our users' previous knowledge of electronic mail and the postal mail metaphor in the design of our workflow package. The team first concentrated on designing the most frequently used functions, and then on refining them.

Our VCA results indicated that we had an opportunity in the workflow area, but that the window of opportunity was quickly closing. To complete our designs and develop customer-specific templates for prototyping, we needed to learn more about our customer's business processes. We used artifact walk-throughs to study three workflow examples: a manufacturing procurement request, a pharmaceutical regulatory submission, and a banking credit approval.

Rather than port the Windows application, the team created a new design using user interface prototyping tools. We adhered to Macintosh guidelines, incorporating standard system fonts, point-and-click selection, standard text selection routines, standard menus and accelerators, consistent button placement, and dialog layout.

Discovering Delighters

Through the discovery process, several of our initial assumptions proved to be inaccurate or misguided. As a result, the team changed plans to better satisfy customer requirements; we learned from the experience and adapted appropriately. The team also discovered that certain product attributes delighted customers.

Button Bar. Surprisingly, the button bar or tool bar within the Team-Links components is a delighter among customers. The buttons provide point-and-click access to frequently used mail and workflow functions, reducing menu navigation and recall of keyboard accelerators. Colorful icons indicate button function. Context-sensitive help is also available as users pass the mouse pointer over buttons in the bar.

Workflow Automation. Data from Contextual Inquiries, artifact walkthroughs, and VCA revealed that business process reengineering and automation is an emerging opportunity within the office automation market. Today, businesses lose time and money tracking materials through approval life cycles. Tools that support workflow automation can potentially yield substantial savings for a corporation. In some industries, trimming one hour from a process can save millions of dollars.

One customer expressed his interest in workflow support as follows: "It will mostly save everyone's time, which is now wasted in tracking down who has the material and who still needs to sign it. It should speed up things, because it doesn't have to physically be sent from office to office (sometimes even different states) for approval. I would think it could save time at year end for summary reports."

The development team capitalized on this information, focusing the corporate office strategy on developing leadership workflow tools. Rather than provide a set of "me too" features, the team decided to concentrate on a specific customer problem and provide a simple, well-done solution. The TeamLinks Routing product is the outcome of these efforts, and the group intends to focus the marketing message on its tracking capabilities. Six months later, leading competitors are now hastening to announce workflow product offerings.

Refinement during Prototype Review

Our VCA results indicated that customers place great value in ease of use. Items from the benefit hierarchy such as: "Make the product usable—match the way I work," "Make the UI consistent within itself," and "Make a product that adds value to my work" were all rated as highly important by our customer partners. Users are specifically interested in minimal key strokes, consistent interfaces and functions across components, point-and-click paradigms, adherence to Macintosh user interface standards, and short-cut keys.

While these principles may be well understood by human-factor professionals, they are not always as obvious to development teams. These principles have a greater impact when a development team hears them firsthand from customers. In addition, their meaning becomes clearer when it is expressed by users in a work context. The result is that a development team emerges with an "applied" understanding of these principles, as compared to a "conceptual" understanding.

The team focused on satisfying these requirements within the TeamLinks components. We employed a design methodology that involved users throughout the development life cycle, allowing users to see product improvements on a monthly basis. During early prototyping, the team conducted one-on-one sessions with users to study concept learning and ease of use. Feedback from these sessions was used to progressively change the design. Subsequent testing revealed that the design modifications improved ease of use. A summary of specific design changes follows.

Redesign of TeamLinks Routing Window. Within the TeamLinks model, users receive workflow packages within the TeamLinks Mail Inbox folder folder. Workflow packages are distinguished from mail message by a special icon and descriptive title. Users view workflow packages in the same way they view new mail messages—by double-clicking on the workflow package. This action displays the TeamLinks Routing window with the workflow package content in view. The original design for Teamlinks Routing Window appears in Figure 4.9.

Prototype testing demonstrated that users had difficulty focusing on important information in this window. The button bar immediately caught their attention and their eyes were then drawn to the distinctive "Routing List. . ." button and the corresponding list of names. Several users overlooked the list of attachments at the bottom of the window. Many users were unable to locate their role instructions, which outlined their specific tasks. Finally, several users commented that important information, such as "What do I have to do with this?" "When do I have to respond?" and "What's my role?" were not visible on the main screen.

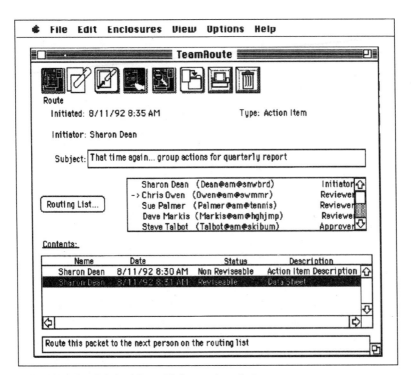

FIGURE 4.9 Original TeamLinks routing design.

Users had difficulty understanding that the window represented a package containing several attachments and signatures. The user interface did not contain any clues to reinforce or suggest a package metaphor. During the testing, we learned that our customers were familiar with mail messages. They easily understood the concept of message attachments and the postal metaphor as it relates to electronic mail. Further, they associated a workflow package with a special type of mail message that needed approval. Unfortunately, the package window did not resemble the familiar message window.

After several design iterations, the package window now appears as shown in Figure 4.10. The team applied the mail metaphor to workflow, rearranging some of the information to create distinct header and attachment areas as seen with mail messages. The header contains Initiator (From), Initiated (Date), To, and Subject fields. Additionally, we added a Role field to the header in response to user requests. Text labels are displayed in a bold font to improve readability and to help users focus their attention.

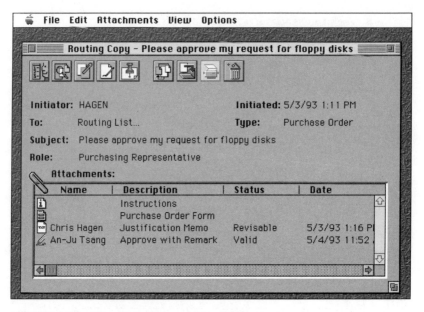

FIGURE 4.10 New TeamLinks routing design.

We simplified the window by removing noncritical information. For example, while the content of the routing list is important, users informed us that is was not essential to include the routing list on the package window as long as it was available via a single mouse click. Therefore, we added an Edit/View-Routing-List button on the left-hand side of the tool bar. Users are also able to quickly view the routing list by double-clicking on the To field. We also removed the Routing List button, which needlessly distracted users.

The graphic designer created smaller buttons and used subtle shades of gray to create a three-dimensional look. Shading was used to invite users to press the buttons. Icons were designed to be understandable in international settings. Below the header, shading was used to define the attachments area, and a paper-clip icon was added to reinforce the metaphor.

To address the difficulty users had in locating role instructions, we placed them in the attachments list. If instructions are present, they always appear as the first attachment and are denoted by a distinct document icon. Users simply double-click on the list entry to find out what they need to do with the package.

In subsequent evaluations with the prototype, customers commented: "I think it's pretty good. Once you get into it, it's pretty easy to use, pretty logical." "I was already somewhat familiar with it because I saw base-level one. It was pretty easy coming back to it. Just from using it the first time, it became familiar. I had some problems with the last one [base-level one], and I think you've solved a lot of the problems with this one [base-level two]." "Anyone familiar with a Mac shouldn't have a problem."

In designing the package window to look more like a mail message, we enabled users to transfer their mail knowledge to workflow. The concept of creating a package could be related to the concept of creating a mail message, namely, addressing the workflow package, attaching documents to the package, and typing in a subject. These changes help to reduce the need for user training.

By simplifying the main window, we enabled users to focus on important information, i.e., their role instructions and the attached work materials. Providing icon buttons for frequently used functions helps to minimize keystrokes and reduce task time.

Terminology Review. The original TeamLinks Routing product used a series of technical terms in the title bars of package windows to identify packages and states. These terms were not very meaningful to users. The original terms are listed in column one of Table 4.4.

Team members working on the Windows and Macintosh platforms agreed to review terminology with the goal of reaching consensus on simple terms that users could immediately identify. The team reflected on the traditional terminology for routing paper packages to develop the new terminology. The new terms are listed in column two of Table 4.4.

By using terms that reflect the paper process, users can immediately identify packages they receive and understand the appropriate actions to take. The terms Template, Original, Carbon Copy, and Routing Copy describe both package type and status in simple familiar terms rather than in technical terms. The package name is placed in the title bar of the package window and is readily visible to the user. The revised terms help to minimize new learning and reduce frustration. Consistent use of terminology across platforms allows all users to speak a common language regardless of their choice of desktop system.

Focus on the Package. The team made a concerted effort to focus on all components of the TeamLinks Office package: mail, workflow, filing, and conferencing. As discussed earlier, the process of iterative

TABLE 4.4 TeamLinks Workflow Terminology.

Original Title Bar	Revised Title Bar
TeamRoute—Template	Template—[document title]
TeamRoute—(Master, routing)	Original—[document title]
TeamRoute—(Master, completed)	Completed original—[doc title]
TeamRoute—(Master, unsent)	Draft—[document title]
TeamRoute—(Master, sent)	Original—[document title]
TeamRoute—(Routing copy, pending)	Routing copy—[document title]
TeamRoute—(Routing copy, sent)	Carbon copy—[document title]
TeamRoute—(Carbon copy, read)	Carbon copy—[document title]
TeamRoute—(Tracking report, read)	Latest copy—[document title]

design yielded excellent results with TeamLinks Routing. Studies of prototypes demonstrated that the use of buttons, color, larger fonts and professional graphics, the mail metaphor, and adherence to Macintosh standards all contributed to ease of use and acceptance of the TeamLinks Routing product.

VCA results indicated that our customers viewed consistency across components as essential to minimizing training and increasing accessibility. Given this information, our goal was to produce a family of products with a consistent look and feel. The team spent six weeks working on mail enhancements and modifying the screens to be more consistent with TeamLinks Routing. For example, the graphic designer created more meaningful icons for the buttons, adding color to reinforce metaphors and make the buttons more distinct from one another. The team agreed on consistent button placement across components, moving all buttons to the top of mail windows. Similar font styles and sizes were used across components to increase readability. Figure 4.11 shows the original mail file cabinet window. Figure 4.12 shows the same window with the enhancements just mentioned.

In addition to focusing on consistency across user interfaces for mail, workflow, filing, and conferencing, the team employed the same graphic for the on-screen "About" boxes and for the packaging and documentation cover designs.

Consistency across product components and with other Macintosh

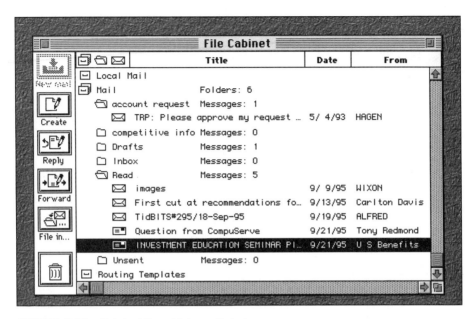

FIGURE 4.11 Original TeamLinks mail design.

applications received rave reviews from customers: "I liked the buttons across the top real well. Real nice." "The fact that it's consistent with other Mac applications is the best news." "Support for point-and-click . . . you did a good job here."

By creating a similar look and feel across components, the team increased the transfer of learning, thus reducing customer training needs. Employing the same graphics for all components created a recognizable product identity for the TeamLinks family.

Filing. The original design to access the remote ALL-IN-1 IOS file cabinet on the Macintosh replicated the TeamLinks for Windows information manager. The VCA process demonstrated that this design would not be competitive, nor would it satisfy customer needs.

The team developed a more viable solution by visualizing the ALL-IN-1 IOS file cabinet as an extension of the Macintosh file system. Team members developed a TeamLinks file cabinet extension. Users connect to the ALL-IN-1 IOS file cabinet through the chooser window. Once connected, a volume (visually represented by a file cabinet icon) appears on the user's desktop. Users double-click on the file cabinet

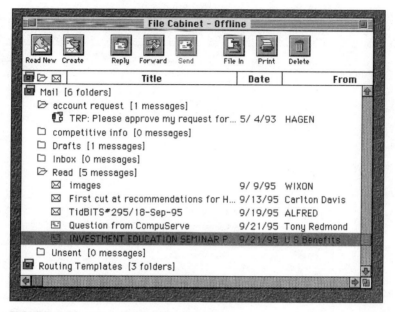

FIGURE 4.12 New TeamLinks mail design.

volume to view the contents in a new window. ALL-IN-1 IOS drawers and folders are visually depicted as their real world counterparts as seen in Figure 4.13. Users can manipulate files in a familiar fashion.

By using the standard Macintosh user interface to manipulate drawers, folders, and documents in the ALL-IN-1 IOS file cabinet, users do not need to learn a new paradigm. This approach minimizes new learning, increases accessibility and ease of use, and adds value. This design is compatible with Apple's Open Collaborative Environment (AOCE) and will create a better return on investment for the program team.

RESPONSE FROM CUSTOMERS

As for the customers, they say it best in their own words:

Major government contractors: "I thoroughly enjoyed testing the product. I am definitely going to buy it . . . our company is committed to TeamLinks . . ." "Excellent adherence to Mac Interface."

Major manufacturing companies: "Simple enough to use and it works." "I'd say yes [in response to a question regarding whether they

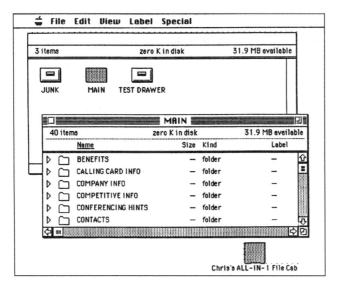

FIGURE 4.13 Browsing the ALL-IN-1 IOS file.

would purchase the product], it ties in well with ALL-IN-1 and meets the needs."

Major pharmaceutical companies: "Logical enough to use without the need to read documentation." "We're very excited and encouraged by these changes. Looks like a Winner!!!!" One customer stated publicly in *ComputerWorld* that TeamLinks/DEC MAILworks is their standard.

Selected government agencies: "Really like mail; like the graphic UI, color, bit buttons, the file cabinet. . ." "Easy to use." "I love this! Our whole branch will want this." "It is exactly what I've imagined and desired for months." "They [customer's users] are going crazy over it. They love it!"

REFLECTIONS

From the perspective of field research methodology we learned several lessons:

1. *Organizational/process factors contribute to the success of a method.* Usability methods cannot be evaluated in isolation. Their

effective deployment requires more than nominal management acquiescence. Management must be an integral supporter and contributor to the process along with the remainder of the cross-functional team. There must be a shared commitment to design the system based on an understanding of the customer's work and to reevaluate plans and goals based on ongoing customer input. This does not mean that management loses control of a project; instead, reevaluations and check points are planned as part of the development process.

2. *These methods save money and time.* In the original plans, close to half the development effort was devoted to creating a "file cabinet" along the lines of Teamlinks for Windows. A relatively small investment in customer visits led to a change in direction that not only saved resources, but increased the product's chance of success. As the development supervisor said: "Without this process we would have spent 18 months and 2 million dollars producing a noncompetitive product."

3. *Methods complement each other.* We used qualitative field research methods, quantitative surveys, total quality methods, and iterative prototyping. Overall, the methods tended to provide the basis for another method. For example, the artifact walkthroughs served as a basis for developing tasks for the prototyping. In addition, methods tended to provide supportive findings, e.g., what we heard in interviews would be confirmed in a survey. Equivalent findings by alternative methods provides particularly strong support for a conclusion.

4. *Open-ended methods should come early; methods oriented around specific questions should come later.* We avoided the pitfall of asking our customers precise questions before we had a broader understanding of their issues and concerns. In addition, our open-ended methods and the strong relationship we had with our customer partners tended to produce more candid results. We also adapted Contextual Inquiry and used it throughout the development process to capture customer feedback. In doing so we departed from the traditional "bottom-up" use of Contextual Inquiry.

5. *Having a single person to coordinate the effort is key.* In this case, one person (Pietras) was responsible for every aspect of the usability effort. The other contributors served as consultants in specialized areas. This not only ensured that the work got done, but also ensured that there was a continuity and depth of understanding of both the customer needs and the product space.

6. *It is impossible to assess the cost-benefit of usability work on this project.* The reason is that the usability work is an integral part of the overall development process. To attempt to separate it from other parts of the development effort would provide a false picture.

The success or failure of any product can normally be attributed to the product's initial plans and the implementation of those plans. For this project, one can evaluate the development strategy against the initial project goals and against the customer needs.

The development strategy satisfied the program's goals. The initial version of the product was delivered in less than a year of development time, and with minimal resources. By-products of the development strategy allowed the team to take additional "informed" risks (seven months into the project, the team received additional responsibility for delivering the mail client), to deliver three separate products with minimal resources, and to better engage and motivate the development team through consistency of purpose.

ACKNOWLEDGMENTS

Many people were involved in the development of TeamLinks for Macintosh, from its inception to its shipment. The authors would like to acknowledge the following contributors: Dave Brown, Dave Burns, Gary Floyd, George Gates, Sabrina Prentiss, Janna Rhodes, Charles Robbins, David Stutson, John Wise, Nam Hoang, and Eunice Zachry (account and support managers); Jennifer Dutton, Nina Eppes, Peter Laquerre, Terry Sherlock, Ricky Marks, Barb Mathers (documentation); Paul Clark, Debbie Christopher, Beth Doucette, Jim Emmond, Mark Grinnell, Steve Hain, Dean Jahns, John Lanoue, Bruce Miller, Stan Neumann, John Quimby, Tom Rogers, Larry Tyler, and Steve Zuckerman (engineering); Peggy Doucet, Mike Pfeiffer, and Beverly Schultz (management); Robert Lehmenkuler, Steve Fink, and Steve Martin (marketing); Phil Gabree and Meg Lustig (product management); Keith Brown, Tina Boisvert, Rick Palmer, Tim Sagear, and Tony Troppito (quality assurance engineering); and Peter Mierswa, for leading the team to develop customer-focused products.

Special thanks to our customers, without whose involvement none of this would have been possible.

A version of this article was originally published in the Digital Technical Journal, volume 5, number 4, Fall 1993.

REFERENCES

Carroll, J. and R. Campbell. 1989. "Artifacts as Psychological Theories." *Behavior and Information Technology*, **8**: 247–256.

Ehn, P. 1988. *Work-Oriented Design of Computer Artifacts*. Stockholm: Arbetslivscentrum.

Gilb, T. 1988. *Principles of Software Engineering Management*. New York: Addison-Wesley.

Gilmore, J. 1991. "A Quantitative Comparative Analysis Technique for Benchmarking Product Functionality and Customer Requirements." *Eleventh International Conference on Decision Support Systems*. Institute of Management Sciences, Providence RI.

Good, M. 1985. "The Iterative Design of a new text editor." *Proceedings of the Human Factors Society 29th Annual Meeting*. Baltimore, MD, Sept 29–Oct 3 1985, 571–574.

Gould, S. Boies, and C. Lewis. 1991. "Making Usable Useful, Productivity-Enhancing Computer Applications". *Communications of the ACM*, **34**(1) 75–85.

Grudin, J. 1991. "Systematic Sources of Suboptimal Interface Design in Large Product Development Organizations". *Human Computer Interaction*, vol. 6, no. 2 (1991):147–196.

Halasz, F. and T. Moran. 1982. "Analogy Considered Harmful". *Human Factors in Computer Systems Proceedings* (March 1982): 383–386.

Holtzblatt K. and S. Jones. 1990. "Contextual Inquiry: Principles and Practice." Technical Report 729. Maynard, MA: Digital Equipment Corporation.

Lakoff, G. and J. Johnson. 1980. *Metaphors We Live By*. Chicago: University of Chicago Press.

Moll-Carrillo, H.J., et al. 1995. "Articulating a Metaphor Through User-Centered Design." *Proceedings of the CHI'95*, ACM, 566–572.

Naur, P. and B. Randall, eds. 1969. *Software Engineering: A Report on a Conference Sponsored by the NATO Science Committee*. North Atlantic Treaty Organization.

Ohno, T. 1988. *The Toyota Production System*. Cambridge: Productivity Press.

Pepper, S. 1966. *World Hypotheses*. Los Angeles: University of California Press.

Sanders, N. 1966. "Participatory Design Research in the Product Development Process." *PDC'92 Procedings of the Participatipatory Design Conference*. pp. 111–112.

Subcommittee on Investigations and Oversight, Committee on Science, Space, and Technology. 1989. *Bugs in the Program: Problems in Federal Government Computer Software Development and Regulation*. Washington, D.C.: Government Printing Office.

Wilson, J. and D. Rosenberg. 1988. "Rapid Prototyping." *Handbook of Human Computer Interaction*. New York: North-Holland. 1988. pp. 859–873.

Wixon, D. and S. Jones. 1996. "Usability for Fun and Profit." *Human Computer Interface Design: Success Cases Emerging Methods and Real World Context*. Los Altos, CA: Morgan Kaufman Publishers, Inc.

Womack, D. Jones, and D. Roos. 1990. *The Machine That Changed the World*. ISBN 0–89256–320–8 New York: Rawson Associates.

The Delta Method— A Way to Introduce Usability

Martin Rantzer

Ericsson Infocom Consultants AB

EXECUTIVE SUMMARY

The Delta Method was developed as a framework for usability activities within software development projects. The method aims to assemble existing usability tools and practices into a usability process that supplements the early phases of traditional system development. The goal of Delta is to be a method for usability engineering that can be used both internally within Ericsson Infocom and sold as a product or service to customers.

The Delta Method focuses on finding and eliciting the requirements of the future users. This is accomplished through interviews, observations in the workplace, and studies of users' interaction with prototypes. The tight integration of the method into the existing system development process raises the usability requirements to the same level as the technical and functional requirements. They are no longer optional or add-ons to the requirement specification.

This chapter will discuss how the method was developed and later integrated into the development process of a customer using a field oriented approach. During the integration the method was used in a pilot project (or field study) to gain the necessary experience, and many of the examples are taken from that pilot project.

BACKGROUND

Ericsson Infocom Consultants AB is a consulting company within the Ericsson Telecom Corporation with approximately 500 employees at four different locations in Sweden. Infocom offers development support to companies within and outside Ericsson, in areas such as Communication Systems, Systems Engineering, and Technical Communication.

The Delta Method was developed as a joint effort by Ericsson Infocom and Linköping University. The method development group consisted of technical communicators and system designers at Ericsson Infocom, and researchers within these fields at the Linköping University. The researchers represented the Department of Computer and Information Science and the Institute of Tema Research, Department of Technology and Social Change. The development was supported by the Swedish National Board for Industrial and Technical Development (NUTEK). The project was a part of the ITYP venture for increased efficiency and skill in the services sector.

The development was initiated by a senior technical communicator who felt desperate from always being called out just before delivery to "correct" the usability problems in a product through documentation. The Delta Method was the first more serious attempt at Ericsson Infocom to introduce usability methods into the company. When the development started in 1992, there was nobody within the company with prior knowledge or experience of human factors and usability. The strategy was to form a method development group that could acquire the necessary usability skills to develop a method with the support of human factors experts from the university, and then to use the method to introduce usability into the organization.

The method was designed to be used by system developers and technical communicators with limited formal knowledge of human factors work, but with experience in areas such as requirements engineering and development of user documentation. This experience, combined with the Delta Method and a genuine interest in improving the work situation for the users, makes it possible to develop more usable computer systems.

THE DEVELOPMENT OF THE DELTA METHOD

In an effort to live as we preach, the Delta Method was developed based on the experiences and needs of its future users—system developers and technical communicators. The development was divided into three separate phases: method inception, field studies, and refinement based on the experience gained during the studies. The field studies were imperative to the success of the method. In order to develop a method that worked in a real design situation, we needed to study both how the development team worked and how they interacted with the users.

During the first phase, the method development group defined the activities constituting the Delta method. These activities were to be built on academically established techniques and ideas. Our task was to use this knowledge and adapt the ideas to the requirements and characteristics of industrial systems design, i.e., cost effectiveness, investments in existing methods, limited resources, and so forth.

In the second phase, the preliminary method inception was used in one of Infocom's commercial projects, which was to serve as a pilot project for the development of the Delta method. The development group (the users) in this project was joined by a researcher from Linköping University working in the team as a system developer. The researcher, apart from working with the design of the system itself, also assembled qualitative data concerning how the method was received and used by the members of the design group.

Finally, the experience gained from the pilot project was analyzed, and a revised version of the Delta method was developed. The result of

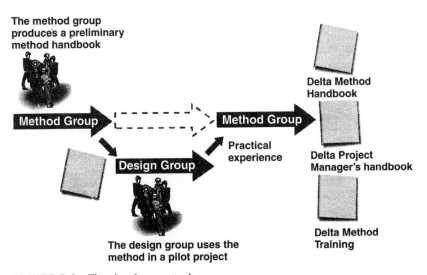

FIGURE 5.1 The development phases.

the revision was a method handbook describing the purpose, the actual steps, and the result of each usability activity. Two new activities, System Definition and Design Preparations, were included in the method as a result of the revision following the pilot project. These activities were not "theoretically" motivated, but were still needed as a way for the customers, users, and developers to form a common understanding of the results so far, and how to use the results during future activities.

A full description of the development of the Delta Method can be found in "A Collaborative Approach to Usability Engineering" by Pär Carlshamre (1994). The Delta Method itself is described in the The Delta Method Handbook (Ericsson Infocom 1994).

THE METHOD PURPOSE

In order to be able to use a computer system in the most efficient way, the system must present an interface that is adapted to the users and their tasks. When designing such an interface, the developers must analyze the needs, requirements, and attitudes of the customer organization (the customer and the users of the system).

The Delta method is a tool for improving communication both within the development team and between the team and the users. It is a way of working with user-centered design, in which the system designers and technical communicators are supported in carrying out the user and task analysis and in designing the user interface.

The traditional (and most common) view of the user interface is to define it as the graphic layout of the program, as it is seen on the computer screen. The Delta Method expands the concept of user interface to have a wider meaning. According to Delta, a user interface comprises three parts:

- The services offered to the user by the system; that is, the functions directly supporting user tasks.
- The actual graphic presentation of the services on the screen (traditionally referred to as the user interface).
- The enabling information (user documentation) needed by the user, in order to be able to use the system efficiently.

This definition suggests a different approach to the early phases of system development. The process of defining the system functionality is influenced by how it is to be presented to the users and the knowledge that is needed to use the functions. All three aspects of the user

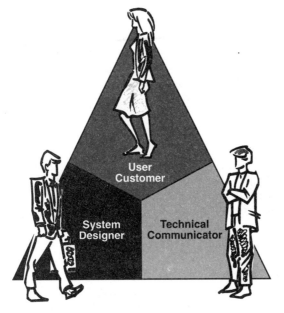

FIGURE 5.2 Three-party relation.

interface are taken into consideration when the requirements on the system are defined. A similar approach, one that defines the user documentation to be an integral part of the user interface, is proposed by Lewis and Reiman (1993). They called it the *extended user interface.*

Because the enabling information is a part of the user interface, it is important that the technical communicators and the system designers cooperate during the design process. This ensures that the different parts of the user interface are designed in a consistent way, and that the services offer a comprehensive view of the system. In other words, working according to the Delta method means that system designers and technical communicators work side-by-side during analysis and design with the aim of preserving the interests of the users.

The Delta Method distinguishes between the customer and the user of the system. The reason for this is that their opinions often differ regarding the nature of the tasks and purpose of the system. Due to this, they often impose different requirements on the system. In general, the customer wants a system that is robust, inexpensive, and easy to maintain, whereas the user rather wants a system that is simple, fast, and that supports the tasks well.

It is important that the requirements of both parties are identified and documented during the analysis. Even if the continued development has a focus on the users, it is important not to ignore the requirements of the customer. The customer is often responsible for the introduction and success of the new system, and in the end is the one that signs the check.

THE STRUCTURE OF THE DESIGN GROUP

Working according to the Delta method means to work in a design group in which a number of different skills are represented, and in which the system designers and technical communicators also are specialized within the field of interface design. It is useful (but not required) to have access to people specialized in areas such as linguistics, psychology, human factors, and cognitive sciences. Such an arrangement increases the group's knowledge of how users receive and interpret information in different environments.

The members of the group should be experienced within their respective competence areas, and should have the ability to listen to and understand the users' needs. They also need the skill to create metaphors, grounding the use of a new technique in the user's present skills and prevailing way of thinking. Other useful qualities are the ability to compromise between conflicting interests and to work with incomplete data. Many of these qualities may seem too universal to serve as requirements on the members of the group, but it is very important that the members can work well work with all types of people, and can understand and describe the users' needs.

THE ROLE OF DELTA IN THE SYSTEM DESIGN PROCESS

The Delta method is not a complete method for system design and development. However, it can be seen as a supplement to prevailing system design methods; it supports the requirements analysis and the initial design phase.

Working according to the method involves performing a detailed analysis of the system's planned functions and its users. The information concerning the users and their tasks is the basis for the design of one or several prototypes of the system. The requirements analysis includes defining requirements for usability as a part of the requirements specification.

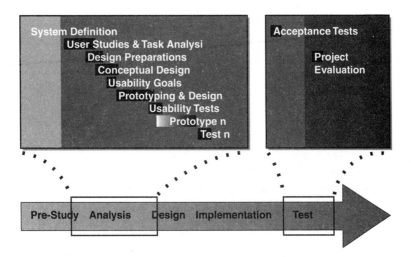

FIGURE 5.3 Integration of Delta.

How to Integrate Delta within Customer Organizations

Every method or tool is in some way dependent on (or at least influenced by) the environment in which it is developed. An organization like Ericsson relies on strict and formal ways of controlling projects, and the development process is primarily driven by documents and specifications. The structure and hierarchy of the documents vary between all the different projects in which Infocom is involved.

It was therefore impossible to create a method that would fit all the needs of different projects and customers. The Delta Method was developed as a general method for user-centered system development, and it has to be adapted to the project or organization in which it is to be used. This adaptation needs to take into consideration issues like existing development process and development culture. The need for flexibility has led to a method that is easy to adapt to many types of organizations.

Delta at Telia Network Management

Telia AB is the largest and oldest Swedish telephone company. The section for Management and Support Systems within the Network Services Division (Telia NM) is responsible for the development and deployment of management and support systems for the phone networks in Sweden. These are often very large distributed computer applications that are used by the regional telephone branches to operate the networks.

Telia NM is responsible for the development of the systems, but they seldom do the actual development themselves. They act as central supplier of new support systems, gathering the views and wishes from the regions and decide how to turn them into requirements for new support systems. A new system is then developed as a project under the management of Telia NM using system developers from subcontractors.

The system development within Telia NM is guided by a Quality System, giving rules and recommendations on issues such as Document Standards, Project Management, and buying external services and products. Telia NM wanted to include an "objective" instruction on how to gather and enforce usability requirements within this Quality System.

Telia NM had no interest in developing a usability method themselves, so (following a study of a number of alternatives) the Delta Method was chosen to be the most suitable of the candidates. The Usability Instruction is still written to be independent of existing usability methods such as Delta. It only states the required results and actions that must be fulfilled at the milestones of projects. This means that Delta is perhaps the method of choice today, but it is possible to integrate other methods in the future.

The good results and experiences from the development of Delta led us to try a similar approach to the development of a document describing the integration of the processes. We planned to develop an instruction named "Delta within Telia NM: Directions for Use" to guide the developers on how to use Delta in conjunction with Quality System. The instruction was then to be used in a pilot project or field study to gain practical experience on how it should be used. The experience gained would then be used to refine the instruction to describe the "adapted" way to use the method.

Due to time constraints for the pilot project, there was no possibility to develop complete "Directions for Use" before starting the project. The directions had to be developed in parallel with the work in the project, so while the development group worked according to the directions for an activity, the Infocom representatives had to outline the directions for the following phase.

The "Directions for Use" stated what usability activities should be carried out prior to each milestone in the development process and how the result should be integrated with the traditional development activities. So, the instruction was basically a way to describe when the Delta activities should be carried out in relation to other activities, and how the result should be used and documented. The all-important document proved to be the requirements specification. The only way to introduce a new concept in the development is to make usability a requirement with the same status as functional requirements.

THE DELTA METHOD—IN THEORY AND PRACTICE

This section contains a general description of the activities in the Delta Method and how it was used in a project involving Telia NM and a subcontractor, Telia Research. The goal of the pilot project was to develop a new generation of software to monitor and manage the hardware and software in local unmanned switches. These three very high-level tasks were to be supported by the system: management of service and upgrades, generation of work orders, and maintenance of an exchange log book.

When the project started there was an existing mainframe application performing the task, and there was also a "renegade" PC program (developed by one of the regions) that was capable of supporting some (but not all) of the required tasks. One objective of the program was to merge the two into one application that supported all the tasks.

Two consultants from Infocom (one system developer and one technical communicator) were included in the design group of the pilot project. They acted both as method support and as observers of how the method should be adapted to Telia's way of working.

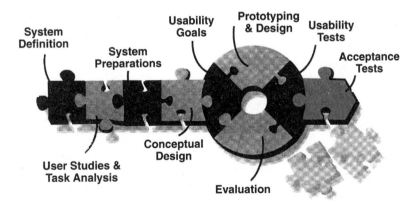

FIGURE 5.4 The Delta activities.

System Definition

The system definition is the initial activity of the method, during which the design group and customer representatives perform an analysis on a high and abstract level. The group makes a rough draft of the categories of users that are to use the system and their requirements for the system. The users are not represented during this activity; its purpose is to gather the customer requirements and set the stage for future, more user-centered work. The customer representatives are typically an upper or middle manager, marketing people, and technical or organizational specialists. During this activity the Delta people also act as "missionaries," explaining the concepts, needs, and activities of user-centered system development.

The activity is divided into three phases:

- *Preparations.* In order to prepare the definition of the system, the design group should have access to adequate background material, such as work descriptions, process descriptions, and organization overviews. As a rule of thumb, all information is useful; it is better to discard it later when the scope of the task is becoming clearer.
- *System Definition.* System designers, technical communicators, and the customer representatives cooperate in the definition of the system. The goal of the phase is that the design group develops a unified view of the scope and contents of the system.
- *System Description.* The result of the discussions is a system description that offers an overview of what the system can offer users and how the users will use the system. The description takes the users' perspective on the system, and the document serves as an excellent way to introduce newcomers to the project, putting them in the user's chair when they try to understand the system.

System Definition In Real Life

The System Definition meeting was held during two days in a remote place, far away from telephones and other distracting elements. The group of customer representatives had all been involved in the prestudy of the project. Present was also the project manager from Telia NM who had the formal responsibility for the development and also controlled the resources. The group also represented a large part of the geographic regions that were to use the system in the future. (This was not a criterion for the initial selection, it just proved to work out that way.) There was a total of eight members in the group.

During the meeting, the group developed an Information Matrix, with preliminary user categories, tasks to be supported, and the information the users need to carry them out. This matrix representation was later converted into a more textual System Description. This document was constantly updated during the entire project, and it represented the customers' requirements on the system and what areas the development group should focus on.

User and Task Analysis

As opposed to system definition (in which the customer's vision is explored), the user and task analysis aims to define the characteristics of the users and their needs. The purpose of the user and task analysis is to describe the user's present work situation and tasks. Special emphasis is put on the user's computer and work experience, need for information, work situation, and work environment, as well as the tasks themselves and how the user performs them. This information is gathered primarily through questionnaires and interviews. The result of the work is a description of the user's present situation and tasks.

User Analysis

The design group (that is, the system designers and technical communicators) need to obtain a good understanding of the users of the system. In order to do so, the Delta method recommends an initial investigation by means of a questionnaire. The design group designs the questionnaire and sends it to the persons, within the customer's organization, who are to use the system and/or have experience of similar systems. A draft of a questionnaire is included in the handbook, but it should only be seen as a template and it must be adapted to the user population.

When the questionnaires have been completed and returned, the result is compiled and analyzed. This is done with regard to aspects such as the users' prior use of computers, education, nature of work tasks, etc. The goal of the analysis is that the design group can distinguish different groups of users with different, or similar, requirements on the system. Even if the bulk of the information can be collected through questionnaires, it is important to verify and supplement the user profiles during the upcoming interviews.

User Analysis In Real Life

The general questionnaire included in the method was adapted to better suit the problem domain and what was known of the users so far. The customer representatives from the system definition activity were used to distribute the questionnaires among the users in their respective region. The System Definition had suggested six preliminary user categories and the questionnaires were distributed to all categories. The selection was slightly "adjusted" to give greater coverage of the larger, more "important" regions.

A total of 51 questionnaires were sent out, and 35 were completed and returned for analysis. The users that replied promptly were promised a small gift as an incentive to fill out and return the questionnaire.

Following the analysis of the questionnaires, one category was regarded as irrelevant and eliminated. Later on the number of categories was reduced even further, and the final design of the prototype reflected only two distinctly different categories. The different characteristics reflected that the system had to support monitoring and maintenance in both urban and city regions.

Task Analysis

When the user analysis has been carried out and a number of user categories have been identified, the design group selects representatives from each category. These are asked to participate in an interview, including a task analysis session. The purpose of the interviews is to identify the users' present tasks, and to obtain an idea of how the users perform their tasks today. The users are also involved in formulating requirements on the planned system.

It is of greatest importance that both the technical communicators and the system designers take part in the interviews. Apart from the obvious reason that one person must take notes throughout the interview, the two often have quite different motives for asking the questions, based on their areas of competence and interest. The interviews are conducted at the workplace of the users. This allows interviewers to observe users performing their present tasks and to capture the atmosphere of the workplace.

During the interview, the user will describe his or her work situation and tasks. The interviewers will try to capture the tasks in an action graph (Figure 5.5) that describes the user's tasks and environment.

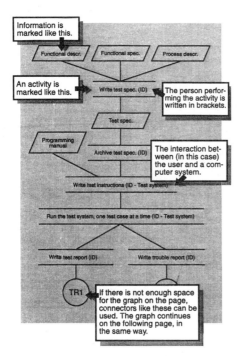

FIGURE 5.5 Action Graph depicting a task.

To verify that the information in the graphs is correct and complete, the interviewers "play back" the description of the tasks to the user. This means that the interviewer describes the work tasks captured in the action graphs to the user. This allows the user to concentrate on correcting the description and adding new information. After the interview, the graphs are given a "finishing touch" and supplemented with any new information that has emerged during the play back.

Task Analysis In Real Life

The selection of interview subjects was based on the user analysis and suggestions from the regional representatives in the system definition group. The development group performed a total of 12 interviews, and the subjects represented all user categories and all geographic regions. All the interviews were performed jointly by a system developer and a technical communicator.

The Action Graphs were used extensively during the interviews. The were some initial problems with drawing the graphs, mostly due to lack of training. The result also depended on the way the users chose to describe their work, and the interviewers' varying skill in capturing the tasks graphically. After overcoming the initial problems, the graphs were considered an excellent way of communicating by both by the interviewers and the users. The number of graphs produced during the interviews varied between one and three, depending on the responsibilities of the users and his or her way of telling his/her story.

Action Graphs describing the same tasks were merged into "super graphs" that were the basis for the continued work. These "super graphs" were also sent out to the users for verification. The graphs were considered to capture and reflect the more serious problems or drawbacks with the organization of the current tasks.

Design Preparations

After the user and task analysis, the design group should have obtained a good understanding of the users-to-be, what their work situation looks like at present, and their requirements and needs. Now the project goes into the phase of creating the future system that, as far as possible, meets these requirements and needs.

Much of the data collected so far deals with the present situation in the workplace, and the result from the interviews includes only vague ideas or hints on how the new system should support the work. The design group develops scenarios describing the future work tasks based on this information, and also develops user profiles stating needed skills and characteristics of the future users. It is very important to verify these scenarios with the users and customer.

The group also develops design recommendations based on the result of the user and task analysis, so as to capture needs and requirements that do not show up in the scenarios.

Design Preparations In Real Life

The Design Recommendations were only defined in general terms, as a collection of rules and recommendations based on the information collected so far and Telia's general guidelines for design of user interfaces, GMMS (Telia AB 1995).

The failure to produce Action Graphs and detailed scenarios describing the future tasks proved to be the biggest mistake during the whole project. They proved to be necessary later on. To avoid this problem in the future, very strict instructions detailing their development were included in the Directions for Use.

Scenarios were developed at a later stage, during the setting of the usability goals and during the tests of the paper prototype. Everyone in the design group felt they had a good understanding of the users and tasks, but the scenarios were still necessary to capture enough details when describing the work.

A scenario would look something like:

When you as a service technician arrive to your job in the morning, you are aware that some automated tests have been performed during the night. Given the ID of your operations and support station, find and analyze the result of the test runs.

As you know, one of the stations has a problem with the XWZ card. Use the inventory register to make the proper arrangements to have it replaced.

Register the actions you have taken in the exchange log.

File the problem as solved.

Conceptual Design

After the activities user and task analysis and design preparations, the actual work on designing a structure of the user interface commences. Initially this work is carried out on a comprehensive, abstract level, deciding which services the system should offer and how they should be structured.

An important issue in connection with the conceptual design is to decide how the services should be presented to the user, and to answer questions like:

- Which conceptual model is the interface intended to convey?
- Should a metaphor be used to exploit the users' background knowledge in different areas?
- Which enabling information is needed for the users to be able to actually make use of the offered services?

The design group then verifies the conceptual model with the users and the customer. The design group uses rough paper prototypes, or "neutral" computer prototypes (that is, prototypes that are independent of the implementation environment) to visualize the conceptual model. The reason for this low-fidelity approach is to move the attention from detailed design items to focus on the general service level.

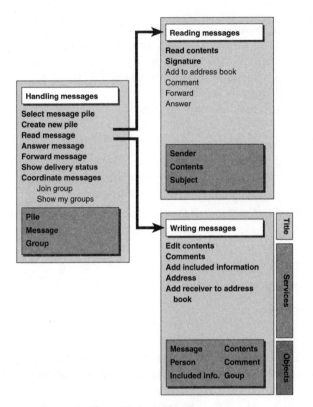

FIGURE 5.6 The UED-Notation.

Conceptual Design In Real Life

The main events during the Conceptual Design activity were two design workshops, each conducted on two consecutive days. The first workshop did not go very well. The design leaders were inexperienced and did not know how to organize the work, and the process was constantly questioned by some of the designers. The lack of scenarios and more detailed data on the users' information needs became very apparent.

The second workshop went better. The Contextual Design process had matured, and the design leaders were more familiar both with the design procedures and the work tasks. The group created a model of the system based on the UED notation described by Holtzblatt/Beyer (1993). The model contained an affinity diagram, descriptions of work tasks divided into areas of focus, and descriptions of services and objects relevant to each focus area.

Formulating Usability Goals

The next step in the process is to specify usability goals for the system. The goals are based on data from the current system, competing systems, or scenarios. The scenarios from the design preparations are used as a base when the design group defines scenarios of typical work tasks that are to be supported by the system. The scenarios consist of fictitious situations (in this case work tasks) that are attempted to be made as realistic as possible. Goals are formulated, illustrating how well the system should support the users in their work. An example of such a goal would be to state the maximum time one assignment is allowed to take. Another one could be to state the maximal number of errors allowed to be made by the user while performing a certain assignment. The goals are often related to the time required to perform an assignment with the present facilities, and the number of errors made at present.

The scenarios and usability goals together form test cases that are documented in the test specification. In order to agree on the contents of the test specification and the new requirements that may have arisen during the activity, the project manager and the customer negotiate the usability requirements in the same manner as when deciding the functional requirements. The result of this activity is a test specification and a usability specification that is a part of the requirements specification.

Usability Goals In Real Life

Just as during the conceptual design, a workshop was the focal point in the efforts to formulate usability goals. The workshop was a two-day session in which, as usual, the second day proved better than the first. During the first day the group tried to set the goals based on business and general process goals that could apply to the task. These goals were not known in detail to the group, so they were of little help.

A second attempt was to focus on the "bottlenecks" of the work processes. That way the goals could at least be used to solve problems in the most crucial areas. This approach was not met by any enthusiasm from the design group, and was therefore abandoned.

At the end of the workshop the group had created 12 usability goals with test cases (scenarios) stating how the goals should be verified. These goals were improved iteratively over time, both regarding the description of the test tasks and the goals that had to be met. Many of the test cases were later iterated with the users, who corrected and supplemented them with more realistic descriptions. They had the detailed knowledge of the domain, and the design group were then able to make the scenarios more opted to their purpose.

Prototype Design

The design group designs a prototype of the interface based on the results from the conceptual design. The structure and realization of the interface are gradually refined during the prototype design. The prototype design work is performed iteratively. At the end of each iteration, the interface is evaluated in relation to the usability goals, and the system is constantly refined. It is important to document the issues discussed during the design work in order to remember why a certain design decision was taken, so it can be reevaluated at a later date.

A possible way of going about to produce the first prototype is to build the structure with adhesive note labels, or to "draw-and-describe" on a whiteboard. The result of this is then transferred onto paper. Thus, the first prototype is a paper prototype that can be tested by the user very early in the development process. When the paper prototype is considered to be good enough, the work proceeds by sketching the layout of "screen windows," using a prototyping tool. At the same time, the structure and contents of the enabling information are outlined in a step-by-step process using prototypes.

The prototype design work is completed when the usability goals have been fulfilled or the planned number of iterations has been reached. The result of this activity is documented in a design specification, of which the prototype is a part.

Prototype Design In Real Life

The first prototype developed was a paper prototype. It was based on the information from the conceptual design and an old existing system that some of members had been involved in designing. The prototype was developed during a two-week period with the help of a designated prototyper that was hired for this one task. The paper prototype consisted of print-outs from a drawing tool on a computer. It reflected the look&feel of the target platform.

The prototype was pilot tested within the design group the day before it was shown to real users. This proved very fortunate, because it was in no way ready for a field run. Several changes and amendments had to be made to improve the structure and capabilities of the prototype.

A computer prototype was developed based on the findings from the usability tests of the paper prototype. The paper prototype was used to verify the functionality and structure of the interface. The computer prototype was more stable, and the intention was to gather more quantitative data during the usability tests. The prototype was developed with a user interface tool that makes it possible to reuse the design during implantation.

All parts of the user interface were available to the users during the usability tests. The prototype included parts of the on-line help system, and a rough user documentation. The user documentation was rather incomplete at the time of the tests, so one of the tests managers acted as a "talking book." If a user selected a relevant topic from the table of contents or the index, the talking book would tell the user the related information.

Usability Tests

The activity of testing and evaluating the interface is intimately connected to the prototype design. By testing the prototype, the design group will find out how well the prototype meets the requirements. Also, the users are given the possibility to give their opinion of the proposed design. Representatives of the user categories participate in the testing. They are asked to carry out a number of tasks ("test cases") with the help of the prototype. The work tasks here are the same as those built during the formulating of usability goals.

The design group records how the user carries out his task related to the usability goals. All experienced difficulties are of importance to the evaluation. Problems and defects found are addressed in the subsequent prototype, which in its turn is tested and corrected. This proceeds until the usability goals are fulfilled, or until a specified number of iterations have been reached. The result of the test and evaluation activity are test minutes describing the result of each user.

Usability Tests In Real Life

The paper prototype was tested by four power users that conducted the tests in pairs. Because the paper prototype was considered to be somewhat incomplete, the tests evolved into a combination of scenario-based tests and discussions on how the prototype could be improved.

One of the test leaders acted as the computer, changing the screens according to the users' actions. The other test leader took notes capturing the discussions between the users. The tests also showed the need for more detailed test scenarios, and the users were involved in improving the realism of the scenarios.

The computer prototype was tested with six users; five of them were typical users, and one of them had previous experience in system development. The tests were conducted over a two-day period in the users' workplace. On the first occasions, the introduction to the prototype was cut too short, and the users were not allowed to play around with the prototype prior to the tests. This proved to be a mistake. The inadequate introduction for the first users led to problems navigating and performing their tasks. This was corrected in the subsequent tests, in which the users were given time to become acquainted to the system.

The usability tests were guided by the scenarios, which now reflected most of the aspects of the different work tasks. All the criteria that were defined as usability goals were monitored during the tests, though some of the were regarded as hard to observe and record. The users were given a questionnaire after the tests to determine their subjective views on the prototype and the scenarios.

SUMMARY

I think that some important conclusions can be drawn both from the work of developing the Delta Method and adapting it to fit the customers' organizations.

The joint venture with Linköping University has been a very good way to transfer knowledge from the academia into our organization. They supplied us with the theories and tools to choose from, and together we tried to ensure that the concepts were viable in an industrial environment. The project in itself raised the general awareness of usability issues at Ericsson Infocom.

The way of developing Delta (inception, pilot, revision) has worked very well within Infocom. It has also been used (with slight variations) during the customer projects. Keys to the success were the field studies during the pilot project, and having a method expert both giving support and observing the use of the method.

It might seem silly, but it is very important to have a method that looks good. There was an enormous boost of credibility when the handbook for the Delta Method was presented as a nice-looking book, instead of the earlier versions with papers in a binder. It was easier to sell as a working method both to customers of Infocom and the system developers doing the actual work.

Some of the important conclusions of the pilot project at Telia were: It is important to integrate a new method tightly with the existing document structure and instructions for project management. The documents and the instructions are the driving force within the development within Telia; and if this integration is done seamlessly, it is easier to introduce the new concepts and tools. The developers feel comfortable recognizing the process as a whole, and only some minor steps and activities related to usability are new to them.

During the trails, we found it crucial to describe, test, and enforce the usability requirements in the same way as for functional requirements. Optional requirements and usability activities will be overlooked when the deadlines of the project are creeping closer.

I believe it is necessary to include the customer representatives in the user-centered design process. The nontypical users (such as power users, domain specialists, and middle management) often have the ability to see beyond today's systems and work practices. It is often a problem with ordinary users that they can give you good feedback on suggested solutions, but fail to come up with the solutions themselves.

In the future, we need to put far more emphasis on the development of scenarios drawn from the users' tasks. The scenarios might well be a good way to make the leap between analysis and design. Today this is considered as the most cumbersome step during the development process.

ACKNOWLEDGMENTS

I am ever so grateful for the help of Cecilia Bretzner and Jörgen Gustavsson with the necessary information on how the Delta work was performed "in real life."

The development of the Delta Method was a joint effort of several people and organizations. The members of the Delta method group were: Cecilia Bretzner, Ulf Idesten, Anders Möller and Göran Sandström of Ericsson Infocom, Jonas Löwgren, Pär Carlshamre, and Karin Mårdsjö of Linköping University. The importance of the contribution from the customers and members of the pilot projects cannot be overstated. They are: Ann Joachimsson and Karoline Wollin of Telia, Heather Forsyth-Rosin, Karin Axelsson, Tomas Jonsson, Jörgen Gustavsson, and Anna-Karin Andersson of Ericsson Infocom.

REFERENCES

Carlshamre, P. 1994. "A Collaborative Approach to Usability Engineering." PhD Thesis, The Department of Computer and Information Science, Linköping University.

Ericsson Infocom. 1994 *The Delta Method Handbook*. Internal Ericsson Document.

Holtzblatt, K. and Beyer, H. 1993. "Making customer-centered design work for teams." *Communications of the ACM* **36**(10), 93–103.

Lewis, C. and Rieman, J. 1993. *Task-centered User Interface Design: A Practical Introduction*. Boulder, CO: Shareware Book.

Telia AB. 1995. *GMMS, Guidelines for User Interface Design*. Telia Internal Document.

Exploring the Design of a Sales Automation Workstation Using Field Research

Robert C. Graf, Ph.D.

Microsoft Corporation

EXECUTIVE SUMMARY

Field work contains many challenges, including clarifying the goals of the sponsoring management, defining the objectives and methods of the study to support management's goals, finding common ground between users' and management's goals to increase the probability of success, spontaneously adapting methods to help users feel comfortable with being observed, structuring large amounts of data for different audiences, and communicating unanticipated results. We addressed all of these challenges in this study. The objectives and methods were communicated and negotiated with the project sponsor. The planned method of observing and video taping users working with the system was not acceptable to many of the participants. Alternate plans were adopted on-site to obtain the desired information. The final report was shaped by the data, and by the needs of the development team and management. It presented design recommendations synthesized from our observations, user interviews, and process and data models. The supporting data was categorized by the users' goals, activities, skills, information and communication needs, software and hardware problems, working styles, and mental conceptions. Flexibility and adaptability were key characteristics of this study.

BACKGROUND

Dun & Bradstreet Software Services, Inc. (DBS), a company of The Dun & Bradstreet Corporation, develops, markets, and supports financial, human resources, and manufacturing and distribution software for large national and multi-national companies. DBS was formed in March 1990 by the merger of Management Science America, Inc. (MSA) and McCormack & Dodge Corporation (M&D). These two companies were intense rivals in the mainframe business software solutions market. Shortly after the merger, the leaders of DBS began an initiative to develop a client-server solution using a Windows-based interface. The Human Factors Department was formed early in 1993 to ensure the new client-server products were useful and usable and followed the Microsoft Windows design guidelines. I was hired in 1994 to help design and evaluate usable client-server applications being developed in the Atlanta office. I also provide support for internal development of business solutions.

The field study described in this chapter was conducted during the months of August and September of 1994. It was the first usability field study that I conducted. My previous usability activities included planning, conducting, and analyzing formal laboratory studies, usability inspections, customer satisfaction surveys, and usability training sessions. Before working at DBS, I supervised the quality assurance department for a statistical software development company and managed software development and design projects.

PLANNING THE STUDY

I was contacted by the manager of a team developing a PC-based mobile workstation to support the internal sales staff after he attended a usability training session that I conducted with my manager. The complete system consisted of a notebook PC, applications, local and central databases, and the hardware and software needed to communicate with the central databases. The project manager's usability goals were vague. He wanted help in making the second release of the existing product more "usable" and "intuitive." The product had been in the field for nearly a year and was receiving very mixed reactions. The goals for the product were to:

1. Increase sales
2. Reduce the cost of sales
3. Provide better competitive information

I met with the project manager and representatives from the development team to learn about their needs, their schedules, the operation of the product, user reactions, and the typical user profile. The team was coming under pressure to improve user acceptance of the product. Obviously, it would be impossible to achieve the three project goals if users refused to use the system. The team had five months to discover and correct usability problems. The user population was diverse. It included marketing representatives, technical product representatives, junior and senior sales personnel, and managers. The working environments, goals, computer literacy, and typing skills differed substantially among users. However, all of these users were instrumental in completing the sales cycle and generating revenues. The challenge was to create a common tool that everyone could use to attain their goals.

In order to further clarify the situation, I composed a list of questions and planned a second meeting with the project development team and the national sales process manager. This list formed the meeting's agenda:

1. Who are the primary and secondary users?
2. What are the distinguishing characteristics of satisfied and dissatisfied users?
3. What skills and knowledge do users possess?
4. What are the users' goals, processes, functions, and tasks?
5. Which functions and tasks can be automated?
6. Which parts of the system are the focus of the inquiry (that is, software, documentation, online help, training, support, etc.)?
7. What are the primary and secondary usability attributes most related to system success (that is, ease of learning, efficiency, resistance to errors, training time, etc.)?
8. What are the criteria for success?
9. How can the system directly benefit the users?
10. How can we make contact with users?
11. Whose approval do we need to obtain in order to contact users?
12. Whom should we contact?
13. What department will bear the cost of the study?

We learned that the primary users were the junior and senior sales personnel, sales management, and marketing representatives. Satisfied users could be classified as individuals who enjoy and embrace technology. The most pressing goal for the sales force was to make or exceed their sales revenue quota for each quarter. Commissions and bonuses were based upon these revenues. The group decided that software was the primary focus of the study. Management expected users to be proficient and self-reliant with the workstation. It had to be easy to learn and easy and efficient to use. Errors had to be easy to detect and correct. Rather than measure these attributes directly, success was to be determined by user acceptance (as measured by a reduction in support calls and complaints). Clearly, user acceptance would be achieved if the workstation directly helped them close more sales. The national sales process manager was the key contact for the accessing users. She would support the project if she became convinced that a usability study would be beneficial.

Considering the wide diversity of users and their need to interact efficiently on a sales cycle that could take 6 to 12 months, we decided to study users in their world. I proposed a study in which I and a team representative would accompany users on actual sales calls. This was rejected by the sales manager as being too intrusive to the sales process. We settled on a plan to interview satisfied and dissatisfied primary users at their site and watch how they interacted with the system. I felt that a field study was essential to obtain a thorough understanding of the realities of sales and the benefits of mobile computing.

I prepared a formal proposal for conducting the study and submitted it to the development team and the national sales process manager. The study was accepted. Funding for travel was to be split between the development group and the Human Factors department. Word went out from the global sales process manager to selected sales regions to prepare for and cooperate with the usability study.

CONDUCTING THE STUDY

The national sales process manager provided us with the names of four regional sales managers. She was an architect of the system, and had a vested interest in its success. The four regions chosen for the study were the Southeast, Southwest, Midwest, and Canada; these regions represented different levels of acceptance to the system. Each regional manager was told to cooperate with our study. We selected several names from each job description at each site that represented satisfied and dissatisfied users. Scheduling was time-consuming, but was facilitated by use of bulk phone messages and e-mail. Every participant was sent a copy of the proposal via e-mail.

I traveled with one of two representatives from the development team to each site over a period of two weeks. We interviewed a total of 16 users. The interviews lasted from one to three hours. My role was to lead the interview process; the team member took notes, asked clarifying questions, and provided answers to technical questions when they arose.

We originally planned to video tape the interviews, especially the parts in which users interacted with the system. However, the first four users made it very clear that videotaping was not acceptable, so we stopped suggesting it. I believe several factors contributed to their reluctance to being videotaped. Sales is a high-pressure job, and being captured on tape while struggling with a sales system is threatening. Some of the interviewees were highly successful sales leaders and managers who usually run the show, and being a subject in a videotape was not comfortable for them.

The data that we collected were not as clean and organized as we originally planned. The interview process naturally progressed in directions that did not follow the list of planned questions. Many users did not want to complete the written questionnaire, but provided verbal responses instead. The bulk of our data involved massive amounts of handwritten and typed notes that were generally based upon our original question list. We planned to organize data into categories by job description to bring some order to the chaos.

ANALYZING AND INTERPRETING THE DATA

Data analysis began on the return flight of the last trip. It was a response to the urgent need to provide structure and meaning to the volume of data that was collected. I felt that the analysis and report had several different audiences: the project management, the higher-level sales managers, and the developers. I wanted to create a format that would enable these different groups to easily access the information they needed to make decisions and do their job. We tried organizing responses and observations by listing and summarizing them under each of the specific interview questions. This approach was unsatisfactory. The interviews were too divergent and the observations were too extensive to be categorized neatly into answers to 11 questions.

After discussions with my traveling companions, I chose to organize the report into three major sections: a summary report, three detailed tasks analyses, and two business models. The summary report summarized the study and presented issues and recommendations that were common to all users. It provided a quick way to provide summary information to management. The task analyses and business models were longer, more detailed descriptions that were designed for use by the developers.

The task analyses provided detailed descriptions of the tasks of the regional sales managers, senior sales executives, and junior sales executives, respectively. We decided that the task analyses should include a day-in-the-life narrative of a typical day, and a description of critical activities and informational needs. The narrative provided the develop-

TABLE 6.1 Data Categories and Examples.

Category	Examples
Goals	• achieve revenue goals • identify qualified leads
Activities	• establish relationships with key personnel • negotiate terms of contract
Crucial Information	• competitive information of competitors • corporate hierarchy of client organization
Physical Environment	• hotel lobby • automobile
Preferred Workstation	• Microsoft PowerPoint
Applications	• Microsoft Excel
Other Productivity Aids	• paper day planner • electronic "wizard"
Benefits of Workstation	• increases productivity by reducing time to share crucial information • provides organization and structure to complex deals
Delighters	• easy access to database of business presentations • ability to fax quotes immediately to prospects
Problems	• data entry is inefficient and slow • inadequate disk space
Requests	• context sensitive help for every required field • a method to transfer data to and from electronic wizards
Training Preferences	• provide timely classroom instruction • train a technical representative for each region
User Comments	• "The workstation stays in my car or hotel. I never type while face-to-face with a client." • "I love to use the workstation to make business presentations."

ers with the background needed to understand the significance of the detailed data. A table was created to categorize the detailed observations and responses based upon the needs of the developers and the natural categories that emerged from the data. This process was akin to creating an affinity diagram, but was performed by reviewing our notes while seated at the airport. The table format allowed developers to easily locate information that was relevant to their needs.

The business models were created by the team's business analyst and included a sales process model and data model. The process model presents all the activities a salesperson needs to manage a deal. The salesperson coordinates a host of different resources and information and converts this into a contract. The data model presents all of the information the salesperson needs to do his or her job.

The following outline shows the organization of the report. The team agreed that the summary report would provide management with an overview of the users' situation and a plan for addressing their needs and requirements. The task analyses and the business models would provide developers with specific data for guiding their development of individual components of the system.

A. Summary Report
  i. Overview of Study
  ii. Purpose
  iii. Method
  iv. General Summary of Findings
  v. Common Needs of Users
  vi. Recommendations
    a. High Priority Enhancements
    b. Proposal for Usability Inspection of the System
    c. Proposal for User-Centered Design Meeting
    d. "The Deal": A Sales-centered Metaphor the Workstation
    e. Future Enhancements
    f. Issues for Additional Research

B. Task Analyses of the Primary Users' Work
  i. Description of the Position
  ii. Data Tables
  iii. Conclusions and Prioritized Recommendations

C. Business Models
  i. The Process Model–see Figure 6.1
  ii. The Data Model–see Figure 6.2

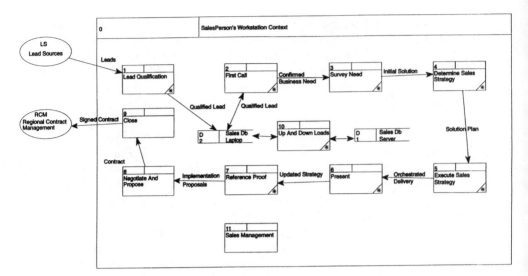

FIGURE 6.1 Business process model of the sales cycle.

IMPACTING THE DESIGN

The report was distributed in draft form to the team members who traveled to the sites and to the interviewees for review and editing. When all the issues were clearly and fairly represented, the final draft was distributed to the entire development team, management, and the interviewees. The report was 24 pages in length and took two weeks to complete.

A usability inspection was conducted shortly after the report was completed. Participants in the review included members of the Human Factors team, users of the system, and members of the development team. A prioritized list of usability issues was produced. This process was greatly enriched by the knowledge gained by the team members who participated in the interviews or who read the report.

The prioritized list of recommendations from the field study and the usability inspection was used to provide enhancements to the forthcoming release of the system. Only enhancements that did not alter the existing structure of the workstation were selected.

It became apparent that only a select group of technically adept users who had access to adequate hardware capacity were truly benefiting from the system. These users had invested their own money and time to customize the system to meet their needs. The individual styles of sales personnel differed dramatically, and the system as de-

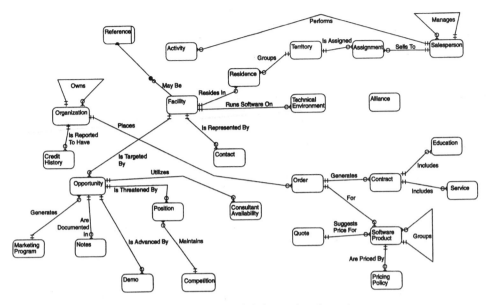

FIGURE 6.2 Data model of the salesperson's informational needs.

livered lacked the flexibility to accommodate these styles. Customization was discouraged by the workstation maintenance group, because
it introduced variability and inefficiency into their work.

The ultimate conclusion of the study was the discovery of a sales-
based, user-centered metaphor, "The Deal." This concept was envisioned
as a software object, like a compound document, that would organize all
of the functions of the workstation into a manageable and comprehensi-
ble system. A participatory design meeting was proposed and planned in
which representatives from each job description would meet with workstation developers, the business analyst, and me to enact a representative scenario of a typical deal using the existing workstation. Deals are
complex and highly interactive. The group was use the workstation to
access, generate, record, and communicate all the information and documents required during a complete sales cycle, from generating leads to
closing the deal. The deliverables would consist of usability goals and a
design proposal that would facilitate the efficient flow of information to
all sales team members throughout the sales cycle. Technical adepts
and novices were to be present for this design meeting.

Unfortunately, the system did not receive additional funding for a
major redesign. The workstation and support systems will be frozen
after the planned enhancements are implemented. Use of the system

will be purely voluntary, and no data will be collected regarding the impact upon the original goals.

ASSESSING THE COST/BENEFIT

The study required six days of travel and lodging for two people at a cost of about $4500. The development team and the Human Factors department invested about four person-weeks of time in the project. The results of the study were well received by all involved parties. However, the timing of the usability study (too late in development) and management changes resulted in the project's termination.

This was our company's first experience with intensive field data collection methods. The costs in dollars and time were considered acceptable. Additional studies are planned for other projects.

REFLECTING ON THE EXPERIENCE

The main problem with the study was getting time in the salespersons' schedule in which they could participate. We expected to conduct the interview in early August, but didn't get to the sites until the end of the month. Unfortunately, these times coincided with the end of a quarter—a very bad time for sales personnel. Quarterly sales goals are often achieved or not achieved during this period. Some hard feelings were generated among the regional sales managers who were told to cooperate.

The detailed plans for executing and analyzing the study had to be modified due to the reactions of the participants. Laboratory control is not possible in the field. Flexibility and a willingness to follow the lead of the participant are essential.

I will continue to attempt to visit and interview users while they are actually engaged in their work. The data gathered in this manner is more representative than that gathered from a user's self-report. However, given the reality of the salespersons' situation, the methodology used was the only acceptable course of action.

I will also try to videotape users in the future. This provides the team members who remain in the office with a more concrete experience of the users' situation. However, videotaping is not a substitute for careful and accurate notes. We found that taking notes sequentially was very helpful for recounting the flow and context of the interview, and for capturing task sequences.

I suggest taking a tape recorder along to the interviews for the purpose of recording personal observations *after* the interview. Due to the large amount of data, important issues can be easily lost during the analysis of field notes that may occur several days (or weeks) after the interview.

I was very excited by the discovery of a user-centered sales-based metaphor, "The Deal," that had the potential for organizing and dramatically increasing the flow of information between all members of the sales force. Although this concept remained undeveloped, it was immediately recognized as potentially powerful by several members of the sales team. I believe that discovering emergent high-level concepts that can be developed into efficient and useful products may be one of the unique benefits of conducting field studies.

ACKNOWLEDGEMENTS

Several people contributed to the planning and execution of this study. I want to acknowledge Chauncey Wilson, Bruce Harple, Jaime Davenport, and Kathy Potts for their role as managers who supported this project. I want to thank and acknowledge my traveling companions, Barbara Pisano and David Pettus, who helped me schedule, conduct, and analyze the interviews. Tara Scanlon and Beth Loring contributed helpful suggestions for conducting effective site visits. Philip Lingo provided technical assistance in installing and supporting software. Finally, I want to thank Dennis Wixon and Judy Ramey for organizing the field study workshop at *CHI'95* that provided the basis for this publication.

REFERENCES

Several usability concepts were mentioned in this chapter, but not elaborated upon. The following reading list will provide more depth to concepts like usability inspection, usability attributes, metaphor, affinity diagram, participatory design, task analysis, and process and data modeling.

Candace, C. and von Halle, B. 1989. *Handbook of Relational Database Design*. Reading MA: Addison-Wesley Publishing Company.
Denzin, N. and Lincoln, Y. (Eds.) 1994. *Handbook of Qualitative Research*. Newbury Park, CA: Sage Publications.

Holtzblatt, K. and Beyer, H. 1993. "Making customer-centered design work for teams." *Communications of the ACM* **36**(10), 93–103.

Mayhew, D. 1992. *Principles and Guidelines in Software User Interface Design*. Englewood Cliffs, NJ: Prenctice Hall.

Muller, M., Wildman, D., and White, D. 1993. "Taxonomy of participatory practices: A brief practitioners guide." *Communications of the ACM* **36**(4), 26–28.

Nielsen, J. 1993. *Usability Engineering*. New York: Academic Press.

Nielsen, J. 1994. *Usability Inspection Methods for Software*. New York: John Wiley & Sons, Inc.

Organizational Considerations in Field-Oriented Product Development: Experiences of a Cross-Functional Team

David E. Rowley

Varian Chromatography Systems

EXECUTIVE SUMMARY

Varian Chromatography Systems, a manufacturer of analytical instrumentation and data systems, uses small, focused, cross-functional teams in the development of its products. This chapter describes the efforts of one such team in the pursuit of a better understanding of the end user's world through the use of Contextual Inquiry. The team faced hurdles in planning and conducting an international field study, making effective use of the data gathered, and incorporating the method into the established product development process. The approaches taken and the lessons learned provide an insight into the issues facing many corporations that are asking product developers to acquire new skills and adapt to new organizational paradigms.

BACKGROUND

Many companies involved with product development are switching from a traditional function-oriented organization to highly focused cross-functional teams. This trend, accompanied by the downsizing phenomenon, has required workers to develop new skills and work in new ways. The shift in the organization away from functional departments can have an impact on field-oriented design efforts. There may no longer be a central repository of expertise in field study techniques (if there ever was one); the motivation and expertise required to perform field studies must now come from within the product development team. Such organizational reengineering may result in engineers, technical writers, and marketing personnel all conducting the sort of ethnographic work once only performed by field study specialists.

Varian Chromatography Systems has made this switch to cross-functional product line teams, and one team's efforts in conducting Contextual Inquiry illustrate some of the advantages and difficulties posed by the new management paradigm. Removing the barriers often found between functional departments results in improved communication and coordination within the team, but the lack of centralization may reduce the scope of impact of field study findings. While it may be easier to impact the design of a product developed by the team conducting the study, it is harder to effect change in the design of products developed by other teams. This chapter will describe how a product line team in this environment approached the task of Contextual Inquiry—how they developed the necessary skills, how they went about conducting a study, and how they incorporated the process into the overall product design effort.

Company Profile

Varian is a diversified, international manufacturer of high-technology electronic devices. Varian's core businesses include semiconductor manufacturing equipment, health care systems, and analytical instrumentation. Chromatography Systems is a division of the Instrument group, which represents a $372 million annual business. The Chromatography Systems factory is located in Walnut Creek, California and has sales offices in over 15 countries worldwide. The majority of sales come from outside the United States.

There are approximately 250 people employed at the Walnut Creek site, including manufacturing personnel. Four product lines are developed by this group: gas chromatographs (GC), high-performance liquid chromatographs (HPLC), GC mass spectrometers (GC/MS), and data-handling products. This chapter will focus on the efforts of the data-handling product line team, who develop data systems used to control chromatography equipment and process chromatographic data into meaningful results. Chromatography is a technique used to detect, measure, and regulate compounds found in a variety of samples. This technique is used in a widely diverse number of applications, including environmental analysis (soil, water and air testing), pharmaceutical manufacturing (quality assurance and new product development), petroleum, toxicology, and industrial hygiene. The vast number of applications of this technology provides significant challenges to developers who are concerned with understanding user profiles and performing task analysis.

MAKEUP OF A PRODUCT LINE TEAM

Like many companies involved in product development, Varian has explored a number of organizational models over the years. Most recently, the chromatography system business has been organized into cross-functional product line teams. These teams are composed of applications experts, engineers, marketing personnel, technical writers, technical support staff, and manufacturing staff. The resulting organization resembles several small companies within the business unit, each focused on a single product line. The exact makeup of the teams varies depending on the nature of the product line. For example, the data-handling product line, which does not develop hardware products, has only one part-time manufacturing representative responsible for installation of software on computers shipped from the factory. Technical support, technical publications, and manufacturing are not purely divided among the product lines; these organizations still represent pools that are managed independently. This hybrid of a functional model and a product line model is a result of resource limitations (there are not enough people to split up into the four product lines) and managerial streamlining (resulting in reduction in overhead, particularly in manufacturing).

As the employees at Varian have adapted to the new organization, the traditional roles played by members of former functional departments have changed. This has been particularly true in the data-handling product line. In the past, it was predominantly members of the marketing department who would visit customers and interact with the field sales organization. Software engineers would rarely have an opportunity to make such contacts, and if they did so, it would be under the guidance of marketing. The purpose for these customer contacts typically would be to solve specific technical problems, or perhaps to function as part of a new product introduction. When the product line teams were established, the roles of the team members blended across functional boundaries, creating the opportunity for greater direct contact between software developers and end users. Along with this opportunity came the responsibility for acquiring the skills and expertise necessary to deploy field-oriented methods effectively. This included not only the skills typically associated with Contextual Inquiry, but a much deeper understanding of the diverse markets served by the products developed by the team.

ACQUIRING SKILLS

Usability engineering methods are not a foreign concept to the data-handling product line team. Prior to conducting Contextual Inquiry, the data handling team had been involved in mobile usability testing, where a makeshift usability laboratory is taken on the road (Rowley 1994). Several other "in-house" usability engineering techniques had also been used, including co-operative evaluation (Wright and Monk 1991), heuristic evaluation (Nielsen and Molich 1990) and user interface walkthroughs (Rowley 1992). All of these efforts emerged from within and directly involved the product development team, and many of the techniques involved some customer contact.

Previous experience with various usability evaluation techniques had resulted in very good feedback, but was limited to portions of the product focused on during the test. Lacking in these methods was a way to capture the *big picture*. Contacts with sales people and customers had resulted in some useful inputs, but none of the big-picture data was being communicated back to the members of the development team. In order to accomplish this, a technique was needed that could acquire some portion of the environment and work habits data gathered at the customer site and vividly reproduce it to the team in such a way that it could support product design. It was important that each person who made design decisions on a product could understand how those decisions would affect the work of the end user.

For this purpose, Contextual Inquiry was selected as the method of choice. It would allow the team to capture very rich information from customer sites while not relying upon a large sample size to generate valid data (Holtzblatt and Jones 1993). Contextual Inquiry was also considered a very feasible and *approachable* technique. A few members of the team had attended tutorials on Contextual Inquiry (Wixon and Raven 1994), while others had already developed some of the skills necessary for conducting semistructured interviews from years of usability testing in the field. Also, appropriate recording equipment (a hand-held video camera) was inexpensive and readily accessible to the team.

GAINING EXPERIENCE

Although the tutorial on Contextual Inquiry had provided hands-on training, real-world experience cannot be taught in tutorials and cannot be acquired without throwing some caution to the wind. As was mentioned earlier, Varian Chromatography Systems sells most of its instruments outside the United States, with roughly sixty percent of sales going to Europe. So when it came time to conduct the first field study, it was decided that an international trip was appropriate. Not only would this provide members of the team with valuable information about various types of labs in several European countries, but would also generate a wealth of experience in the cultural implications of field study techniques.

PLANNING AN INTERNATIONAL STUDY

Members of the European field organization had requested meetings with the development team to discuss ideas for new products. Two members from the team planned to visit sales specialists in the field for this purpose. This would also provide them with an opportunity to set up visits with customers in the area. In planning this trip, the product line team described a customer profile about which they wished to gain more firsthand knowledge. The sponsoring sales specialists were notified that the two visiting team members wished to visit labs matching this profile, but the choice of the specific sites was left up to the specialists. Control over the site selection would give sales specialists the opportunity to show good will to customers with whom they wished to foster a close relationship.

There were two overall goals the team had hoped to accomplish by conducting this study:

- Gather general information, preferably on video tape, of typical laboratory environments in which Varian instruments were used. The purpose of this data was to give software engineers, technical writers, and other team members a real sense of the flavor of the user's world (Brun-Cottan and Wall 1995).
- Investigate the requirements for specific new products that would fit into this environment. This second goal would shape the direction of the interviews and observations.

To help refine the focus of the observations, the team used affinity diagrams to derive a small set of focus statements from a large list of questions, assumptions, and ideas they had about the customers' work patterns (see Table 7.1). Three focus areas were selected:

1. Who are the people in the lab and what roles do they play?
2. How do these people communicate instructions, status, and results to each other?
3. How do these people use their data systems to accomplish their work?

The two team members hoped to talk to individuals who worked in various roles in the labs to get their firsthand insights into these issues. They also had prototype software that could be shown to the customers to get feedback and to investigate future scenarios.

As mentioned previously, a hand-held video camera would be used to record as much of the site visits as possible. Because many of the customers would be pharmaceutical laboratories (who often have strict regulations on recording equipment), it was unclear exactly how many sites would allow such equipment on the premises. The sales specialists had been given advance warning of this, and many of them were skeptical about whether recording devices would be allowed into the labs. Instead of attempting to get full authorization from the customers, which may take months in some cases, the "surprise attack" approach was favored, hoping it would be easier to show up at the door with a video camera than to struggle with multiple layers of red tape (it's easier to beg forgiveness than ask permission).

The two members of the product line team who would make the trip were both project leaders—one with a software engineering background, and the other with a background in chemistry. They would be accompanied by a hosting salesperson at each customer site. At the time they left on the trip, it was not known exactly how many customers would be visited. The trip would last two and a half weeks (including travel time) and would target four countries where Varian had a significant presence: England, France, Switzerland, and Germany. One of the team members spoke fluent French and some German, and the sales specialists all spoke fluent English. The amount of English spoken by the customers was likely to vary greatly.

CONDUCTING THE STUDY

Concerns about the use of video equipment in pharmaceutical labs were justified—the first several labs visited would not allow the use of a camera. Without any other recording device, the team resorted to

TABLE 7.1 Refining the focus using affinity grouping.

Original Questions, Grouped by Affinity	*Focus Statements Derived from Groups*
• Who uses the instruments in the lab?	
• What are the responsibilities of the various lab workers?	
• What restrictions apply to various job	
• What job titles are used?	Who are the people in the lab and what roles do they play?
• Who recalculates results?	
• Who calibrates instruments?	
• Who generates graphical images?	
• Who generates automation lists?	
• How is information communicated between lab workers?	
• How is connectivity implemented?	How do these people communicate instructions, status, and results to each other?
• Where do the lab workers get their directions?	
• Where does the data go after it leaves the lab?	
• Are instruments shared?	
• How many types of analysis are performed?	
• How much time is spent recalculating results?	
• How are graphics used?	How do these people use their data systems to accomplish their work?
• How many injections are typically made of each sample?	
• How often is calibration done?	
• What type of calibration is done?	
• What type of reports are generated?	

taking copious notes during the interviews and observations. Once inside the customer sites, they would typically be introduced to the laboratory manager. They revealed to the manager the nature of the visit and the three areas on which they wished to focus. A loose agenda was set up for the visit, always concluded with a question-and-answer period. The customers invariably had a list of inputs and questions about current products that the interview team were obliged to address. Most site visits lasted half a day.

The interview with the lab manager would give a general understanding of the cultural topography of the lab, and an overview of the processes used by the various individuals who worked there. It was no surprise to find that each individual lab, even labs in the same industry, had different job titles, procedures, restrictions, and requirements.

Following an initial interview session, the team asked to go into the lab and talk to some people doing real work. In several cases, they were very successful in getting a glimpse into the day-to-day issues of the lab. There was a tendency on the part of the users (and even the sales specialists) to treat the observation like a presentation—they would describe in general terms how work might be done. The interviewers constantly had to reiterate that they wanted to observe actual work. In some cases, partially due to the language barrier, the sales specialist who assumed the role of host would stand between the interviewers and the user and explain how the lab operated. It sometimes required constant, gentle prodding to get the sales specialist to step aside and allow the user to tell the story (or better yet, act out the story).

The team finally did encounter a few labs that would allow the use of video equipment. Two of them happened to have a special relationship with each other, so their combined observation helped illustrate some important aspects of their workflow. One was a chemical manufacturer that produces materials used in the manufacturing of pharmaceuticals. The team observed a quality-control lab that tests samples taken from manufacturing batches at regular intervals. This lab works in interrupt mode, having to respond to samples coming from the production area very quickly. The second company observed was the distributor used by this chemical manufacturer. Truckloads of the product are sent to the distribution company to be transported to the manufacturer's customers. The distribution company checks the incoming product to ensure that it meets the acceptance criteria of the customer, and to protect against contamination of the distribution company's storage facility. During the visit, the contents of the truck being tested was marginally out of spec, and required a verbal approval from the manufacturer before acceptance. Observing the two companies consecutively allowed the team to see how the companies worked together and how they resolved problems. Also, because videotape was used, some of the sights and sounds of a busy, crowded QC lab contrasted with the experience of pulling samples from a tanker truck could be brought back to the development team.

Even when allowed to use the video camera, the quality of the recording left a lot to be desired. Most of the labs visited were filled with fairly loud instruments in close proximity, with very little room to move around. Hand-held video cameras typically have a narrow-angle lens, making it difficult to get a good view of the entire lab. Most of the shots of users and instruments were extreme close-ups. Also, the built-in microphones in most video cameras are very good at picking up every sound in a room, obscuring the voice of the person you want to hear. Although the team had a lapel microphone to use during inter-views, it could not be employed practically while following subjects around the lab, especially if they had to run outside to take a sample from a tanker truck. The result is a rather poor-quality video with a noisy audio track. An experienced camera operator is a valuable asset here. The team's relative lack of experience with the camera resulted in many minutes of inaudible tape with the subject's face off-camera. With experience you learn to always keep the subject's mouth in view when they are talking—the lip-reading cues are essential when the audio is poor.

INTRODUCING PROTOTYPES

As mentioned earlier, prototype software was used to explore future scenarios—trying out new tools to accomplish tasks observed during the visit. At most sites, the team had the opportunity at least to demonstrate portions of the prototype and get some feedback. The pro-totype review was typically done after the observation portion of the visit. The prototype software only served to illustrate how the user would interact with a new product; there was no real functionality implemented. For many customers, the lack of functionality was a problem. They could not get a good idea of how the product might influence their workflow. There were a few customers who provided some very good inputs, and some possible new areas of development were explored that had not been considered prior to the study.

The prototype did afford one interesting observation that has had a fundamental influence on the marketing and development strategy taken for this new product. A prototype had been developed with the U.S. petrochemical industry in mind. A trend in this industry (as well as many others) is the employment of instrument operators who have limited chromatography experience. They are instructed on basic oper-ation of the equipment, and are restricted from making any changes that may affect the results. The prototype was developed to support these restrictions. At many of the European sites visited, it was found there was an adverse reaction to the positioning of this product. Most of the customers visited were proud of the high level of training the operators had received, and the operators were given a greater amount of freedom to make modifications to the analysis procedures than had been expected. Although the prototype product could still add significant value to their work, the *spin* that had been put on it was definitely wrong.

In one case, the team decided not to show the prototype software to the customer. The customer had been working with Varian on developing a custom interface to the data system used in a quality assurance lab. The customer had changed their standard operating procedure to use the new customized interface, and (after months of tuning) they were very satisfied with the solution. The prototype software provided an alternate interface to the data system, and also introduced a new workflow model. While the future system that was prototyped might have very well fit the tasks performed at this lab, it was decided (on the spot) that introducing a new interface to this customer would send a mixed message about Varian's commitment to the current offering. Stability in this type of organization is critical, and it was decided that showing a prototype would not be well-received by the customer, nor fruitful to the observers.

KEEPING THINGS IN PERSPECTIVE

Whenever customer visits are used as a mechanism for gathering requirements for a new product, there is always a concern that the specific requirements from one customer may skew the impression of the requirements for the entire market. During this study, the team was well aware of this phenomenon and attempted to keep each customer's input in perspective within the overall market. It seems clear that a good understanding of the market segments is required to effectively make these judgments. The interviewers used their own experience in the industry (along with the input from the sales specialists) to apply weight to the data points gathered. This approach is not infallible (you can always make false assumptions), but it becomes more reliable as you gather more data. The organization of the product-line team seems to help in this area. The team is able to use their experience with the application to help discern outliers from market trends, where an independent field research organization (having presumably less experience with the application) may find that differentiation more difficult.

One adverse situation was encountered that could have potentially affected the objectivity of the study. The situation was related to the sales specialists picking the customer sites. Some sales specialists used the customer to make a point about a particular issue or feature they wanted to emphasize. While it is very important to take into account specific feature requests during the visit, it can sometimes get in the way of collecting more general workflow data. This situation is difficult to avoid. One possible solution is to ensure that an alternate mechanism exists to collect this sort of data, and to encourage the field organization to use this mechanism. For example, change request forms can be distributed to the field for their use, and completed forms can be logged by the development team. The status of the change request can then be sent back to the sales person or customer who initiated the request. It is also worthwhile to spend time with the hosting salespeople and let them know exactly what you wish to accomplish with the customer. In several cases during this study, that was limited to the time spent in the car on the way to the customer's lab. Despite these efforts, it is possible that hidden agendas will arise at the customer site. Part of the experience of conducting field studies is recognizing when pet issues have been set up, and being able to deal with them gracefully.

TOO MANY NOTES

At the end of the two-week data-collection portion of the study, the two-member interview team had visited 15 customer sites in four countries. Many of the interviews conducted involved some sort of interpreter (a situation that we had hoped to avoid), and there was relatively little videotape to show for the hours spent observing customers. However, the two objectives established when entering the study were met:

1. Videotape and artifacts were gathered that could be used to help illustrate users' workflow to the rest of the development team. Although the best example of this data came from companies in one market segment, the environment and issues surrounding these labs are quite typical of other markets.
2. Specific requirement inputs, along with more general strategic marketing inputs, were gathered for new products.

The process of analyzing the information gathered was long and somewhat overwhelming. Immediately after the trip (on the plane ride home), preliminary analysis began. An overview of the site visits and immediate recommendations for product development were quickly generated. This initial report was followed by a more careful study of the videotape and the creation of a composite tape. The tape was shared with members of the product line team as well as members of other product line teams that may use such techniques in future customer visits.

The recommendations made from the analysis of the study were documented in the change control system used by the development team to track feature requests and bug reports to closure. A change control board consisting of members from the product-line team review the submitted changes and determine their priority. By putting the recommendations directly into the change control system, the data from the observations was quickly assimilated into the teams' routine mechanism for managing design changes. No special procedural accommodations had to be made for these field inputs. Members of the change control board considered these inputs simply as highly informed change requests, and typically gave them a higher priority than change requests submitted by internal sources. That the changes were based on well-documented observations no doubt enhanced their credibility.

The information in the preliminary report had an impact on products currently under development. Several of the inputs submitted to the change control board were implemented. Other inputs changed the approach to the development of new products. The team's experience with the software prototype reviewed during the study indicated that the positioning of this product needs to be reconsidered before proceeding.

The overall impact of the study was disappointing. There were just too many notes taken at too many sites to effectively consolidate them without investing a tremendous amount of time and effort. Because both interviewing team members were project leaders whose primary charters were to schedule and manage software projects, sufficient time never became available. While the recommendations provided valuable inputs, the goal of bringing back a vivid picture from the field was not satisfactorily filled. The interview team gained insights, but dissemination of those insights was not particularly effective or widespread. The impression of the study on the development team was not much better than when customer visits were made by members of the marketing department in the past organization.

OPPORTUNITIES FOR IMPROVEMENT

If Contextual Inquiry was going to become a routine procedure during product development, several changes would have to be made to the way in which it was implemented. The two biggest problems with the first study were the inability to process the overwhelming amount of raw data gathered from the site visits, and the inability to adequately convey the big picture to the rest of the team. The first problem, that of too much data all at once, was mostly due to the lack of organization prior to the study. If the interview team had a way of organizing the data as it was collected, the task of analyzing the observations would be much easier. Certainly the team's lack of experience in this sort of data gathering technique was a major contributor here. Also, the fact that so many sites were visited in such a short period of time (without any time between visits to digest the incoming material) made the sheer volume of data a barrier to its analysis.

The second problem (not being able to effectively reproduce the experience of the visit) cannot be addressed so easily. Even with very good video quality, there is no way to capture everything that goes on. With the recording restrictions encountered at so many customer sites, it seemed unlikely that video could be used on a regular basis. The only way to get the full impact of the visit was to experience it first-hand. However, unless customers could become far more accessible, this could not be feasibly accomplished.

THE PRODUCT DEVELOPMENT PARTNERSHIP

It became clear that it was necessary to have direct access to customers who would consent to site visits and be willing to participate in design activities. While giving sales specialists the choice of which customers would be visited involved them in the process, it added an extra layer between the development team and the end user. To eliminate the layer meant some other mechanism for recruiting customers would have to be established. Also, the team would have to track which customers were interested in hosting site visits, what types of activities were performed at those sites, and what specific interests those customers had. If all of this information could be directly available to the development team, then contacts could be made with little advance notice, and the team could focus on customers who did the type of work being targeted for investigation.

And so the Product Development Partnership was formed. Brochures were sent out to registered data-handling customers asking them to participate in a co-development relationship with the product line team. Site visits were mentioned as one of several possible types of encounters that might occur as a result of the partnership. On the return mailer, customers were asked some basic questions about the type of work they do and any special interests they might have. In less than three weeks, over ten percent of the brochure recipients responded, some of them quite enthusiastically.

A database was set up documenting all contacts with the partners, starting with the responses in the return mailer. Follow-up telephone calls and e-mail were sent out asking more detailed questions about which parts of the data system were most important to them. This information would provide screening parameters to help select site visits for specific studies. The database provides a framework for logging all information collected at a customer site. Also, the fact that the observations are logged into the database makes them immediately accessible by anyone on the product line team.

The Partnership, which currently only targets U.S. customers, was created with the buy-in of the U.S. sales manager. In order to keep the sales force in the loop, copies of all written correspondence with customers is sent to the customer's sales person. Salespeople are also invited to attend site visits if they choose. Limiting the Partnership to U.S. customers is partially a result of access to registered customer information; names and addresses of non-U.S. customers are not directly handled at the factory. The scope of the Partnership will be expanded outside the U.S. once it has been well established locally.

The goal of the Partnership is to facilitate frequent, focused Contextual Inquiry visits with customers who are willing to invest some time toward the development of superior products. By finding customers close to home, travel costs can be minimized, eliminating at least one barrier to frequent contacts. By organizing customer background information in a database, sites can be found that match any given study focus. The brochures acted not only as a device for recruiting partners, but also provided some background on the techniques that might be used. Partners were therefore more informed about the relationship, and only responded to the invitation if they were sufficiently motivated to collaborate.

The impact of the Product Development Partnership cannot be accurately measured yet, but the initial responses seem promising. Several field visits have been conducted since the establishment of the Partnership, and the amount of effort required to plan these studies and organize the results is far reduced from that of the initial European trip. Site visits have been planned based on customer profile information stored in the database, as well as geographical location and other specific application interests collected from the brochure return mailer. Other product line teams are making use of information in the Partnership database as well, because many of the participants own products from more than one product line. The increased customer access provided by the Partnership is helping to make Contextual Inquiry a routine part of the product development process.

ASSESSING THE COST AND BENEFIT

The people with the data-handling product line both sponsor and conduct Contextual Inquiry studies, so there is no interdepartmental controversy over the cost of these efforts. The methods used and resources expended are solely the responsibility of the product line. Because customer visits by representatives of the factory are occasionally requested by members of the field sales organization, some sort of visit will be conducted regardless of the techniques employed. By taking the opportunity to visit customers and collect contextual data, the product line team feels that they maximize the return on investment.

Certainly there are measurable costs associated with performing field-oriented methods such as Contextual Inquiry, and these costs can cause any team to think twice before embarking on such a program. In the case of the international study described in this chapter, the two team members who conducted the study invested two-and-a-half weeks of travel and data-gathering time into the initial stage of the effort. Associated with that time is the cost of travel and accommodations for the trip—a significant expense not to be dismissed lightly. The second stage of the effort, data reduction and analysis, was primarily conducted by the two members who performed the observations. The duration of this stage is more difficult to measure, as the initial analysis was done over a period of several months while the team members also participated in other activities. Much of the videotape analysis and composite tape construction was done after hours at home. The third stage of the effort, effecting design changes, was conducted as part of the team's existing change control process, and only represented a fraction of the time spent reviewing change requests from other sources. As it turned out, relatively little time was spent in change control meetings discussing design changes from the study—the credibility of the source reduced the controversy that often contributes to the amount of time spent determining priorities.

The value of the information gathered in the international study is also difficult to quantify, but is generally regarded by all parties involved as worth the investment. The team learned an important lesson from the experiences with the prototype shown to customers. It is unclear whether other requirements-gathering techniques would have revealed the inappropriate fit of the proposed product in the European markets encountered in the study. The result of not discovering the problems in the product's positioning could be complete failure of the product in some of Varian's most important markets. While this might not affect other product lines directly, the failed opportunity could have a significant impact on the future of the data handling product line.

The Product Development Partnership was established to facilitate customer contacts and allow the team greater flexibility in scheduling site visits, as well as to provide greater control over who they were going to visit. In order to keep traveling costs down, proximity to the factory is a consideration for potential customer sites; but keeping such a program running involves a commitment from the product line team. Participants in the Partnership expect to be engaged in some design activity. By offering this opportunity to them, the team has committed themselves to following through. If the team does not communicate with the participants on a regular basis, they will lose interest and be less likely to grant a site visit in the future.

Any data-gathering technique that puts members of the development team into customer labs has many associated benefits. When these contacts involve sales specialists, who often feel isolated from the factory, those salespeople get an opportunity to help define the direction of new product development. They also get to see the issues and tradeoffs that have to be made during the development lifecycle. This enhanced level of understanding helps set expectations about product schedules and specifications. Customers who are visited by members of the development team usually view the experience as a form of respect and appreciation; but the greatest benefit has to be the insights it provides to the development team. Software developers are often faced with the prospect of having to make educated guesses when designing a product. By having direct experience from the field to draw upon, these decisions are more likely to match the needs of the users.

TABLE 7.2 Adapting to the challenges of field-oriented design.

Field-Study Challenges	How They Were Addressed
Many sites did not allow the use of recording equipment.	• Instead of showing up at the door with a video camera hoping to be let in, provide more information to the customer in advance of the visit to allow them to gain appropriate authorization.
When recording equipment *was* allowed, the quality of the video was disappointing.	• Practice camera technique. Try to record all of the work environment, not just the computer screen. • When sound quality is poor, keep the speaker's face in view so that lip-reading cues can be used. • Use a lapel or wireless microphone.
The video was no substitute for "being there."	• Plan short, frequent visits using as much of the development team as possible.
The amount of raw data collected during the study can be overwhelming, sometimes hindering the analysis effort.	• Plan a scheme of organizing the data before beginning the study. • Avoid prolonged periods of data collection without some time to analyze and reduce the data. • Anticipate that data collection may constitute only a fraction of the time required to analyze the data and generate design inputs.
Impacting the design can be difficult if field-oriented methods are not an accepted part of the development process.	• Use existing channels, such as a bug-tracking and change control system, to feed design inputs into the project.
Gaining direct access to customers can be difficult.	• Use direct mail to solicit product development partners from a list of registered customers. Keep track of customer profiles and contacts in a database to facilitate future studies.

LOOKING AHEAD

The success of a cross-functional development team is highly dependent on the team's ability to acquire new skills and perform tasks that have been previously considered outside their job description. Part of the responsibility for gaining these new skills belongs to the company.

A broader scope of training must be provided to the people who will be asked to broaden their field of expertise; but a large portion of the responsibility belongs to the individual. As a member of a cross-functional team, you must be prepared to accept new roles and to work with people who have very different backgrounds than your own. In the case of the product-line team described in this chapter, software engineers and project leaders became directly involved in a program that would have been considered the sole responsibility of the marketing department in years past. Any of the traditional stigma attached to marketing activities by engineering staff would have prevented this effort.

New types of training are also being considered by the data-handling product-line team. Because customers rarely have enough time to allow visitors to observe them for a prolonged period, the full story is not directly revealed. In an attempt to experience the pressures and tasks of a chromatography lab more directly, an extended roleplaying exercise is being planned. In this exercise, members of the development team will act as technicians in a lab re-created at the factory. They will be given assignments based on those observed during customer visits, and will be expected to deliver results as they would if they were employed by the lab. Time will be allotted at the end of each day to discuss the experiences of the day, and to brainstorm possible new products and changes to existing products that better support the activities just completed. The exercise is expected to last several days, to give a complete impression of various aspects of the lab technician's job.

Although Contextual Inquiry is a relatively new method for the product line team described here, many things have already been learned about the process (see Table 7.2). For example, you cannot rely solely on video tape to bring the experience of a field visit back home. The amount and quality of video tape actually recorded is often disappointing. Instead, steps have been taken to get more of the team into the customers' labs, to experience the users' work firsthand. The advantage of Contextual Inquiry, and the very reason it was chosen by the data-handling product line, is that a tremendous amount of information can be gathered from relatively few sites. This certainly has been the case. In fact, the sheer volume of notes collected can be an obstacle to a thorough analysis of the findings. A plan for organizing the data as it is being collected can help a great deal. By organizing customer information in a database before the visit, not only can the team do a better job of selecting qualified sites, but they have a place to put their data as the studies are being conducted. Control over site selection provides the team with the ability to focus on fewer sites more regularly during the product development life cycle, instead of attempting to visit as many sites as possible in a very short period of time.

Contextual Inquiry will continue to play a major role in product development for the data-handling product-line team at Varian. Other usability engineering techniques will be used as well, and new types of training for members of the team are being explored. Cross-functional teams like the one described in this chapter need to consider the expectations placed on its members. Members of the team need to be prepared to take on new responsibilities and explore techniques from disciplines with which they may have little previous experience. It should be the goal of the team to create an environment that is constructive and supportive of this process. The obstacles and barriers that had to be overcome by the team described here may be specific to this particular organization; other teams will no doubt have other obstacles and barriers to negotiate. The team's ability to learn from experience and adapt field-oriented methods to the culture and needs of the organization has a direct bearing on the long-term success of such techniques. Regardless of the features of any particular organizational landscape, effective institutionalization of a field-oriented method such as Contextual Inquiry requires a long-term commitment by those who sponsor it.

ACKNOWLEDGMENTS

The author would like to acknowledge the members of the Varian data-handling product-line team, with particular thanks to Jean-Louis Excoffier, who spent many hours gathering information, analyzing data, and applying the findings. Additional thanks to the individuals who reviewed this material, especially Dennis Wixon, Diane Brown, and Larry Wood, who provided many thoughtful inputs. Greatest thanks go to the customers who participated in field study exercises. They accepted the sometimes awkward situations posed by the observations, and appreciated the efforts of the observers and the value of the experience.

REFERENCES

Brun-Cottan, F. and Wall, P. 1995. "Using Video to Re-Present the User." *Communications of the ACM* **38**(5), 61–70.

Holtzblatt, K. and Jones, S. 1993. "Contextual Inquiry: A Participatory Technique for System Design." *Participatory Design: Principles and Practice*. Eds. Namioka, A. and Schuler, D. Hillside, NJ: Laurence Earlbaum Associates.

Nielsen, J., Molich, R. 1990. "Heuristic Evaluation of User Interfaces." *Proceedings of CHI'90*. Seattle, Washington: ACM, 249–256.

Rowley, D. E. 1994. "Usability Testing in the Field: Bringing the Laboratory to the User." *Proceedings of CHI'94*. Boston, Massachusetts: ACM, 252–257.

Rowley, D. E., and Rhoades, D. G. 1992. "The Cognitive Jogthrough: A Fast-Paced User Interface Evaluation Procedure." *Proceedings of CHI'92*. Monterey, California: ACM, 389–395.

Wixon, D., and Raven, M. 1994. "Contextual Inquiry: Grounding Your Design in User's Work." *ACM, CHI'94 Tutorial*. Boston, Massachusetts.

Wright, P. and Monk, A. 1991. *Co-Operative Evaluation—The York Manual*. York, UK: University of York.

A Day in the Life of a Family: An International Ethnographic Study

Susan M. Dray

Dray & Associates

Deborah Mrazek

Hewlett-Packard

BACKGROUND

Within the Information Technology (IT) business sector, fierce competition is the rule. In order to compete, many companies have found that there must be a very short product lifecycle so that they are able to bring new products to market quickly. Historically this has been slightly easier than at present, because the markets for most IT manufacturers have been either the business sector or sophisticated consumers (such as high-technology laboratories). As the business market has matured, however, many IT manufacturers have sought other markets, such as the home and family. This puts particular pressure on product designers, who must learn how to design for a new and different type of user.

Whenever a company enters a new market, it is important that they understand the characteristics of that market. Traditionally, this has been the role of Market Research departments. These departments are well-positioned to understand the factors that influence the buying decisions of a target market, as well as the demographics, habits, and lifestyle of the target market. Optimizing design and business tradeoffs requires a many-faceted picture of the customer and their needs. This is critical information, because the decision to purchase a product is required for success.

However, designers must be concerned with more than simply designing a product that people will want to buy. Designers must also design a product that people will be able to use, especially because ease of use and "user-friendliness" are becoming increasingly important factors in customer loyalty. For designers, therefore, another type of information is also needed (information about how that product will be used) so they can optimize the ease of use of their designs. This kind of information is not readily available simply by asking people, as one would do in a focus group, because people are usually rather poor at accurately verbalizing what they do when they are not doing it. Instead, this information is best obtained by contextual methods that allow observation of users doing tasks in their real-world environment.

This, then, was the situation in which Hewlett-Packard (HP) found themselves. Like many other IT manufacturers, HP was seeking growth in the family market. To better understand this global market, we conducted a major contextual research study of families in the U.S. and Europe. We used a number of methods in this research, including naturalistic observation (Suchman 1987), Contextual Inquiry (Wixon et al. 1990), ethnographic interviews (Spradley 1979), and artifact walkthroughs (Raven & Flanders 1996) This chapter will chronicle how this study was done.

Because the data generated is considered to be proprietary at this point, we will not discuss the specific findings or the process of analysis. The results have, however, helped the division to set some new "directions" for design.

PLANNING THE STUDY

HP regularly uses User-Centered Design (UCD) techniques to involve their users and customers in their design process (Mrazek and Rafeld 1992; Rideout and Lundell 1994.) Many companies involve users during the design and testing phase of design projects, but HP believes it is also important during the conceptual stages. To gather this kind of information so early in development requires somewhat different skills from the more traditional focus on product testing. Conceptual design information typically is far more qualitative and contextual. There is no substitute for actually watching behavior as it unfolds in natural settings to discover important insights. Therefore, when HP wanted to gain insights as to how families use computer technology, they decided to go to the homes of representative families in the U.S. and in Europe to see firsthand.

Cross-organizational Links

Building on previous work by HP's Market Research department, the Human Factors team (aided by a consultant) set about designing a contextual study of families. We recognized early on that it was very important that this entire study have organizational ownership beyond the Human Factors group, because other groups would actually have to use the findings.

The key disciplines that were most involved in this particular new product development effort were Marketing and Engineering. Therefore, we worked closely with both Marketing and Engineering to make sure that we were gathering information that would be helpful to them and the entire organization. For instance, the protocol was developed jointly by Marketing, Engineering, and Human Factors. Each area contributed "pet questions" to which they needed answers. We also worked closely with other internal researchers in this process in an attempt to leverage efforts wherever possible.

In addition, we designed a study to utilize observation teams from each of these disciplines. Marketing, Engineering, and Human Factors personnel all participated on these observation teams. The teams were themselves ad hoc, and varied in their familiarity with each other prior to these visits. We tried to arrange for cross-disciplinary teams of observers wherever possible. This allowed us to both gather information relevant to each during each visit, and also to facilitate cross-organizational communication as a result of the visit.

Together these methods provided a way to bring the learnings from this study directly to those who would most need them, and to provide another picture of the customer to the organization to complement those views that were already available. Because this study was part of an ongoing effort, this was effective.

Logistics (US)

In a major study such as this, the logistics are quite time-consuming, but also critical to the overall success of the project. We will focus on those elements with the largest impact on success.

Recruiting. We chose four medium-size cities in the U.S. that are not primarily high-technology in focus. These were chosen to be representative of typical markets, and were easy to reach from both Portland and Minneapolis. Because the consultant was the continuity, visits were scheduled sequentially.

We used a market research firm based in Portland to locate three families for us in each of these locations, which turned out to be a cost-effective strategy. Over the course of the recruiting, they became very familiar with typical responses to the screener, and were able to recruit an excellent sample. This same firm made all of the arrangements for payment, got instructions on how to reach the home, and confirmed the visits in writing. Their professionalism helped to allay concerns about the unusual situation of having strangers visit for four hours while both audio and videotaping.

The consultant called each family the night before the visit for final confirmation. This contact with the family helped to ease the initial discomfort of the first few minutes of the visit.

Family profiles. Each family had a computer with Windows 3.1, a printer of any variety, and at least two children. In the U.S., we had up to eight children in the family, and there were often additional family members and friends present during at least part of the visit.

Team roles. The consultant coordinated all of the communication to the teams of HP folks, and made sure that they were briefed ahead of time as to how we would be working the visits. One of them was assigned camera duty and was responsible for learning how to use the video equipment. The other person typically was responsible for bringing along all of the release forms and the HP logo gifts, called "spiffs," including coffee mugs for the parents and Frisbees for the children. We covered all of their questions, and reviewed the protocol.

Logistics (Europe)

Recruiting. In Europe, we used a German market research firm to make all of the arrangements for the families. Because of the very strict privacy laws in Germany, they were not able to "cold call" the way the American firm did. Rather, they posted advertisements on electronic bulletin boards and in the "personals" section of the local paper. This worked very well, although it was much slower and more tedious. The recruiting effort, therefore, was somewhat more expensive in Germany. Overall, we visited six families in Germany.

Even with the professionalism of the recruiting firm, several German families expressed concern about the visits. Initially, one did not want us to videotape certain works of art, and another took great pains to show us their burglar alarm system when we first arrived. This unease was certainly understandable, yet posed a particular challenge for us in building rapport.

In France, the German firm subcontracted to a French firm which arranged for two families in the Paris region. These were families where one parent had participated in focus groups in the past and had indicated a willingness to be contacted in the future.

Family profiles. As in the U.S., all families had a PC, a printer of any variety, and children. In Europe, all families had Windows 3.1 available, but not all used it. In addition, each family had two children.

Team roles. The visit team in Europe consisted of the two authors and a local translator. The translators had been arranged for by the market research firm and in both countries, we had very gifted people who worked well with us. In France, we conducted significant portions of the visit in French. We also were joined by an HP Marketing manager on one visit in Germany.

CONDUCTING THE STUDY

While there was some variation, depending on the size of the family, whether food came at the beginning of the visit or later, and factors specific to each family (such as infant nap schedule, etc.), we followed this same basic pattern for all visits.

Phase 1: Entry

In a visit like this, the most crucial part is the initial few minutes. It is during this time that rapport is built, and therefore we spent the time to establish a strong positive rapport with each member of the family. This was especially critical in the families who were anxious about our presence. We used a number of techniques to build rapport.

We began each visit with a brief introduction of the team and reiterated the purpose of the visit, which had previously been communicated by the recruiter and confirmed by letter. For most families, this was followed by a dinner that we brought with us or ordered soon after our arrival. We used the food as an ice breaker, and this turned out to be an excellent decision. Not only did it free the family from having to think about dinner, it allowed us to have a natural conversation with the family during those critical moments of entry. In addition, we were able to schedule over dinner time, which allowed us access to the entire family early in the evening, before children had to go do homework or be put to bed.

We were concerned about how the food would be received in Europe, because it is very unusual for visitors to bring food along. However, perhaps because we were Americans, or perhaps because the whole study was so unusual, we found that bringing the food worked very well there as well. In Europe in particular, the families were often quite curious about us, and we found that bringing dinner was an especially effective way to put the family at ease.

In addition to eating with the family, we talked about the goals of the study, and had the parents and any children over 18 sign a confidentiality statement and limited release form to allow us to videotape. All families had been told about the study in advance and had been told that we would be videotaping, so this was no problem. In addition, we agreed to turn off the camera if there was anything which the family did not want to have filmed. This seemed to allay any remaining concerns about being filmed.

Phase 2: Formal Data Gathering

After dinner, we moved to the location of the computer and had the children begin by showing us what they did with the computer. We began with the children partly to get their input before their interest waned. However, we found that this also gave us increased credibility with the parents. They appreciated the fact that we asked their children to participate and showed so much interest in their accomplishments on the computer. We asked them to print us a sample if they were old enough to do this. In one case, we asked a four-year-old if he ever printed and he said he didn't know how, but he would figure it out, which he proceeded to do while we watched. He proudly showed us the printouts which he then allowed us to take with us.

The visit became an ongoing conversation with each family member in turn. Guided by the protocol developed jointly with Marketing and Engineering prior to the visits, and using an adaptation of Contextual Inquiry, we watched how each used the computer and printer, and how they described their use. We collected print samples whenever possible. If these had been printed previously, we did an artifact walkthrough with the family member and had them reconstruct the circumstances of its creation.

We also asked the children to draw a picture of what computers and printers would be like when they were as old as their parents ("THAT old?!" they said). We provided Mr. Sketch brand "smelly" markers, which were a particular hit in Europe (where they were not yet available). This served two purposes: It provided us with additional information and it occupied the children while we talked with their parents. After they were done, we asked them to explain their drawing "for the video camera" and we labeled specific items as they described them. This allowed us to capture more fully their meaning, and to engage them in a conversation about the role of technology in both their current and future lives.

We photographed the location, and each family member using the computer. We also catalogued the location and condition of supplies, documentation, and other equipment such as fax machines, copiers, etc.

Phase 3: Informal Discussion and Close

Once each family member had demonstrated their skills on the computer, and we had reviewed the drawings and covered the questions on the topics list, we let the family control the discussion more. We tried to answer any of their technology-related questions. We waited until near the end of the visit to disclose our opinions, so as to minimize our influence. As the visit drew to a close, we took a snap-shot of the family (pets and all), gave each family member a small token gift, thanked them for their time and information and closed with their honorarium. We later sent a copy of the photo to the families with a thank-you note.

Each visit took roughly four hours, although some (especially in Europe) lasted much longer. One of our French families was so interested in showing us what they did with their computer that we were there for over six hours, and almost had to be rude in order to extricate ourselves. Most of the German families brought out the good wine, the family's special Christmas cakes, or even champagne at the end of the visit, and wanted to hear more about us. This is an indication of the strength of the rapport. This was also particularly surprising to the German market research firm, who had been privately skeptical that we would be able to get these very formal German families to open up and share with us.

Phase 4: Team Debriefing

In addition to photos, video tapes, and audio tapes, we each took notes, and (in Europe) used checklists to gather the data systematically. After each visit, the team debriefed on the process and key findings. Each team member completed a debriefing questionnaire that focused on the critical insights from each visit. We used this as the basis for a debriefing discussion. We also did a city debrief after the final visit in a city. Again we used a summary debriefing questionnaire along with team discussion. This was very helpful, because the volume of data collected was massive. We also identified things that we wanted to change or follow up on with future families, and this flexibility allowed us to shift as needed over the course of the study (although the basic protocol did not change during this time).

Some time after each visit, a thank-you card was sent to each family. Included in the card was a copy of the family snapshot so they could remember our visit. This also turned out to be a very positive thing. When we followed up with the German families a month or so later, most of them mentioned this note and were extremely positive about the visit. Our attention to rapport building had clearly been successful.

Once all of the visits were completed, the data was analyzed and presented in a variety of formats and models. As mentioned in the beginning, however, this chapter is focused on how we did our study, not what data was collected or how it was analyzed, as this information is considered proprietary.

REFLECTING ON THE EXPERIENCE

We learned a tremendous amount doing this study, in addition to learning about the specific things we were studying. First of all, we learned that it is possible to do such an ambitious study internationally in a relatively short time, and to involve a cross-section of the organization while doing so. The planning, all the logistics, and the data collection for all 20 homes took less than three months. Cross-organizational alignment and data analysis have been ongoing.

Success Factors

In retrospect, there were a number of things which were important in the success of this research:

Food. The food worked extremely well, both in the U.S. and in Europe. It set an informal and friendly tone, and allowed us to overcome the natural reticence that most teams encountered. For this reason, it was most effective when brought at the beginning of the visit.

Formal debriefing. The formal debriefing was also important in the success of the project. Each team was able to process the visit immediately, when details were fresh. Then, at the end of the visits, they could reflect on the trends and patterns they saw. This made the eventual analysis much easier.

Cross-cultural visit teams. The visit teams each represented at least two and in many cases three very different perspectives. This turned out to be another critical success factor for this study. People with different professional perspectives naturally see the same event somewhat differently. Having Engineering and Marketing people on the same visit , therefore, made for lively debriefing sessions.

Gender. Gender of the visit teams also was important. In the U.S., we had at least one and sometimes two women on the team. This was not perceived as an issue or to have any particular valence, positive or negative. In Europe, however, we speculate that having two American women proved to be important, although this is based on subjective impressions of our German colleagues and ourselves. Because we were clearly not European, we could ask "dumb" questions, which often proved to be very important for understanding the aspects of technology that make for ease-of-use. We were also able to elicit valuable information from both the men and the women. We were able to get them to talk about their concerns about technology, as well as to brag and show us their technical "triumphs." Again, the European Market Research firm we used had been privately skeptical that women would have such success, especially in Germany. Gender, which they had originally thought to be a liability, we believe proved to be an asset.

Initial focus on children. Our initial focus on the children also proved to be important. By focusing our attention on the children, we instilled confidence in our legitimacy with the parents, allowed the children to show off and allowed shyer parents to share their opinions through their child. ('My son's work would be much better if. . . .') The drawing activities later in the visit kept the children occupied, yet involved in our visit.

Collecting artifacts. The scrapbook of snapshots and collections of sample print-outs are a tangible mental tie between the visit teams and the families. For those involved in the design who were not able to attend a visit, the snapshots, children's drawings and sample print-outs added another dimension of reality to the summarized findings.

Continuity. The consultant was the facilitator and provided continuity across all 20 visits. This turned out to be very important. Having different teams in each city, we were able to have the benefit of having "fresh eyes," along with the cross-disciplinary synergy that cross-functional teams bring, and still have the continuity that comes from having a single person or team. This blend led to very powerful findings.

Risk factors

Burn-out. The biggest difficulty was the intensity and focused energy that each visit required. Maintaining a focus for four hours in what was often a very chaotic environment, especially in the large families with children of many ages, pets, phones ringing, etc. was very difficult and required practice. In addition, travel to and from the families lasted between 20 minutes and two hours for the round-trip, and the debriefing often took over one hour. We visited families every day, and in one case, made two visits. This proved to be extremely difficult, because while on the visit, each team member was always in an energy-demanding "learning-mode." This made for a very demanding schedule.

Logistics. In addition to the level of intensity, the logistics were very challenging. We had to rely on a number of people, and if a single detail was forgotten, the entire visit was more difficult or even at risk. A mug with a broken handle, a forgotten videotape, or a worn-out battery in the cassette recorder could all impact the visit. This was even more critical in Europe, where we were in an unfamiliar setting. For instance, many of the addresses in Germany were poorly lit, and in one case, the taxi could not find the street number. Given the German concern for punctuality, we were concerned about the possible impact of our lateness. We planned for extra time in case this happened, after we realized that it was an issue.

Limited team size. Because we were visiting people in their homes, we had to limit the size of the visit teams. This meant that not everyone who wanted to participate was able to do so. Luckily, there have been subsequent family visits that have given more people the chance to be exposed to this very interesting market. These visits were modeled on our study and used the same type of protocol and method. Predictably, they were also very well-received.

No "Grand Debrief" for all teams. It would have been ideal if all of the visit teams had been able to meet soon after the visits to do a "Grand Debrief," but this was not possible due to logistics. By the time we were able to do so, most team members had moved on to subsequent projects and were unavailable.

CONCLUSIONS

Despite the challenges, this study was extremely useful. It confirmed once again that there is no substitute for contextual studies, especially in the conceptual design phases of product development. Exposing people across the organization to real-world customers, in their natural settings, doing their own activities in their own particular way is a powerful way to discover business insights.

The results of this study have influenced many design decisions and specifications for new products. They have also proved to be valuable during user interface inspections and usability evaluation as well.

Through this study, we gained valuable insights on how families use computer technology. These insights were gained in an efficient and cost-effective way. Most importantly, these insights were gained "in context," and because of this context, they will stay fresher longer.

ACKNOWLEDGMENTS

We would like to thank the following people for their contribution to this study: Lauren Deming (U.S.) and Norman Dyer (Europe) for their excellent recruiting, Michaela Rossberg and Marie-Jeanne Valberg for their translations and co-facilitation of the sessions in Europe, the Engineering and Marketing people from HP who participated as observation team members, and, of course, the families most of all, for opening their doors to us so we could catch a glimpse of how we could make technology fit better for each member.

REFERENCES

Mrazek, D. and Rafeld, M. 1992. "Integrating Human Factors on a Large Scale: Product Usability Champions." *Human Factors in Computing Systems, Proceedings of CHI'92*, Monterey, California, ACM, 565–570.

Raven, M. and Flanders, A. 1996. "Using Contextual Inquiry to Learn About Your Audiences." *SIGDOC Journal of Computer Documentation,* in press.

Rideout, T. and Lundell, J. Hewlett-Packard's Usability Engineering Program. Michael E. Wiklund, Editor. *Usability in Practice: How Companies Develop User-Friendly Products*. Boston, MA: AP Professional, 1994.

Spradley, J. 1979. *The Ethnographic Interview*. New York: Harcourt Brace Jovanovich College Publishers.

Suchman, L. 1990. *Plans and Situated Actions: The Problem of Human Machine Communication*. UK, Cambridge: Cambridge University Press.

Wixon, D., Holtzblatt, K., and Knox, S. 1990. "Contextual Design: An Emergent View of System Design." *Human Factors in Computing Systems, Proceedings of CHI'90*. Seattle, WA, ACM, 329–336.

The Challenges of User-Based Design in a Medical Equipment Market

Diane S. Brown
ATL Inc.

EXECUTIVE SUMMARY

Field studies and user-based design are vitally important in improving the usability of medical equipment. However, the medical industry poses three unique challenges to the use of field research: organizational resistance, the nature of the work, and the hospital environment. As a result of these challenges, our methods for conducting field studies and analyzing the results has evolved. The methodology used in two field studies is reported, and samples of the results are presented.

BACKGROUND

ATL builds medical ultrasound imaging systems, which doctors use to diagnose many diseases. A small hand-held probe is placed on various parts of the patient's body, and sound waves are transmitted and received by the system. The received data is transformed into a picture of a cross-section through the organ or vessel of interest. The systems have a hardware control panel, with additional controls and functions accessed through a software interface (Figure 9.1).

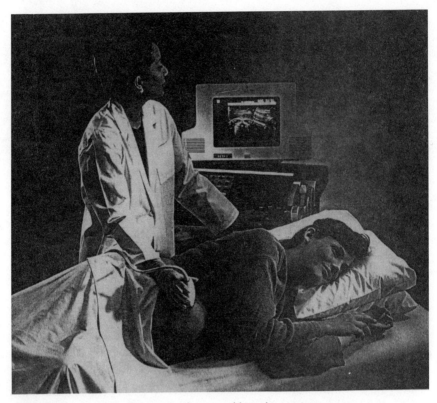

FIGURE 9.1 An ATL diagnostic ultrasound imaging system.

The systems are sold around the world, primarily in North and South America, Europe, and Asia. Within the United States, Canada, and a few European countries; trained technologists are the primary users of the systems. Physicians (mostly radiologists) also use the systems, although less frequently. However, in many countries outside the U.S., physicians are the primary users. Radiology, cardiology, and obstetrics are the main medical specialties in which diagnostic ultrasound imaging is used. The advantages of ultrasound over other imaging modalities are the ability to see what is happening in the body in "real time" (rather than from reconstructed images), the relatively low cost, the portability of the system, and its noninvasive nature (it involves no incisions or injections). For these reasons, operating rooms, emergency departments, and critical care units are just a few of the places where ultrasound is becoming more prominent.

Early ultrasound systems were built by engineers and physicists. They looked remarkably like the tools used by engineers, such as oscilloscopes (Figure 9.2). Besides the styling of the systems and the addition of new features, surprisingly little has changed over the years in the types of controls presented to the user and the overall interaction style.

Many ultrasound companies are still focused on technology. They have not yet adopted a user-centered design process. Consequently, many of the needs of the users remain unmet (Skytte 1994). New technologies continue to be added to the systems to improve diagnostic performance, but these technologies only add to the complexity of the human-system interaction.

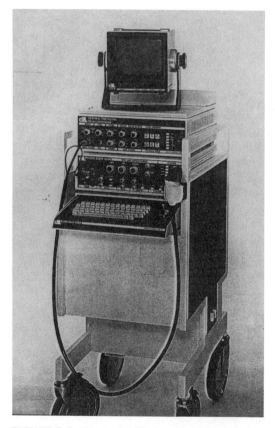

FIGURE 9.2 An early ultrasound system.

Organizational Challenges

For many years at ATL, software and hardware engineers built the user interfaces based mostly on requirements and evaluations by former users who now work in the marketing department. As pointed out by Keil and Carmel (1995) and Grudin (1991), this approach to requirements gathering and subsequent design is often high-risk in meeting user needs. Ultrasound systems have been sold over the years primarily because of their image quality, not their usability; but because of many complaints from our customers about the usability of our systems, ATL management (albeit with some skepticism) agreed to create a group in Product Development focused primarily on the usability of our products. The Human Factors Design group is responsible for promoting usability; however, that does not necessarily mean always having authority to impact design, because organizational change does not happen easily (March 1994; Mayhew 1994).

WHY DO FIELD STUDIES?

Being tasked with improving the usability of our systems, we asked ourselves, "What *exactly* about our systems is hard to use?" Our investigation began by asking the sales and marketing people about feedback from our customers. We were also invited by our marketing department to observe focus groups with our customers in which they were asked how we could improve the usability of our systems. Both the customers and marketing department gave us input in the form of design solutions, rather than stating the actual problems. For example, some stated, "We need a larger monitor. . . ," or, "It's too hard to get to the function I want. . . can't you put it on the first menu?" or, "This line on the screen needs to be green. . . ," etc. If we asked them to explain the problems, they talked in abstractions and generalizations.

In looking for design solutions from these focus groups, we used an exercise where we gave them pieces of felt in the shape of several different controls and asked them to design their ideal control panel. We chose felt because it can be moved around easily, yet does not slide out of place. Each person then gave a brief description of the rationale behind their design. After the sessions, we documented each of the designs by putting them online using a drawing program; then we began our analyses. It was quickly obvious that no new design solutions had been generated—the designs were mostly what they were using now with slight variations in control positions. Also, the focus was only on the hardware controls, with the software interface completely overlooked. However, the exercise stimulated some fascinating conversation among the users about their work.

Another avenue we pursued in trying to understanding our users' needs was talking to ATL luminary physicians. Most ultrasound companies have formed symbiotic partnerships with a few key physicians. The physicians are usually quite prominent in their fields, and often do research with the company's equipment. This research, in turn, is published in prestigious medical journals. Because these partnerships are valuable for companies (and they are key in moving the applications of ultrasound forward), the physicians' input about a system carries a great deal of weight. Their likes and dislikes are often reflected in our designs, and these types of users can be very demanding (Sellers 1994). Although they provide highly valuable input, they rarely represent our typical users, particularly in their intents and work patterns.

At this point it was clear that we needed to pursue new ways of understanding the *context* in which the problems were encountered, as well as gain a *detailed* understanding of what the users were trying to accomplish in order to better support their work. This was the primary reason we began our field work.

CONDUCTING THE FIELD STUDIES

To date we have undertaken several field studies, each with a different focus. On reflection, the studies fell into three different categories. At times, we needed to answer a very specific question about a sequence of steps the user takes to accomplish a task. For example, do the users erase the text they typed on the screen immediately after they print a picture, or do they leave it on the screen until they are ready to type new text? We found these field studies the easiest to perform for these reasons:

- Narrow focus
- Small amount of data to gather and analyze
- Short duration of time at the user sites

The goal of our second type of field study was to incorporate current work tasks into our system functionality. For example, many users attach external cameras to the systems for taking pictures of the anatomy. Integrating the functions of the cameras into the system can be beneficial, because the cameras have separate user interfaces that might require the user to focus attention away from the ultrasound system, interrupting their work. While more extensive in scope than answering one or two specific questions, in most cases we found these studies straightforward because there were well-defined work models with which to study and make comparisons. It was mostly a matter of integrating already-defined steps or procedures into our systems, with incremental improvement in current usability problems.

The third type of field study is currently underway. Our goal is to "rethink" the human-system interaction from first principles in an effort to make major steps forward in usability. The scope is broad, both in the types of users studied as well as the questions we want to answer. For the rest of this chapter we will focus on this field study, because it is the most challenging study we have undertaken and it presents unique problems and results.

The First Site Visits

The intent of our first site visits was to "see how they use the systems." Because of our inexperience, we did not know to narrow the focus as much as possible, nor did we carefully choose the target users. We simply asked our marketing department to set up some site visits, and went with pencil and paper in hand to watch. We visited fifteen to twenty different hospital radiology departments across the U.S. that were primarily general abdominal ultrasound scanning centers. Some of these sites were key physician sites that research new applications of ultrasound. We collected data by taking high-level notes that reflected only what we knew how to interpret, or what the users took the time to tell us (which was usually their likes and dislikes). However, we did begin to understand the general steps they took to complete their work. We also observed several competitive systems being used, which led to two critical observations:

- None of the currently manufactured ultrasound systems were easy to use.
- Most of the users' work was cognitive and internal, not physical and observable.

We noticed that the user interface designs of ultrasound systems are mostly based on the physical placement of the most frequently used controls, and the systems use the same basic interaction style. (This is not surprising, because it is far easier to capture tangible physical actions than extract elusive cognitive processes.) Additionally, each system has hundreds of controls and functions from which to choose, but only about ten to twenty percent are used overall.

With each introduction of a new ultrasound system into the market, we noticed that it was basically a rearrangement of the same set of controls along with some added features. Functions and paradigms were being carried over for years without a revisitation of old requirements and constraints. The fact that a control was frequently used did not mean it was essential to their work; it was often a workaround to a system limitation. It seemed that no one had stopped to asked the questions "What are they *really* trying to accomplish with all these controls?" and "Has their work changed over the years?" In turn, we asked ourselves, "How do we reduce the complexity of these systems?"

Refocusing our Field Study

At this point we refocused our field study, and our goal became how to "rethink" rather than "relayout" the same set of controls with the same interaction style. Instead of general questions like "How do they use our systems?" we began to ask more concrete questions:

■ How can we capture the cognitive work of the users?

We had observed the users visually scanning a picture on the screen then changing controls based on their assessment. What decisions were they making prior to taking physical actions?

■ How can we capture their intents without interrupting their work?

We were familiar with the "talk-aloud" method (Beyer and Holtzblatt 1995; Hotzblatt and Jones 1993) of having users talk about work while they are doing it, but we were dealing with sensitive, noninterruptable situations: sick people, operating rooms, intensive care units, and demanding physicians, just to mention a few. In addition, the users' work can change significantly if disease is found, yet it is inappropriate to talk out loud about it in front of the patients.

■ Who should we target for study?

We wondered how to resolve the dilemma of designing for a broad range of users with limited time and resources for field studies. Somehow we needed to narrow our focus—but what risks do we accept as a compromise?

■ What common knowledge do our users have that we can take advantage of in our designs?

We noticed a strong mismatch between their medical-based knowledge and our engineering-based designs.

■ How can we capture the detailed information we need for design?

The users moved so quickly at times that we could not capture the detailed steps by taking notes.

Choosing the New Sites

Setting up new site visits was the first step we took in tackling these questions. We chose ten new sites in the U.S. (both cardiology and radiology departments) in medium to large urban hospitals, two sites in Europe (England and Germany), and six sites in Asia (China and Korea). Again, we relied on our marketing department for most of the sites, but we were more concrete in communicating our criteria. From prior experience we learned the following:

■ Include users in all major ultrasound markets (e.g., general imaging, cardiovascular, and OB/GYN).
■ Study only a few key physician sites (they are not representative of typical users, but their feedback is important).
■ Most users in the U.S. expected to be paid for their time.
■ There are strong customer loyalties to ultrasound manufacturers. These loyalties can bias the feedback from users and cause some users concern about our observations of their work on competitive systems.

An interesting dilemma we discovered is that there are not a lot of users or sites to study—substantially fewer than the consumer software market. Therefore, we found we had to compete with other ultrasound manufacturers for users. In addition, the manufacturers offer money for the user's time (in the U.S.). We found we were not only having to pay the users but also outbid the competition. We were having to compensate many physicians even more for their time than the technologists.

Three of the U.S. sites came from contacts made on our prior studies. This time we arranged the site visits ourselves, and made sure that the users understood what information we were looking for. We arranged some studies to run concurrently with clinical evaluations of new features run by the marketing department. Although this gave us access to additional sites, we learned that it was difficult to get the information we needed for two reasons:

- The user's work was interrupted by the clinical evaluations, because it required the use of new features or products.
- Additional observers increased disruption to the lab work flow.

We arranged the international site visits through the sales department's country managers. Our systems are sold through distributors in each of the countries and someone from the distribution company accompanied us on the visits, also acting as interpreters. Cultural differences, etiquette protocols, and the language barriers all challenged our methods. Other issues worth noting are:

- Their work hours can differ from those in the U.S. This is important to know when planning site visits to avoid waiting long hours before users begin their work.
- We lost information during translation because the interpreters did not understand our goals. Next time we are going to take a written script of our goals and what we would like users to do, and give it to the interpreters *and* the users.
- At some sites the examination rooms were too small for more than one observer, or for setting up a tripod for the video camera.
- Voltages and access to electrical outlets are often unknown, so it is safer to use batteries for the video camera.

New Tools and Methods

To capture the detailed information we need for design, we decided to videotape the studies. The goals of using videotape were threefold:

a. Collect a detailed record of the users work practice that could be used in generating design requirements.
b. Provide more rapid communication of what we had observed to those not participating in the actual field studies.
c. Because we have a small pool of users and sites from which to study, and field studies are time-consuming and expensive, we elected to create a video database that would allow us to reuse the tapes to answer design questions in the future.

The technologists were surprisingly cooperative about our video-taping, as long as the patient consented. Sometimes they required the patient or hospital to give a written consent. In general, physicians in the U.S. were apprehensive about videotaping, and we could not video-tape at any military hospitals.

We carefully considered the video equipment we bought, because we had to tape in very dim lighting (the lights are turned off or down during exams so that it is easier to see the picture on the ultrasound system screen). We took notes and added very brief but specific questions at the end of the exams. We found it much easier for two people to do the field studies per site: one to run the camera, and one to take notes. Also, it was extremely advantageous to have two perspectives for comparing and validating the data. It was remarkable how often one person missed relevant information that the other person caught. We felt we had a more complete set of data with two people per site doing the study. Three people may have posed some problems, because the exam rooms were small and more people could make the patients uncomfortable. Because the patients must partially disrobe at times for most exams the patients were less reluctant for a female than a male to be in the room observing the work.

We included some of the software developers in some of our site visits after briefing them on our goals and methods of doing field studies. This did not work well because they seemed to lack the interest in doing a field study and did not have adequate human factors training or interpersonal skills to gather the information. For example, after briefing developers on interviewing and observing techniques, and the goals of the study, one developer never asked the user a question (or even brought a pencil and paper for taking notes).

In these new studies we still faced the problem of trying to extract the intents and decisions of the users. Even when we tried to schedule time for interviewing after the exams, after work, or during lunch, we frequently found that the users simply did not have time. New patients were often added to the schedule, or the technologists were reluctant to have another person do extra work in order for them to take time for interviewing. In retrospect, studying the lead or supervisor reduced this problem because those individuals could delegate work more easily, and they were expected to schedule time for "management" activities. However, many of the supervisors do few exams and are more management-oriented in their work. For example, at one site the lead technologist carefully monitored how much film he used, because he was responsible for justifying and budgeting money. He took extra steps in his work to reduce film usage. These steps were not reflected in the work of the people who worked for him.

We decided to try a new approach to capture the users' cognitive work. We scheduled two sessions: the first session was held at their site to observe and videotape two to four hours of their work; in the second session, the users came to our site for an interview. We intentionally removed them from their work environment so they would feel less time pressure. We scheduled the interview at their convenience, which usually meant on weekends or in the evenings. The interviews lasted from three to six hours, including lunch or dinner, and we paid them for their time. We structured the interviews so they began talking about their work at a high level, then we redirected the questions to capture more detail:

[Transcript of PM being interviewed by DB about how PM begins an ultrasound examination of the adult heart.]

DB: How are you notified that a study needs to be done?

PM: I either get a phone call from the physician or I receive a paper request from the clinic. Sometimes I check the schedule on the computer in the hospital.

DB: So you receive a piece of paper from the clinic?

PM: Yes, from the receptionist who scheduled it.

DB: Or the physician calls you directly and requests the study?

PM: Yes, but then I have the receptionist schedule the study. I ask the doctor a lot about the patient because I want to make sure the exam is justified. I need more information than just that a study needs to be done.

DB: What kind of information do you need?

PM: Well, I don't want to be biased by being told by the doctor that "I want you to do the exam because the patient has a bad valve. . . " I want to be unbiased, open to all possible pathology. Maybe it's something completely different causing the problem.

DB: So you ask the physician certain questions.

PM: Yes. I ask the physician, "Why are we doing this?" The doctor may tell me the clinical indications of the patient, like shortness of breath, or that the patient has a history of valvular disease. I even challenge them sometimes by asking, "Didn't they just have this?"

DB: So you want to make sure it makes sense to be doing this type of study?

PM: Uh-huh. I don't want to do an exam to "go fishing"; I don't want to feel like they're looking for something in the heart as a last resort, or that this isn't the right type of diagnostic procedure.

We transcribed the audio and videotapes at a very detailed level, and put the data into a hierarchical outline that began with their high-level goals, the decisions they make, and the actions they take in reaching their goals. Every high-level goal or intent led to another level of goals, decisions, and actions (Figure 9.3).

For a pilot test, we used one or two internal marketing people who formerly worked in the field. Although their mental models were not highly representative of typical users, this exercise was extremely valuable for us—it helped us learn crucial terminology and allowed us to build a hypothetical model to test against. It provided a good foundation of knowledge for our team so when we went into the field we felt better prepared to understand the user's work. We also documented distinct differences between internal and external users, and hope to use this to convey to our management the critical importance of doing field studies rather than solely relying on internal sources for requirements.

Using custom-developed video logging software, we time-stamped the videotape as the user made comments or initiated actions. As time-consuming as this was, we felt it necessary due to the highly specialized nature of the work the terminology, and our goal of creating a database. The transcription took approximately three to four days per user.

ANALYZING AND INTERPRETING THE DATA

With about half of the field studies completed, we began listing the observations, as bullet items and grouping them by affinity. After we organized the observations, we reviewed the interview transcripts and extracted the goals of what they were trying to accomplish. We looked for what the users do versus what they think they do, and why there might be a mismatch between the two. This proved to be a reasonable approach unless unanticipated situations emerged during their work (for example, if the patient began to have problems, the technician found unusual disease, or there were equipment problems). Not surprisingly, these exceptions were not captured in the interviews, thus

4.3 Look at structure and function of heart by following set protocol of views.
    4.3.7 Parasternal short axis view
        4.3.7.1 Assess the structures: look for abnormalities
            Δ Start in the middle of the left ventricle and scan down as far as you can to the apex. Then go back up to the mitral valve.
            Δ Make sure the mitral valve opens up okay.
            Δ Go up to the base of the aorta.
               – Look at the tricuspid valve.
               – Look at the pulmonary artery.
               – Look at the pulmonic valve.
               – Look at the aortic valve—tri leaflet.
        4.3.7.2 Assess the function
            Δ Look at the flow throughout the valves.
            Δ Go into Pulsed Doppler to look at RVOT.
            Δ Use CW through the pulmonary artery.
            Δ Want to pick up higher velocities that may show up with abnormalities like:
               – branched stenosis
               – valvular stenosis
               – valvular regurge
               – in pediatrics, bicuspid valve in aorta
               – aortic stenosis (calcification)
            Δ See how well you can narrow down on the abnormality.
            Δ To see it up closer:
            Lower the DEPTH.
            Increase the ZOOM.
            Δ To see better resolution of the structure:
            Decrease the number of scan lines (LINE DENSITY) (better frame rate).
            Increase the GAIN or decrease the GAIN if you have thick, calcified leaflets.
            Δ Is it good enough?
             Eliminate all possibilities that can be negatively affecting the picture.
             Like:
               – TRANSMIT FOCUS
               – Patient position
               – GAIN
               – DEPTH
            Δ It depends on how well you feel you can see it.
            Δ It's learned from experience.

FIGURE 9.3   An example of a hierarchical outline format of interviews.

we could not extract their intent. In these cases, we intend to review the data with the user, if possible, and have them interpret their actions. If this is not possible we will use our internal clinical sources as interpreters, because we do not have sufficient knowledge to do the interpretation ourselves.

Recently we began modeling the data based on the contextual design methods developed by Holtzblatt and Jones (1993). Although we had already produced models of a large portion of the data, the contextual design methodology added a dimension of organization and graphical description that had been lacking in our methods. We anticipate that this will also help in solving the problem of communicating our field data to product-development teams. A team of two people analyzed the data by walking through the audio and video transcripts while concurrently recording observations and comments on small pieces of paper, and tracking the information flow and physical environments on flip charts. We consolidated the artifacts from each site into a model, and attached these to our site visit notes.

One aspect of the users' work we felt was important (and one that was not captured by contextual design methods) was the element of time. From our studies, it was clear that the time it took to complete the work was of primary importance. Therefore, we specifically focused on the length of time that elements of their work took to complete. We needed a tool for quantifying and communicating this data to our management and development teams. Because our data showed that the nature of the work done by our users can differ significantly depending on what part of the body they are examining, we wanted to graphically represent the differences and similarities in the patterns of their work. Based on these goals, we developed a tool for graphically showing patterns of work over time.

The tool is based on a musical composition metaphor using "staffs" and "measures" (Figure 9.4). Each of the five sections of a staff represents an element of work the user performs. The bottom staff shows the type of imaging technology being used, like color technology to see blood flow, or a two-dimensional black and white picture to see anatomical structure. The middle staff shows the associated controls that are used with a particular imaging technology. The top staff shows nonimaging technology activities, like making a measurement (of a fetal head, for instance), entering patient information into the system, or taking a picture for documentation purposes. Each "measure" comprises 60 seconds of activity. Each measure of activity shows, for example, the duration of time the user spends entering patient information into the system. Each element has a distinct symbol or is color coded to differentiate the

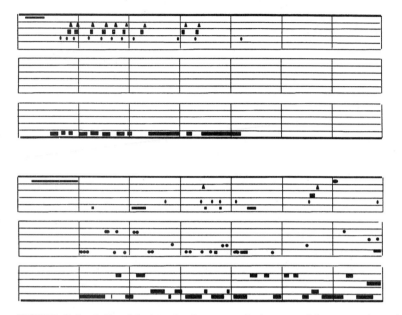

FIGURE 9.4 A Graphical tool using a musical composition metaphor, showing work patterns over time. The upper picture shows work patterns during part of an ultrasound study of a second-trimester pregnancy. The lower picture shows work patterns during a part of an ultrasound study of a normal heart.

patterns. This tool also shows the multitasking nature of work elements that overlap in time. For example, the user may be simultaneously making measurements, recording data to a VCR, and asking patient history.

Even at a glance it is obvious that the obstetrical study has almost a "rhythm" to it. It appears quite repetitive and simple. On the other hand, the cardiology study looks complex and highly involved. With this tool it is easy to see the frequency, duration, and patterns of work. We intend to continue to explore and evolve this unique tool.

GENERATING DESIGN REQUIREMENTS

Most of our design requirements came from direct observations. The affinity diagramming of the observations worked well as a tool for organizing the specific details of the users' work and served as the basis of our designs. Additionally, we evaluated any design suggestions that came from our users and their potential for solving specific usability problems that we had identified. The artifacts we gathered were often "workarounds" to problems the users encountered; thus we focused on how our requirements could eliminate these workarounds.

Even though we were the designers, we still had to communicate, justify, and document our design requirements to other members of the development team. We wrote a requirements document that listed both the high-level requirements and the supporting detailed requirements. This method alone did not reduce "requirements churn" (Hutching and Knox 1995), a process in which requirements are repeatedly revisited because the context in which they were generated was not communicated. Consequently, we included context of use scenarios at the beginning of the document, and after each requirement we added a brief description of our observations and the rationale that led to the requirement. This seemed to help somewhat, and it documented the history behind our decisions.

IMPACTING THE DESIGN

We are not in the design phase for this project yet, and we still have additional studies to complete. However, a common thread in the way the users described their work was in anatomical and physiological terms. For example, we often heard "I'm turning this (control) up because this is a small vessel and the blood flow is really slow. . . " or "There's a lot of (tissue) motion so I need to turn the (control) down. . ." They changed several controls, in a flurry, based on the anatomical or physiological characteristics they perceived. From this information, a more appropriate design schema may be to adjust the system based on anatomical and physiological characteristics rather than "engineering-oriented" controls that abstractly relate to these characteristics.

For other projects, this is the point in the process that we included other members of the development team. We generated several design concepts and evaluated each for the following:

- Meeting the design requirements (which came from field studies, marketing, management, etc.)
- Trade-offs required
- Constraints

We narrowed down on one concept and documented our rationale and decisions in a "User Interface Concept Document," which was circulated for review by the developers and the product manager. We documented the design in a "User Interface Design Specification," which was also given to the developers. This heirarchical "hand-off" of documents left gaps in communication between the designers and developers.

ASSESSING THE COST/BENEFIT

Our management has been relatively supportive of our work. Some managers remain quite skeptical of the need, while others understand the importance of usability but not necessarily the methodology behind field studies. If we had sole authority and impact on design, we could gain buy-in more rapidly. There are many other influences on the final designs (key physicians, marketing, management, developers, etc.); therefore it is very difficult to show the direct pathway that led to successful (or unsuccessful) design and how field studies were either crucial to the process or may have prevented problematic designs. However, our field studies continue to give us invaluable data to support our decisions. For example, we can state with confidence the number of users we observed that took a specific action or encountered a specific problem. Quantifiable data like this is very convincing in a technical environment. We anticipate that the results from our current studies and their impact on future designs will make a convincing case for incorporating field studies as part of the product-development process.

The time the studies take and the communication and management of large amounts of data remain our biggest problems. People rarely take time to read written transcripts (or even requirements documents), and the context of work from which the requirements were derived is lost with this method. Videotapes convey context and capture rich data, but are time-consuming to review.

The users we studied were delighted that an ultrasound manufacturer cared about their work. However, during our early studies, some users became disillusioned because they felt they spent a lot of their time giving input but did not see changes made to the equipment. Because we were the designers, they expected us to quickly change our system design. We learned to quickly clarify that, for many projects, we have long product development times compared to the consumer software industry.

REFLECTING ON THE EXPERIENCE

In retrospect, we learned many valuable lessons from our field studies. We continue to pursue new tools and methods for solving the problems we have encountered.

Preparing and executing the field studies:

- Choose the target sites and users carefully. There are few things more frustrating than spending time gathering irrelevant data.
- There may not be a lot of sites or users to study. Unless studies are extended geographically, there may not be users that fit the criteria for the study.
- We could reduce the sample size (number of sites studied) if three well-chosen sites turned out to be highly homogeneous in their work.
- The number of international users are increasing, but the logistics of doing field studies, and narrowing the scope of users to study remain problems.
- Because the marketing and sales departments' focus is on what makes a product sell, they rarely know details, intents, and patterns of work that are representative of the users and crucial to design.

Methodology:

- Transcribe the data after each site visit. We waited until half our studies were complete, which resulted in too much time spent transcribing.
- Two people were not enough for doing the transcription and analyses. This extended the time significantly.
- We cannot interrupt the users while they work, and the "talk aloud" method failed in our studies. Retrospective review of the videotapes by the users seems worth pursuing as long as they can spend the time needed.

Other issues:

- We still ponder how to capture all the ways work patterns change if disease is found, or how significant this is to design.
- We had not anticipated the fatigue factor of field work—three site visits in three consecutive days is our limit.
- Communicating our data to different audiences was difficult.

Cross-functional teams and contextual design models can reduce communication problems (Mayhew and Bias 1994). Even though we were not successful with software developers doing field studies, we still believe it is vital that they are involved from the beginning. Weekly briefings on our findings as we complete a study might be a way to keep them involved early and often without requiring them to do the field work.

■ The in-house usability testing with individuals and focus groups was appropriate for answering certain questions about current designs, but was not an adequate substitute for field work. We could not realistically simulate the users' environment and work, nor could we meet our goal of looking for deeper insights rather than rearranging current functionality.

In spite of the issues noted above, we are convinced of the necessity of field studies. Not only does the data serve as a solid foundation for design, but also the data provides a crucial understanding of when and how to make the necessary design tradeoffs. We have applied data from field studies in many ways to our designs, and we (the designers) know how critical it is to the success of our designs. When there are problems with design, the most frequent cause is that the design has not been grounded in the users' work. Our main hurdle is to make our methods and results visible enough in our organization to show concrete positive results, and thus gain widespread support.

ACKNOWLEDGMENTS

We would like to acknowledge the following people for their time and support of our field work: Jacques Souquet, Gary Schwartz, Helen Routh, Rick Dugan, Lisa Butler, Joe Ungari, and especially Sonja Takatori for her patience, understanding, and insight. We would also like to thank the users who participated, particularly Pat Martin and Joe Roberts, who gave a great deal of time and effort.

REFERENCES

Beyer, H., and Holtzblatt, K. 1995. "Apprenticing with the Customer." *Communications of the ACM* **38**(5), 45–52.

Grudin, J. 1991. "Interactive systems: Bridging the gaps between developers and users." *IEEE Computer*. April 1991. 59–69.

Holtzblatt, K., and Jones, S. "Contextual Inquiry: A Participatory Technique for System Design." *Participatory Design: Principles and Practice*. D. Schuler and A. Namioka, Eds. Hillsdale, NJ: Lawrence Erlbaum Associates.

Hutching, A. and Knox, S. 1995. "Creating Products Customers Demand." *Communications of the ACM* **38**(5), 72–80.

Keil, M., and Carmel, E. 1995. "Customer-Developer Links in Software." *Communications of the ACM* **38**(5), 33–44.

March, A. 1994. "Usability: The New Dimension." *Harvard Business Review*. Sept-Oct 1994. 145–149.

Mayhew, D., and Bias, R. 1994. *Cost-Justifying Usability*. Boston, MA: Academic Press 1994.

Schuler D., and Namioka, A., Eds. 1993. *Participatory Design: Principles and Practices*. Hillsdale, NJ: Lawrence Erlbaum Associates.

Sellers, M. 1994. "Designing for Demanding Users." *Interactions*. July 1994. 55–64.

Skytte, K. 1994. "Engineering a Small System." *IEEE Spectrum*. March 1994. 63–65.

"You've Got Three Days!" Case Studies in Field Techniques for the Time-Challenged

Kristin Bauersfeld

Netscape Communications Corporation

Shannon Halgren

Claris Corporation

EXECUTIVE SUMMARY

Recently, the Interface Design Group at Claris has had the opportunity to conduct field studies to help define the direction of new products. This opportunity has come at the price of short time frames in which to conduct, interpret, and apply the results. Many of the traditional field study techniques do not lend themselves to these time constraints. Therefore, we have developed three field study techniques (adopted from traditional methods) that work within our time schedule. These techniques are described, then discussed in the context in which they were executed.

BACKGROUND

In order to fully appreciate and understand the motivation behind developing our new field testing techniques, it is first necessary to understand a little about Claris Corporation and the role our group played within it.

Claris Overview

Claris Corporation, a wholly owned subsidiary of Apple Computer, Inc., has grown during the past three years to become one of the world's 10 largest PC software vendors. Its greater-than-industry-average growth is largely due to its focus on a consistent mission: To create and publish award-winning, "simply powerful software" to propel business, education, and home users to even greater creativity and productivity.

Claris applications are best-sellers in several Macintosh categories, and for the past two years Claris has been the world's largest Macintosh software vendor (measured by units shipped). This fiscal year, Claris will ship more than 4 million units (excluding upgrades), including more than 1 million Windows units.

User Research History at Claris

Few software companies have achieved a well-integrated user research-design program, with up-front buy-in from marketing and engineering groups. Claris has been working toward this end, and recently took another step in its direction with the mounting of field research efforts.

Prior to this step, user involvement in the design process at Claris was limited to formal, in-lab usability testing. This was largely due to our development cycle's tight time frame. Usability tests were run near the end of the implementation phase, when most of the functionality had already been defined and there was limited time for fixing usability bugs. While this approach is effective in uncovering design and usability flaws in an already-designed product, it is not an effective method for creating conceptual designs, design metaphors, etc. This type of usability test is directed at evaluation of a design, whereas we were increasingly interested in discovering how people worked to generate a design.

On a few occasions, designers ventured into the "real world" and interviewed end users. However, these interviews tended to act as reality checks for the interaction designer, and did not necessarily have a formal impact on designs. Rarely were these interviews performed after receiving buy-in from engineering and marketing teams, and interview results were not formally shared with these teams.

Field Research Opportunity Knocks

Recently, Claris has started to develop several new products. These new products are targeted at a set of users that we had not yet researched. Due in part to this fact, the Interface Design Group was involved at the conceptualization phase of these products and participated in decisions regarding product goals and feature sets. While the opportunity for involvement in these decisions is present, and it is understood that field research is necessary, incredibly tight time frames make it impossible to employ traditional field research techniques (which often take several weeks or months to execute). Often our schedules require that our research design, execution, analysis, and application to designs must be completed within one to two weeks.

Developing our Field-Testing Techniques

Because our aggressive product schedules eliminate most traditional field methodologies, we had to search for new ideas. After careful review of the literature and discussion with several user research colleagues in other companies, we adopted three field-research techniques. These techniques were selected to fit into our tight time frame and answer our specific research questions. Most of our current field testing uses a combination of these techniques. A brief description of each technique is presented below, and then discussed in more detail in the case studies to follow.

TECHNIQUE 1: CONDENSED ETHNOGRAPHIC INTERVIEW

Information Gained. This technique provides a deep understanding of a culture (in our case, a customer's environment). We wanted to understand our users' work processes, work responsibilities, tools used, time sinks, frustrations, and needs. Workflow models and ideas for new or improved products and features can be derived from this data.

Background. Based in anthropology, ethnography is the science of studying and attempting to understand and describe a specific culture by conducting numerous in-depth interviews (Fetterman 1989). When researching a culture, ethnographers constantly strive to keep an open mind by not making any assumptions regarding the culture. Several excellent "how to" and ethnography background references are available (see Larry Wood's chapter in this book; Fetterman 1989; Spradley 1979).

Our Methodology. Our interviews focus on the user's daily responsibilities or tasks. Users are asked to begin discussing their daily activities. For each regularly performed task mentioned that we are interested in, more detailed questions are asked. For example, users are asked to describe and demonstrate the processes they use to accomplish the task, and the tools required for task completion. Users are also asked about their frustrations with their current processes and tools, and asked to describe how their process could be improved. We also ask to see various tools and artifacts mentioned by the user. Figure 10.1 lists an example line of questioning for discovering how one individual uses her bicycle. First, the user is asked very broad questions regarding the use of her bicycle. Notice the question does not assume the user rides her bike, but rather keeps the question open and asks how she uses her bike. The next set of questions probes into one of the parts of the bike the user mentioned she uses: the handlebars. Because the interviewer is interested in this tool, he probes into how this tool is used, and asks the user to discuss how well this tool is currently working and how it could be improved.

Sample Questionnaire

Current Processes

Please describe how you currently use your bike.

Could you walk me through a typical use of your bike? Please be specific. (Tester probes for details).

Steering the bike

What is the current method you use to steer your bike?

How satisfied are you with this method? (1–10)

Ideal Processes

If you could design the perfect way to steer your bike, what would it be?

FIGURE 10.1 Example line of questioning about using a bicycle.

Equipment Setup. The interviews are conducted in the user's environment so that a deeper understanding is gained by seeing the tools and artifacts discussed. We usually videotape the interview.

Time in Field. 30 to 90 minutes.

Time to Analyze Data. 60 minutes per user.

TECHNIQUE 2: PASSIVE VIDEO OBSERVATION

Information Gained. Using this technique, insight is gained into how users work in the absence of a researcher. Usability problems and time sinks or frustrations can be clearly seen using this technique. Sometimes passive video observation is able to uncover more problems than can be seen in formal lab studies or traditional human observation, where a researcher is typically present.

Background. There currently exist several work-observation techniques that require a researcher to shadow a user through his or her work day and carefully record significant events (see Karen Holtzblatt's chapter on Contextual Inquiry in this book for an example). Some observation techniques allow the researcher to be more active and ask questions of the user to clarify what she is observing, while other techniques require the researcher to be a strictly passive observer. Both active and passive observation of this type have the disadvantage of having a researcher present, which might affect the user's behavior. The rationale behind video observation is that a video camera shadow is less intrusive than a human shadow. A video camera's vigilance also exceeds that of a human observer, and more hours of work observation can be conducted. This video observation technique is based on a technique currently used in the Human Interface Design Center group at Apple Computer, Inc. We are grateful to Dave Schroit, Bonnie Nardi, and Michael Tschudy for their informative advice, and Kent Boucher for the use of his lab's equipment.

Our Methodology. A video camera is set up in a user's environment to capture the area view. A second camera or scan converter is used to capture the user's computer screen or desk surface. The two images are mixed and recorded. The user is told to ignore the video cameras as much as possible and go about work as normal. We attempt to pick a time for taping when the user does not anticipate having any meetings or unusually long interruptions. Nonetheless, we encourage the user to perform their job as they normally would, even if that means leaving the view of the camera for an emergency meeting. Each user is taught how to turn off the video camera if he or she must discuss a confidential or private matter that they don't want caught on video tape. Users are taped for approximately 2 to 3 hours. After taping, the researcher returns to the site and removes the equipment.

Equipment Setup. One video camera is pointed at the user's work area (the computer, desk, and chair). This camera view is necessary to get an idea what the user is working on (their computer or papers on their desk) and if any other people are in the work area. A second camera or a scan converter is used to capture the user's computer screen. Both these views are mixed onto one screen using the mixer. This mixed image is then displayed on the TV monitor and recorded by the VCR (See Figure 10.2). We have found that it is very useful to have the monitor showing the image being recorded, not only to help us set up the mixed image, but also to show the user what images are being recorded.

Time in Field. 30 to 45 minutes for equipment setup and removal.

Time to Analyze Data. 4 to 8 hours per user.

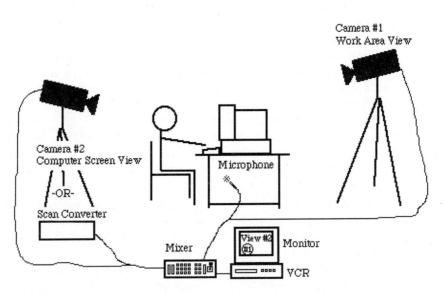

FIGURE 10.2 Equipment set up for Passive Video Observation.

TECHNIQUE 3: INTERACTIVE FEATURE CONCEPTUALIZATION

Information Gained. This technique produces a visual representation of how the user thinks about his or her work processes. This data can be formally analyzed with cluster or MDS analyses, or it can be informally studied to determine a generic user mental model. This technique also captures users' terminology, which can then be used in naming product features and in the documentation and help systems. Finally, tool, artifact, and software feature importance information is captured, which can be used in product and feature decisions.

Background. This technique was developed in-house based on our investigation of ethnography and Contextual Inquiry, as well as by our need to capture users' mental models of their work processes and to validate proposed feature sets.

Our Methodology. This technique best follows the condensed ethnographic interview technique. During the interview, tools, forms, processes, and software features that the user mentions are recorded on sticky notes. At the end of the interview, all sticky notes are placed on a flip chart. The user is first asked to go through and rate each item for its importance to their job with an A (Very Important), B (Important), or C (Somewhat Important). Any item that isn't an A, B, or C is placed in the trash section located at the bottom of the page (See Figure 10.3a). The user is next asked to rearrange the items into categories that make sense to them in the context of the process they just described. No restrictions are placed on the user regarding how many categories they should create or the number of items that should be in each category (See Figure 10.3b). Finally, this user is asked to label their categories using sticky notes of a different shape and color. When applicable, we bring a stack of pre-made sticky notes containing the various features we are considering including in our product. We hand the user one feature slip at a time, describe what it is, and have her give it an A through C rating or place it in the trash. If the feature received a letter rating, we ask the user to place it in one of their categories.

Equipment Setup. A video camera is used to capture this process. The sticky notes are arranged on a large sheet of paper, which is either attached to a flip chart or taped to a wall. The sticky notes used to label the different categories are a different color and larger than the sticky notes containing the individual item names. We bring medium-

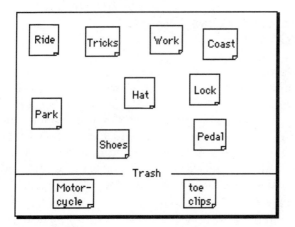

FIGURE 10.3a Interactive feature conceptualization flip charts before sticky note arrangement.

point black markers for writing on the sticky notes so they can be read from a short distance.

Time in Field. 30 to 45 minutes.

Time to Analyze Data. 60 minutes per user.

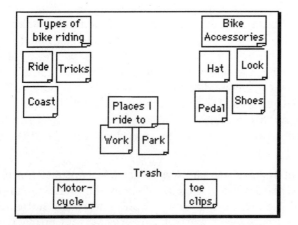

FIGURE 10.3b Interactive feature conceptualization flip charts after sticky note arrangement.

CASE STUDY 1: UNDERSTANDING USER PROCESSES

Study Overview & Goals

This study was initiated by the lead interaction designer of a new Claris technology that might eventually encompass several products. In order to create quality designs, she felt that there was a need to gather more information about her target users as well as to get their feedback regarding this new technology. It was determined that a field study would be the best way to approach the problem. Because the questions being asked were so open-ended, an open-ended technique was needed that would allow study of these questions in a meaningful way. The interaction designer enlisted the help of the testing specialist, and (together with product team members in the Interface Design, Marketing, and Product Development groups) arrived at the following goals for the study:

- To gain a better understanding of the daily goals and tasks of a specific group of Claris customers.
  - How are daily tasks being accomplished?
  - What are customers' biggest time wasters?
  - How do customers manage switching between tasks?
  - What are the commonalities between different professions and different work locations or companies?
- To get an initial customer reaction to our new technology.

Our uses had a wide range of profiles, and we decided that if we could find commonalities in style or process between this diverse user group, we would be able to use this information to create truly useful products. We chose the following research techniques:

- Ethnographic Interview
- Passive Observation

We decided that two different field testing techniques were required in order to fully address the goals of the study. The condensed ethnographic interview would be used to understand users' work processes and get customer feedback on our technology. The passive video observation would be used to capture users' time sinks and task-switching behavior, and to augment information gathered during the interview. The combination of active interviewing combined with passive observation seemed to provide a symbiotic combination.

A TYPICAL VISIT

Each customer was called by one of the two testers directly. During the initial phone conversations, we took care to explain the type and quantity of equipment we were planning on setting up in their environment. We wanted to alleviate or discuss sooner, rather than later, any anxieties the customer might have about being videotaped.

The two researchers split the responsibilities of conducting the study. Both were present for two practice sessions conducted in-house and for the first field session, but then took turns conducting the remaining field sessions (of which there were ten).

What We Brought

The following equipment and supplies were brought along on each customer visit:

- 2 video cameras or 1 video camera and 1 scan converter
- Video mixer
- 12"–13" video monitor
- VCR
- Microphone
- All necessary cables, extension cords, converters, etc.
- Interview questions
- Claris nondisclosure form
- Cheat sheet with schematic of equipment setup

Setting Up

When we arrived at a customer site, it generally took 15 to 25 minutes to set up our equipment. As we worked, we explained the function of each piece of equipment and encouraged questions about the setup. We also took time to show each user how to stop and restart the camera should she want to hold a personal conversation off-camera. When visiting customers in a work setting, often times colleagues had been informed of our visit. More often than not, this generated a considerable amount of curiosity, and a crowd gathered to watch the equipment being set up.

Condensed Ethnographic Interview

Because the goal of this investigation was to gain an understanding of our customers' work culture, the interview focused on the user's daily responsibilities and tasks. For each regularly performed task the user discussed, we asked about the processes used to accomplish the task and the tools required for task completion. We encouraged users to walk us through tasks, demonstrating the steps. Users were asked about frustrations with current processes and tools, and asked to describe the perfect futuristic environment where all daily problems could be solved. With this approach, we hoped to get a sound understanding of most aspects of the user's environment within a relatively short time. Anytime the user mentioned an artifact such as a database, a paper form, a project board, or an invoice, we asked to see it. For most artifacts we asked if we could make a copy of it, or if it was too big to photocopy, we asked to take a picture of it.

For consistency, we created a list of questions to be used as a guideline during the interview. However, we remained flexible and often allowed the conversation to go off on tangents if an interesting and relevant issue was brought up by the user. Before completing the interview, we confirmed that the five or six major interview areas we were interested in had been covered.

Passive Video Observation

After the interview, the researcher left the user work site with the cameras in place to capture the user's work area (usually the camera was facing them from across their desk or across their shoulder) and their computer screen. The cameras were set to record before the researcher left. The researcher returned again in 2 to 3 hours to turn off the cameras and take the equipment down.

Data Analysis

The data we gathered were notes and videotapes of the ethnographic interview, artifacts from the user's environment, and videotapes of user's performing tasks on their computer. From the interview notes and videotapes, we organized our data by task and tools.

For each significant task for which a user was responsible, we noted the following:

- Task goal
- Steps needed for task completion
- Tools used for task completion
- Time sinks in current process
- User's comments about the current process

- User's ideas how the process could be improved
- Our observations about the process

For each significant tool the user discussed, we noted:

- Tasks the tool helped accomplish
- How the tool was used
- Tool strengths
- Tool weaknesses
- Users' comments about the tool
- Our observations about the tool

The interview and passive observation tapes provided a significant volume of data. Unfortunately, we did not account for the time it would take to view and take notes on the tapes once the visits were completed. We relied heavily on the interview tapes, using them to clarify and augment the notes taken during the visit. This left little time for the passive observation tapes before the required end of the study. As a result, subsequent use of this data was based primarily on the interview tapes.

The organization of the interview tape data provided by the above breakdown of task and tools allowed us to get a clearer understanding of a typical day. This information was then used in numerous brainstorming and design sessions to keep a user-centered focus. Although no formal analysis and presentation was made of this data, the experience and knowledge base proved invaluable.

Lessons Learned

- *The condensed ethnographic interview proved to be useful in a short time frame.* We were able to conduct one customer visit nearly every day. In our relatively short time with the user we were able to get a fairly accurate view of the major tasks, goals, and responsibilities of the user.
- *Allow ample time for video review.* We ran out of time to watch all the work observation videotapes that we recorded. It will be important to plan in several days of video review next time we use this technique.
- *Avoid trying to learn too much.* The scope of this study was too broad. We attempted to study a vary large population of users. It would have been better to either narrow our focus to a particular industry or profession, or to narrow it to a few specific tasks.
- *Get buy-in from product teams before you go.* This particular study was primarily meant to be an exploratory, information gathering

activity for use by the designer when building future interfaces. We have learned that all types of user research, even exploratory, benefit greatly by involving engineering and marketing groups early in test-preparation phases, especially if they are to be the recipients of any of the data collected.

Study Successes

In general, we felt that using field study methods were appropriate for our situation. Because the products are still under development, we are unable to talk about in detail about the results. However, we can tell you that the open-endedness of the method allowed us to address our technology questions without bias toward any existing technology. In addition, the ethnographic interview questions allowed us to really understand our users' processes and correlate them with artifacts used to help accomplish those processes.

CASE STUDY 2: USER PROCESSES, CONCEPTUAL MODELS, AND FEATURE VALIDATION

Study Overview and Goals

This study differed from the previous field study in that it was focused on a single product and not a technology. The features of the product had already been determined by product marketing, and the interface design group was tasked with designing the interface to encompass the dictated features. Again, it was decided that field research was needed before design could begin. In addition, we had one week to complete the study and translate the data into preliminary designs. The user population studied was the same group as in the previous study. However, data from this study did not provide the required depth in particular task areas. After several discussions with the product team members, the research was approved and everyone agreed upon its goals:

- To understand users' processes for a well-defined set of tasks.
- To validate the proposed product feature set.
- To capture the users' conceptual model of their work.

Research Techniques Chosen

- Ethnographic Interview
- Interactive Feature Conceptualization

As one of our research goals was to quickly learn about user's current work processes, we again chose to use the condensed ethnographic interview due to our success with this technique. The interactive feature conceptualization task was selected to address the feature validation and conceptual model capturing goals. As we had learned in the last study, buy-in from the rest of the team is very important. Therefore, we were sure to include team members in the technique selection decision and asked them to accompany us on the customer visits.

What We Brought

The following equipment and supplies were brought along on each customer visit:

- Interview form
- Two different colors of sticky notes (preferably different sizes as well)
- Two or three fine-tipped markers
- Two or three sticky notes with our feature set (1 feature/paper, different color than other sticky notes)
- Portable flip chart with paper
- Video camera and tripod
- Regular camera
- One marketing product team member

Setting Up

This study didn't involve as much setup time as the last study, because we only had one video camera. As the video camera was being set up, we thanked the user again for letting us come visit and expressed how excited we were to hear about his or her job. We also explained the reason for videotaping the interview and its potential uses.

Condensed Ethnographic Interview

The interview was conducted by the interface designer, who had experience conducting field interviews. The marketing product team member was seated near the video camera, and was charged with keeping the camera focused on the action and taking notes on sticky notes (see next section). The marketer was told not to ask the user any questions until the ethnographic interview had been completed. We began the interview by asking the user to explain his or her environment and general processes within the environment. We then quickly jumped into more specific questions about the task processes in which we were interested. The interview lasted between 30 minutes and one hour, depending on how talkative the individual was and how effectively we were able to keep them on track.

Interactive Feature Conceptualization

During the interview, the second team member (usually the marketing representative) noted every artifact, process, tool, and software feature that the user mentioned on sticky notes (one per sticky note). Typical items recorded on the sticky notes included *invoice, project folder, word-of-mouth referrals, customer database*, and *fax log*. Around 30 to 50 sticky notes were created for each user.

At the end of the interview, the sticky notes were placed on the flip chart paper and the user was asked to rate each item with an A, B, or C. This step generally took about 10 minutes, with some time going to clarification of what was written on the sticky note. Once the items were rated, the user was asked to group the items in terms of things which "go together." Finally, the user was asked to add a label to each group. This process took between 15–20 minutes.

The final step involved handing the user, one at a time, the papers with our proposed features written on them. The user was asked to first rate each feature using the A, B, C scale, then place them in the appropriate grouping. Items that were not important were placed in the trash.

Data Analysis

Each item noted on a sticky note was placed into a database. We captured the category name, each item within the category, its rating, and whether it was an item they mentioned or a feature we gave them (see Figure 10.4). We were then able to look at the data at three levels.

First, we had to develop a quick summary to give to the product-marketing team. This involved looking at the broad groupings created by the users and pulling out similarities and differences across users. We also drew heavily on the interview notes for a general understanding of process similarities and differences across subjects.

We were then able to compare this broad overview and conceptualization with the dictated product requirements. In this case, the product marketing conceptualization and the user conceptualization of tasks and product requirements were very different. As a result, significant changes were made by marketing to the direction of the product based on this data.

At a second level, we compared individual data points across subjects using a cluster analysis. We were hoping to build a generic conceptual model based on common and unique data points. Although we were able to successfully perform a cluster analysis on the data, there were two problems with the results. First, there were too many unique data points between users, and even our attempt to provide some normalization did not help. Second, we only had enough data to begin building a model, and more data was needed to begin seeing trends across users. We feel this will be a useful technique as we gather more data points in subsequent studies, or normalize the data by having all users sort the same set of items.

Finally, data from both the sticky notes and interview notes was used to put together a process flow model during the brainstorming design stage. Each case was tested against the model for validity. This process helped us clearly understand the similarities across user processes and where the deviations fit in. Design of the product was going on in parallel with process flow model generation, and each complemented the other.

Interactive Task Conceptualization Database

Participant Number 1	**Priority** ◉ A ○ B ○ C ○ NR
Item Name Bike Helmet	
Category Name Safety Equipment	**Origin of Item** ○ Participant ○ Interviewer
Notes participant always wears a helmet.	

FIGURE 10.4 Sample information recorded in database.

Lessons Learned

- *Both techniques provided useful data.* We were very pleased with the information gleaned from both the interview and conceptualization techniques. Both met the requirement of being quick to perform and analyze and both met their research goals.
- *Take good notes.* Once again, a short time frame did not allow us time to look at the interview video. However, if you take good notes, as we had, you will seldom have a need to go back to the tapes.
- *Include team members.* Inclusion of the product team members proved invaluable during decision making because we had a shared knowledge base from which to draw.
- *Carry paper in a tube, not a flip chart.* We decided that a flip chart was too difficult to carry to each customer site. Since this study, we have begun carrying pages of flip chart paper in a poster tube and hanging the paper with masking tape on any flat wall or desk surface we can find in the user's work space.

Study Successes

The data collected during this field study proved incredibly useful. As mentioned above, the data significantly influenced the direction and definition of the product and subsequent Claris products. The technique itself was very portable in that the materials required were simple and few, and the preparations needed were minimal.

CONCLUSION

We developed three field investigation techniques (the condensed ethnographic interview, passive video observation, and interactive task conceptualization) to address our research needs. We have used these techniques in various combinations to suit our specific research problem and, more importantly, our tight time frame. Of the three techniques, the condensed ethnographic interview and interactive feature conceptualization (techniques 1 and 3) proved most successful. We've found the advantages to these techniques are:

- The interview provides depth of knowledge and understanding in a short time frame.
- The feature conceptualization provides a concrete visual representation of users' mental model and process structure.

- The feature conceptualization technique allows for the breakdown of information into discrete data points that can be analyzed in several ways.
- Both techniques allow for participation by all project team members.
- Both techniques assist with the creation of process flow models.

The third technique we developed, passive observation, was not as useful to us in influencing an actual product design. This was, in part, due to some unique aspects of the study in which this technique was employed (i.e., the broadness of scope of the study, lack of buy-in by the product team, and limited time to process data). We would recommend this technique in instances where time is not an issue and the research is focused around getting a detailed understanding of how a user performs a set of tasks and finding "real world" usability issues.

Although we experienced considerable success in turning data into design in Case Study 2, there is still more refinement necessary to this process. First, a more efficient way to compare subjective data across users needs to be developed. This may, in part, be helped by the forms used to record data. As more information is obtained on the data, the collection becomes more efficient. Our forms did not facilitate this process very well. Second, much of our effectiveness in turning data into design drew upon the process flow model, which seemed a natural fallout of the data collected. However, it's unclear how this technique would work given a less process-oriented environment. Finally, an efficient and systematic way needs to be developed to pull out the most relevant data for communication. Retrospective viewing of the videotapes would most likely uncover a wealth of information missed during our less-refined processes; nonetheless, time does not often permit this step.

FUTURE WORK

The primary goal of this research is to aid in the development of highly effective and usable products. Future work will focus on refining our current techniques as well as developing new ones. This will include promoting and evangelizing the success of our methods across Claris and getting other team members involved. Our goal is to increase the impact of these studies on the development cycle and product design.

REFERENCES

Fetterman, D. 1989. *Ethnography: Step by Step*. Newbury Park, CA: Sage Publications.

Spradley, J. 1979. *The Ethnographic Interview*. New York: Harcourt Brace Jovanovich College Publishers.

11

User-Centered Design in a Commercial Software Company

Stanley R. Page

Corel Corporation

EXECUTIVE SUMMARY

A cross-disciplinary team was formed to do customer research as input for a new version of the WordPerfect word-processing application. The Contextual Design process was used to gather and analyze the data. When the process began to produce positive results, additional research teams were formed within the company to provide customer data for the design of other applications. An overall team was established to coordinate the research and synthesize the data. The Contextual Design techniques used by these research teams are discussed along with methods used to facilitate communication between the teams. Lessons learned in the process are also discussed.

BACKGROUND

WordPerfect was born in the basement of the Orem City building. Alan Ashton and Bruce Bastian had been hired by the city to write a word-processing program for their new Data General computer. Ashton and Bastian would write code in the basement of the city office building and take it immediately upstairs to try it out on the secretaries who would be using it. They would watch as the software was used, and get immediate feedback about needed features and ways to improve the software. They would then return to the basement to implement the changes.

Ashton and Bastian probably did not think of what they were doing as field research, but that is exactly what it was. The early success of WordPerfect was largely due to its having been designed in the field to meet the needs of real users doing real work.

As WordPerfect became more successful and the company grew in size, it became impossible to retain the same kind of intimate contact with end users that Ashton and Bastian had benefited from in the beginning. One method used early on to retain contact with users was the customer support system. WordPerfect offered all registered users of their products toll-free phone access to customer support personnel. These phone calls were used to help customers learn to use the products and to provide input for improving the products. Suggestions for enhancements and problem areas were reported to the development teams on an ongoing basis.

Other methods of obtaining customer data have also been used including usability testing. It has been eye-opening for many developers to see users struggling in the usability lab with the features they developed. Additional sources of user data have included formal lab experiments (Johnsgard et al. 1995; Page 1993) and informal focus groups.

One problem with these methods was that they came late in the development cycle. Usability feedback was obtained only after the product was designed and large amounts of code written. Information from customer support would have to wait until future versions to be implemented. Focus groups could be used early in the design process, but they removed the users from their actual work and work environments. There was a desire to find a way to get back to the same quality of customer data that had been used to design the word processor for the secretaries at the Orem City offices.

PLANNING THE STUDY

The Executive Vice-President of Development established a small team and gave them the charge of doing customer research as input for the next-generation word-processing application. The company had already had some success with limited field research, and the feeling was that field research was the right way to gather data for the new design.

Scope

The scope of the research was purposely kept very broad. The team planned to study the work practice surrounding the making of documents. We wanted to learn about how documents were conceived, how they were created, how they were reviewed and approved, and how they were distributed.

Team Makeup

A cross-disciplinary team was formed to do the research. Team members had expertise in WP development, human factors, documentation, marketing, and usability testing. They were freed from their other responsibilities so that they could dedicate themselves full-time to the research effort.

CONDUCTING THE STUDY

The Process

The team used the Contextual Design process as taught by Karen Holtzblatt and Hugh Beyer of InContext Enterprises (Holtzblatt and Beyer 1993). The basics of the process were developed at Digital Equipment Corporation (Holtzblatt and Jones 1993; Whiteside, Bennett, and Holtzblatt 1988; Wixon, Holtzblatt, and Knox 1990) and had been refined and expanded by Holtzblatt and Beyer. The value we saw in the process is that it leads the research team systematically through all the steps required to go from data gathering to product design. It pulls together a number of techniques from different disciplines. The techniques have been modified to flow together as a seamless process.

Team members participated in three weeks of training from Holtzblatt and Beyer, spread over a six-month period. Each week of training was followed by four weeks of work by the teams, in which they applied what they learned in the training. For example, during the first week the team learned how to do interviews and initial interpretations of those interviews. The team spent the next six weeks capturing interview data so that the data could be used during the second week of training.

Selecting Participants

We determined that we needed a broad cross-section of user characteristics. We wanted participants from various professions and geographic locations at both small and large companies. We wanted to observe people using our software products and competing products, as well as people who were not using computers at all in their work. Data about the market distribution of our products was used to make certain we included participants from the industries that have been important to our success.

The following sources were used to locate potential participants:

■ Data from our marketing research group
■ Lists of registered users
■ Regional sales representatives
■ Contacts (friends and acquaintances) known by team members

As the data was interpreted for each round of customer visits, we found that we had a better understanding of the types of participants needed for the next round of visits. It became a refining process. Holes in the data became obvious during the interpretations, and we would plan the next set of visits to fill those holes.

Once a contact person was identified at a suitable company, we would give them the information about the type of individuals we wanted to meet with and the time commitment required. We made these contacts by telephone, and for longer-distance visits we would follow up with a letter explaining our intentions.

Problems Encountered

Even though we were careful to explain that we wanted to do one-on-one observations of people doing real work at their own workstations, we would occasionally find on arrival at the site that they had scheduled their people for a joint focus group. Some rearranging of schedules was often needed after we arrived at the site.

Some people thought we were there to help them solve problems with their software. They wanted us to spend our time helping them rather than gathering data. We would have to find a way to accommodate them, or get them in touch with someone with the company who could help them, and then move on to our data-gathering needs.

We were not always able to get in to see the types of people we desired. We wanted a cross-section of job types, but sometimes found it difficult to get to observe people at higher levels of management. Even if we scheduled them far in advance, we would often arrive to find they were too busy to meet with us. We would then be offered the time of their administrative assistant or secretary as an alternative. As a result we got more information in the support job categories than we needed, and not quite as much as we would have liked in others.

The Observation/Interview

All members of the research team participated in conducting interviews. Each observation/interview lasted between two and three hours. It was important that each interview be conducted in the user's own workplace, where the artifacts and context of the work were readily available to stimulate the interview.

An attempt was made to make the person being interviewed feel like a partner in the process. We wanted them to feel like they could end the interview or refuse to answer any questions they were uncomfortable with. We let them know that anything they told us would remain confidential. We tried to get them to engage in typical tasks, and then took notes furiously to capture everything that was pertinent. At points of particular interest in their work, we interrupted and asked questions. We also noted the physical layout of their workplace and collected as many artifacts as possible.

We generally took a tape recorder with us and asked if we could tape the interview. The tapes were handy if there was going to be an extended period of time before the data was interpreted. If the data from the notes was interpreted soon after the interview (within 24–48 hours), we found it was not worth our time to go back and listen to the tape.

Analyzing and Interpreting the Data

Initial interpretations of the interview data were done with the entire team. The person who conducted the interview would review their notes with the team. The other team members asked questions to draw out important information. One team member was assigned to capture each important fact identified by the team from the interview data onto electronic "cards" (Figure 11.1). Other team members drew the following types of diagrams on large flip-chart pads as appropriate information was identified:

Workflow Model. The workflow model shows individual roles and the flow of work (communication and artifacts) between them (Figure 11.2). Roles are represented by circles and artifacts are represented by

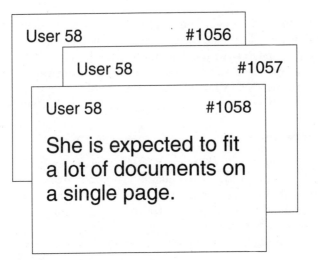

FIGURE 11.1 Individual fact cards captured during an interview interpretation.

rectangles. A workflow model was drawn for each individual interviewed.

Sequence Model. A sequence model lists the steps the participant
took to accomplish a given task (Figure 11.3). It includes the trigger
that caused the sequence to begin and the overall purpose or intent of
the sequence. Several sequence models were often generated from a
single interview.

Physical Model. The physical model is a map of the participant's
environment. It shows the physical layout of the workplace and can be
either of an office (Figure 11.4) or an entire work site.

Context Model. The context model was designed to show how people
within the organization exert influence or authority over each other.
While we felt that being aware of the cultural influences in the organizations was important, we did not feel that this model represented
them in a useful way. Although contextual models are considered part
of the contextual design process, we did not use them.

STRUCTURING THE DATA

The following methods provided ways to organize the wealth of data
collected so that it was understandable and usable.

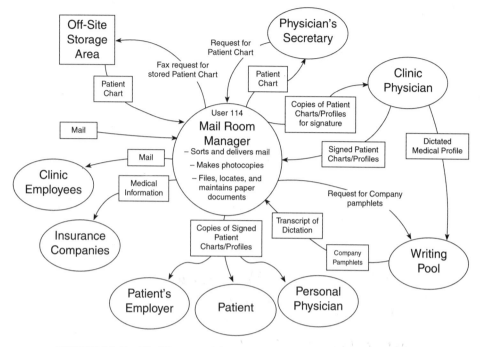

FIGURE 11.2 Workflow model.

Affinity Diagram. The electronic cards containing data captured during the interpretations were printed out and sorted according to similarity. Natural categories emerged from the data, and eventually a giant outline was formed, which told the story of the work. Figure 11.5 shows a small portion of our affinity diagram with the headings and subheadings that were added as the cards were grouped.

Consolidated Models. The models generated during the interview interpretations were compared and common aspects identified. The consolidated models represented these key common elements in generalized ways. A consolidated physical model was generated that represented a customer's individual office, and another that represented the entire work site. Several consolidated sequence models were generated from groups of similar sequence models (for example: adding a graphic to a document). The various workflow models were consolidated into a single model that showed all the roles people were assuming in the work we observed.

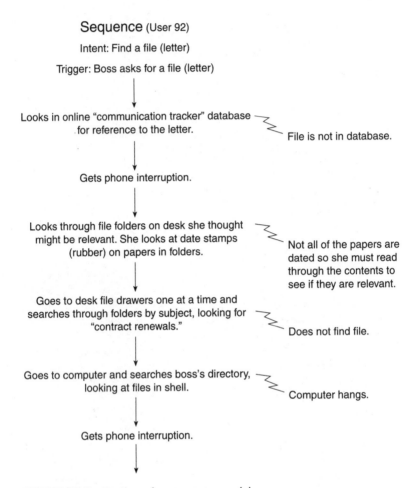

FIGURE 11.3 Portion of a sequence model.

Redesigned Work Models. The customer's work was redesigned based on ideas generated from the consolidated models and affinity diagram (Figure 11.6). The goal was to streamline the customer's work by eliminating steps and avoiding breakdowns. Emerging technologies that might help streamline the work were identified and studied at this point.

User Environment Model. The User Environment Model (UE) is a blueprint of the system from the customer's point of view. It presents

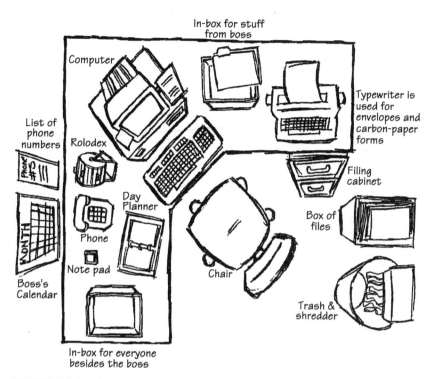

FIGURE 11.4 Physical model.

functional requirements of the system in a way that is independent of the user interface or platform implementations. The UE was generated from the redesigns and consolidated models.

User Interface Designs. Rough paper prototypes were used early in the process to test concepts of the user environment models with users. As these concepts became more solidified, running prototypes were created using ToolBook and Delphi. We found the running prototypes especially useful for communicating ideas to our management and development teams.

EXPANDING THE FOCUS

When there began to be indications that the research being done by the word processing team was showing promise the decision was made

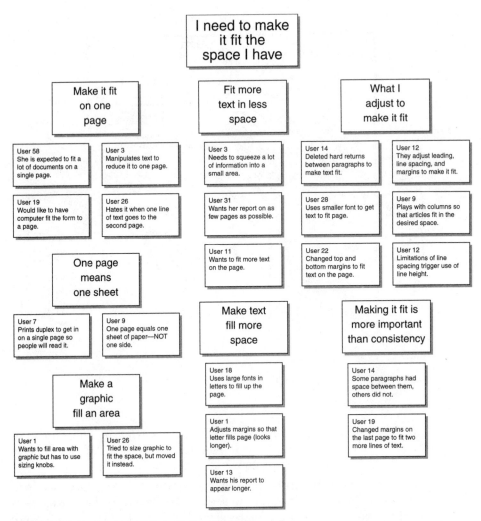

I need to make it fit the space I have

Make it fit on one page

User 58
She is expected to fit a lot of documents on a single page.

User 3
Manipulates text to reduce it to one page.

User 19
Would like to have computer fit the form to a page.

User 26
Hates it when one line of text goes to the second page.

One page means one sheet

User 7
Prints duplex to get in on a single page so people will read it.

User 9
One page equals one sheet of paper—NOT one side.

Make a graphic fill an area

User 1
Wants to fill area with graphic but has to use sizing knobs.

User 26
Tried to size graphic to fit the space, but moved it instead.

Fit more text in less space

User 3
Needs to squeeze a lot of information into a small area.

User 31
Wants her report on as few pages as possible.

User 11
Wants to fit more text on the page.

Make text fill more space

User 18
Uses large fonts in letters to fill up the page.

User 1
Adjusts margins so that letter fills page (looks longer).

User 13
Wants his report to appear longer.

What I adjust to make it fit

User 14
Deleted hard returns between paragraphs to make text fit.

User 12
They adjust leading, line spacing, and margins to make it fit.

User 28
Uses smaller font to get text to fit page.

User 9
Plays with columns so that articles fit in the desired space.

User 22
Changed top and bottom margins to fit text on the page.

User 12
Limitations of line spacing trigger use of line height.

Making it fit is more important than consistency

User 14
Some paragraphs had space between them, others did not.

User 19
Changed margins on the last page to fit two more lines of text.

FIGURE 11.5 Portion of the affinity diagram.

by management to expand the scope of the project. The team was divided in half and additional people added to each "new" team. One team was to continue the study of work related to the creation of word processing documents. The other team, known as the "Overall Team," was told to expand its scope to include all business work practice. This was partially fueled by the fact that application suites were becoming an ever more important element in the software market.

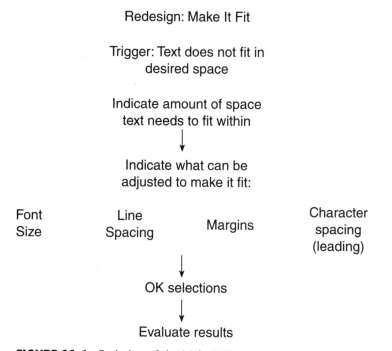

Redesign: Make It Fit

Trigger: Text does not fit in
desired space

Indicate amount of space
text needs to fit within
↓
Indicate what can be
adjusted to make it fit:

Font	Line		Character
Size	Spacing	Margins	spacing
			(leading)

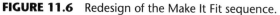
↓
OK selections
↓
Evaluate results

FIGURE 11.6 Redesign of the Make It Fit sequence.

The Overall Team

The new members of the overall team included people with expertise in the various application categories that WordPerfect was interested in. People with experience in the following areas were added to the team: spreadsheet, electronic forms, graphics/presentations, communications, and document management. The task of the overall team was to understand business work practice in general, and to figure out how all the pieces of a suite of software applications should fit together to facilitate the work.

One member of the team also belonged to the company's software process committee. As the overall team was refining its field research and design process, he was helping to determine how these methods could fit into the new company-development process. As a result, the Contextual Design process has become an approved part of the company's product life cycle. User environment models and other consolidated models are accepted as deliverables for the requirements phases of development.

Subteams

As specific areas of work were identified by the overall team, subteams were established to study the details of that work. In addition to word processing, areas of work studied by subteams have included: graphics, charting, forms, slide shows, and others.

Some of the subteams were able to dedicate resources to the research process full time for a short period of time. Other teams worked only part time on research because of other commitments. Because of these variations, many of the subteams only completed part of the process. They found that even if all they did was the interviews, interpretations, and affinity diagram that it was still worthwhile. Many design ideas can be generated from the affinity diagram alone.

Training Team

A two-member training team was formed to train new teams in the process. One member of the training team had a background in human factors and skill in field research techniques. The other member of the team was a programmer analyst with expertise in software development processes and object-oriented software design.

COMMUNICATION BETWEEN TEAMS

One of the biggest challenges we faced was to find ways to ensure that frequent communication and coordination occurred between the various teams. The following techniques were used to facilitate the communication.

- *Liaisons.* Members of the overall team were assigned as liaisons with the subteams. Liaisons were to meet with the subteams on a weekly basis for two-way sharing of status information. This was only marginally successful because information shared at the liaison meetings was not detailed enough and as teams became busy it was easy to postpone or cancel liaison meetings.
- *Mentors.* We found that an effective way to get a new team up and running quickly was to have a member of the overall team act as a mentor for the new team. The mentor would spend half or quarter time with the new team and help them avoid repeating mistakes in the process. This proved to be a more effective means of communication than the liaisons. The down side was that the

overall team lost the services of that member while they were acting as a mentor for the new team.

■ *Model sharing.* Most of the consolidated models and the user environment model were put into electronic form so that they could easily be shared with other teams as needed.

■ *Open Houses.* Occasional open houses were set up where members from other teams were invited to a specific team's design room for a sharing of work progress. Visiting team members would be asked to review models and identify issues and concerns.

■ *Bulletin Boards.* In-house electronic bulletin boards were used to post weekly team progress reports and as a forum for discussion.

■ *Design Reviews.* When teams were ready to pass design specifications off to implementation teams, design reviews were held where detailed walk-throughs of the design documents took place.

IMPLEMENTING IDEAS

We knew from the start that it would not do us any good to gather a lot of customer data and come up with great new designs if we couldn't get the development teams to accept them. As soon as we had our first affinity diagram and consolidated models built, we started having open houses within the company. These open houses were used to introduce management and development teams to the processes and to sell them on the value of the data being generated.

In some of the subteams, the developers who would later implement the ideas were part of the team. In those cases there was an easy transition from design to implementation. When the research and design team was separate from the development team, we would try to introduce the design ideas to the development team before the concepts were fully developed. Involving the development team in the design of the final details helped them to feel ownership of the ideas. We found our developers very supportive of the process, and the only real resistance to ideas was because of schedule constraints.

The following are examples of features in current products that are the result of our field research:

Make It Fit

When the word-processing team was doing their initial research, they found that people often had the need to fit text into a certain space. Sometimes they needed to shrink the text to fit it on one page. Other times they wanted to expand the text to fill in blank space on a page, or to make a report longer. This need became evident from the affinity diagram and sequence models. The Make It Fit feature was implemented in WordPerfect 6.1 for Windows (Figure 11.7) and has received favorable reviews (Lombardi 1994).

QuickTasks

In planning the PerfectOffice 3.0 suite there was a desire to begin to move users away from an application-centered view of software, and toward a more task-oriented approach. One idea to accomplish that goal was QuickTasks. QuickTasks automates a series of steps across multiple applications, prompting the user for input as needed. Data from the overall team was used to determine tasks that would be useful to include. Individual as well as the consolidated sequence models provided detailed information about the steps required to accomplish the tasks. QuickTasks has received a lot of favorable press. One reviewer noted that "The QuickTasks feature in Novell Inc.'s PerfectOffice is a good example of how a suite can go beyond being just an assortment of mainstream applications" (Bethoney 1995).

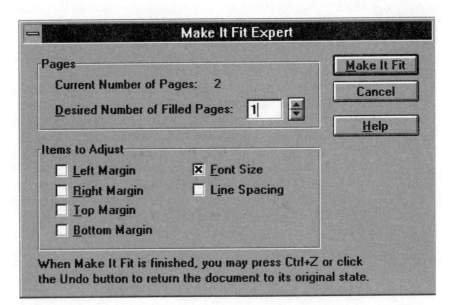

FIGURE 11.7 Make It Fit feature in WordPerfect 6.1 for Windows.

LESSONS LEARNED

The following is a miscellaneous collection of lessons we learned and insights we gained during the course of the process. Hopefully these will help other teams avoid some of the mistakes we made and improve their processes.

- *Having a cross-disciplinary team greatly enhanced the effectiveness of the team.*
- *The output of the research does not have to be perfect.* Most members of the research team were perfectionists by nature. We found that too much time was being spent trying to make the output for each stage in the process perfect before moving on to the next step. We learned that it was better to force ourselves to work quickly, iterate often, and to clean up later (if necessary).
- *Have daily process checks.* Taking a half hour at the end of each day to identify what went well and what didn't go so well helped us to constantly improve the process and our work patterns. This information was recorded in a journal and in a "process check" document.
- *Don't get hung up on the process.* The results are more important than the process. Occasionally we would get into long and heated arguments in the team. These arguments were never about the data; the data almost always spoke for itself. The arguments were over how to best represent the data, or whether we were following the process correctly.
- *Go back to the users often.* We were most productive and most creative when we were frequently going out to visit customers, either to validate our ideas or to gather new information.
- *Taking time away from research to report findings and sell your ideas is important.* We fell into the trap of becoming so involved in the research and perfecting the data that we forgot the importance of sharing our findings. Management began to wonder if the project was ever going to deliver any usable ideas. We corrected the problem by suspending our research for a time and concentrating on selling and communicating.
- *You must sell your ideas in ways that communicate effectively and appeal to management* (e.g., running user interface prototypes). We tried selling our concepts to management by talking about the User Environment Model and showing them rough paper prototypes, but it was only after we had a running prototype that our ideas began to gain wide acceptance.

■ *Use the process to help sell your ideas.* Development teams were less likely to argue about ideas when they knew that they were generated from real customer data.

CONCLUSIONS

The Contextual Design process has given us a logical, systematic way of studying our users. It has allowed our design teams to thoroughly understand the customers for whom we are designing. It has been exciting to see how easily design ideas are generated when we understand the real work intents of our customers and the struggles they encounter to accomplish those intents.

It has been valuable to have multiple application teams using the same research process. It has given us a common vocabulary when discussing customer needs, and has allowed us to share a common vision for the future of our products.

The user environment model has become an effective long-term blueprint. It has helped us see how our various products should work together to support the customer's work. At the same time that the long-term vision is being worked on, individual features (like Make It Fit) can be implemented. The user environment model shows how these individual features fit into the overall picture.

Because of the success of these research efforts, funding has been provided to continue doing customer research. We have begun to rotate new members through our research teams to give more of our designers and developers the opportunity to get a firsthand look at our customers at work.

REFERENCES

Bethoney, H. 1995. "Novell's QuickTasks Option: How suite it is." *PC Week*, 16 January 1995. p. 75.

Holtzblatt, Karen and Beyer, Hugh. 1993. "Making customer-centered design work for teams." *Communications of the ACM* **36**(10), 93–103.

Holtzblatt, Karen, and Jones, Sandra. 1993. "Contextual Inquiry: A Participatory Technique for System Design." A. Namioka and D. Schuler (eds). *Participatory Design: Principles and Practice*. Hillsdale: N.J.: Lawrence Erlbaum Associates.

Johnsgard, Todd J., et al. "A comparison of graphical user interface widgets for various tasks." *Proceedings of the Human Factors and*

Ergonomics Society 39th Annual Meeting. San Diego, California, October 9–13, 1995. Santa Monica, CA: Human Factors and Ergonomics Society.

Lombardi, John. 1994. "WordPerfect 6.1 heats up Windows war of words." *InfoWorld*. 14 November 1994. p. 192.

Page, Stanley R. 1993. "Selecting colors for dialog boxes and buttons in a text interface." *Proceedings of the Fifth International Conference on Human-Computer Interaction*. August 8–13, 1993. pp. 208–213. Amsterdam: Elsevier Science Publishers.

Whiteside, John; Bennett, John; and Holtzblatt, Karen. 1988. "Usability Engineering: Our experience and evolution." Martin Helander, ed. *Handbook of Human Computer Interaction*. New York: North Holland, 1988, pp. 791–816.

Wixon, D.; Holtzblatt, K., and Knox, S. 1990. "Contextual design: an emergent view of system design." *Proceedings of CHI '90*. Seattle, WA: ACM, 329–336.

Using Field-Oriented Design Techniques To Develop Consumer Software Products

Dianne Juhl

Usability Group, Microsoft Corporation

EXECUTIVE SUMMARY

Microsoft has used a number of techniques to infuse user's input into product design, including paper prototyping, laboratory testing, monitoring of field test sites, and systematic tracking of product support calls. Interviewing and observing users in the field is an extension of this work. Understanding how people do or could use computers at home provides a new opportunity to use field-oriented techniques and user-centered design activities. The company sponsored a research project to collect data about home or family tasks, projects, and leisure activities. There were several stated goals for the research project:

1. Build a comprehensive understanding of home activities and how they are accomplished.
2. Systematically examine home activities for new software product opportunities.
3. Determine ways to improve usability and increase customer satisfaction with Microsoft's consumer software products.
4. Complete the project and report results in 60 days or less.

215

This project was collaboratively defined and conducted by the Microsoft Usability Group with product teams who develop consumer software products. Home sites for interviews were carefully selected using existing marketing profiles. Contextual Inquiry (CI) was the field study technique deployed to accomplish this research project. It provided a structured process for collecting data about customers in the context of their own environment, and then analyzing it. A total of 19 people in six households were interviewed, and this resulted in over 2,000 data points and 200 work models. The data points were structured into an affinity diagram. The work models were organized in terms of four types, and then data from like models was consolidated. Together, they provided a coherent understanding of the customers' issues and a tangible statement of their work practices and leisure activities. The project's deliverables were an overview of the 20 most common home tasks or activities, and a report on software product-development opportunities. Subsequent to the project's completion, the results have been entered into a database and drawn on by multiple product teams.

BACKGROUND

Microsoft develops both generic software tools for the corporate or business domain and task-centered applications for the consumer domain. The company works with a variety of users from both domains throughout the entire product design and development process. In general, we recognize that partnership with users is important, and that users are the experts about their domain. The company uses the expertise of usability specialists, program managers, and product planners to collect the data, make sense of it, and then infuse that data into the software's design and product-marketing plans. We also continually adapt and customize our user-centered design activities so they can be used within the constraints of Microsoft's rapid product-development cycles.

The Microsoft Usability Group creates a variety of situations in which users can give us input on the company's software product design. In the planning stage of the product-development cycle, we use field-oriented techniques such as Contextual Inquiry, which focuses on understanding customers' work practice. Early in the initial design stage, we conduct rapid, iterative usability studies with paper prototypes either at the customers' sites or in the usability lab. At this point, we seek users' input about the system model. As we move further into the development cycle, we typically conduct usability lab tests with on-line prototypes to get data about users' performance and satisfaction with the product's interface. Finally, during the quality-assurance stage of the product-development cycle, we often install beta software at field sites and monitor its usability over time. The customer's input collected from field studies is used in the planning stage of the next product cycle. After the product is released to the marketplace, we systematically track product support calls to determine if our user-centered design activities and usability testing have resulted an a more usable product overall. All of these strategies depend upon an ongoing conversation with the user. All these strategies provide a means for Microsoft product teams to work closely with users over time in a relationship that helps us make informed product-design decisions.

Microsoft's product teams have used a number of these strategies when developing task-based software titles for the consumer market. However, because the consumer market is a relatively new one for Microsoft and our company's software designers are just beginning to understand this target audience, herein lies the opportunity for using field-oriented data-collection techniques and user-centered design activities. While we believe it is useful to observe people interacting with software products in a lab or field setting, it can be even more useful to gather extensive, detailed information about these customers' work or leisure practices in the context of their own environments. So, typically, product teams work with users in home, small business, nonprofit, or educational settings and engage them in conversations about work practice and product design. Contextual Inquiry (CI) is one technique that has provided these teams with a well-defined, structured process for gaining an understanding of the users' tasks and activities. If applicable, the teams then employ user-centered design activities to roll that understanding into the software's design.

The research project described in this chapter employed the Contextual Inquiry technique to meet its study's objectives. The sponsoring organization for the project described in this overview was the Microsoft Works Business Unit. The research project was conducted in the summer of 1994. The goals of the project were to gain a better understanding about home activities and how they are accomplished, uncover new software product opportunities, determine ways to improve usability, and increase customer satisfaction with Microsoft's consumer software products.

PLANNING THE STUDY

Four people comprised the core research project team, which included two Microsoft program managers, one product planner, and one usability specialist. Throughout the project's duration, the project team solicited input and help from many product teams.

The project team's first order of business was to decide which research technique to employ. Because the sponsoring organization was interested in observing peoples' home activities (regardless of whether they were done on the computer), we believed that going into the home environment and engaging consumers in a dialogue would be more useful than traditional interview or focus groups methodologies. This called for a qualitative research methodology using participant-observation techniques. The Contextual Inquiry (CI) method provided the structured field methodology that the research team wanted for collecting and interpreting this data. In addition, CI facilitates building and communicating a shared understanding of the customer.

Next, the team refined the project's broad objective into a succinct focus statement and a checklist of ten issues to investigate. While the general objective was to determine the main activities and projects that people do at home, the research team chose to focus, in particular, on the integration or connection between these activities. For example, the team's checklist of issues included the following:

- How family members communicate with each other, e.g. notes on the refrigerator, grocery lists, phone messages, events penciled on the calendar, etc.
- How the family manages scheduling for events such as grocery shopping, dance class, piano practice, soccer games, doctor visits, etc.
- What hobbies the family members do together.
- How a family plans and manages "life events" (graduations, weddings, family reunions, etc.).
- What information or professional advice the household gathers when working on an activity or project.

Once the project's scope was determined, the project team outlined the logistics of recruiting participants, training interviewers, collecting data, and analyzing the findings.

The team planned to conduct five home-site visits. The site profile for this study was developed by the core project team in collaboration with Microsoft marketing personnel. It was important that the home sites matched profiles used in previous consumer marketing research (i.e. focus groups or phone surveys), because it was believed that it would help build confidence about the data collected. The description of the homes to be selected for this study was fairly specific:

- Households that owned their own home and a computer.
- Households in which the partners of the home were between the ages of 35–65.
- Three of the five households should have children living at home, between the ages 6–17.
- Two of the households should have no children living at home.

Additional parameters were used to further define the "ideal" home site, and these included:

- Some family members in the selected households do volunteer work for nonprofits, school clubs, community groups, or some special-interest groups.
- Some of the homes are connected to libraries, bulletin boards, etc. via the Internet.
- Some children in the selected households used computers at school.
- Some of the homes regularly played games on their computer (adults as well as children).
- Some wage earners in the selected households operated a home-based business, full-time or part-time.

Once a site profile had been composed, Microsoft Usability Group Test Coordinators recruited the families using the Usability Group's database of participants' names.

By design, the core team planned to send several investigators to a site, pairing up one investigator with each family member in each home. This meant that a group of two to six Microsoft personnel might be dispatched to a site. Because the core team only comprised four people, the project team was expanded to include adjunct team members. This expansion helped balance the workload of the core team and created larger shared customer understanding. Ten additional employees were recruited. These additional ten people represented a variety of functional areas in Microsoft: program management, product planning, user education, testing, and product support.

All interviewers/observers were trained in Contextual Inquiry techniques. A two-hour training session was conducted by the usability specialist on the core project team. The philosophy of CI and basics about conducting an inquiry were presented in this training session.

Also, because some of the investigators had little or no expertise in interviewing children, a usability specialist with experience in this area provided specific training for the research team. So that the team could practice their Contextual Inquiry skills, an additional site visit was scheduled. This "pilot" site visit provided the team with a valuable "trial run," as it not only gave the team a chance to practice their newly learned CI skills, but it provided a means of evaluating whether our focus statement, our checklist of issues to be covered, and our logistical plan for conducting the inquiries were on target.

It was estimated that a site visit would be approximately three hours in length. The data would be captured using field notes, audio tape recordings, and photographs. The investigators' key objectives were to conduct an inquiry about the activities and projects of each person in the home, and to bring back a record of the observation/interview, which would be shared in the debriefing meetings.

Debriefing meetings were scheduled and open to all interested Microsoft personnel. The core research team published the schedule at the beginning of the project, and sent out weekly reminders. Training on conducting a CI data-sharing meeting and creating user work models was done during the debriefing meeting. Core team members attended all debriefing sessions. Their role was to moderate the meeting and facilitate the data-recording process.

When communicating the findings to Microsoft management and product teams, the project team specifically planned to employ work-modeling techniques for concretely representing the customers' work practice. An affinity diagram would be built to illustrate the scope of issues important to the customers. In addition, a report would be written that detailed the 20 most common home activities and explained what software product-development opportunities were discovered. Finally, all the data would be made available to all Microsoft product teams so that everyone could capitalize on the understanding gained from this research project to build consumer software applications that better support user's home activities and tasks.

CONDUCTING THE STUDY

The project team scheduled the site visit with each household at a time when everyone in the family would be at home. After arriving at the home site, one person on the project team introduced the investigators and the study's purpose. The team made the focus statement explicit to the family, stating that the team was interested in finding out about the family's activities, projects, hobbies, and upcoming life events. We explained that by getting a sense of how families manage and track all the things they have to do in a given week (and year), Microsoft could use that understanding to design consumer software and future products that better meet the family's needs. The family members were assured that specific information shared with the research team would be kept confidential, and permission was obtained to use audio recorders and cameras. Finally, the team set the user's expectations about how a Contextual Inquiry was conducted, noting that it would different from a traditional interview in that the family member would be doing most of the talking while investigators took notes, occasionally interrupted with a questions to clarify understandings, or asked permission to photograph a particular artifact.

Once introductions were completed and nondisclosure forms were signed, the general structure of the site visit session was explained. The team explained that we wanted to pair each family member with one investigator. The schedule was also outlined: 15 minutes to generally describe "regular" household activities, one hour for family member-investigator pairs to "tour" the home, and 30 minutes at the end in which all family members were brought together into a common room with the investigators to participate in a concluding discussion.

During the site visit, the project member talked with their assigned family member about his or her activities and projects (both long-term and short-term), what strategies they used to accomplish them, and why they choose to work on certain activities in lieu of others. The investigators usually assumed an "apprentice" role, reinforcing the concept that each family member was "the expert" about their individual and household activities. The investigators asked the adult family members to imagine that they were showing someone how to run their household for a week. Children were asked to show the investigators the places in the home where they spent the most time and explain what activities were done in those places. Everyone was asked to describe their plans for the upcoming year. The key to a successful site visit was getting each family member to take Microsoft team members on a "tour" of the home, showing us all the places where he or she worked on activities, projects, and hobbies.

RECORDING AND ANALYZING THE DATA

The project team gathered and recorded the data according to plan. Debriefing meetings were held within 24 hours of the site visit. A transcript was created for each interview with a family member. We used a CI group analysis process (called an interpretation session) in which the investigator, plus two or three other team members, were present for the debriefing meeting. While the investigator read aloud the data he or she had collected, a transcript of the interview and the conversation of the attendees at the debriefing meeting were recorded.

This transcript included the following five elements:

1. Data about each family member's activities·and projects.
2. Interesting characteristics of the work.
3. The team's insights and interpretations about the user's activities.
4. Design or product ideas sparked by the spoken observations.
5. Questions for future contextual inquiries.

In addition to the transcript, five types of work models were generated for each family member. The flow model depicted the type and amount of communication and coordination that occurred between each family member and other people. In addition, this model showed work objects (any object facilitating communication or coordination) which were passed between a family member and others in accomplishing a task or activity. The sequence model detailed the step-by-step actions the individual took to accomplish a specific task. A third model showed artifacts created and used by the individual in the process of doing an activity or project. The context model showed the influences upon the individual. The fifth work model was a caricature of the home's physical environment. Similar to a "blueprint," this model depicted the layout of the home and how it facilitated or hindered the activities of family members. Although no video-taping was done at the time of the site visits, photographs were taken and subsequently used to provide richer detail on the both the physical environment and artifact models.

It took one month to complete all the site visits and debriefing meetings. During the 30-day survey of the activities in the home, the project team observed 19 people in six households, recorded over 2,000 separate data points on the interview transcripts, and created a collection of 200 work models.

After all site visits and debriefing sessions were completed, the project team built an affinity diagram from the 2,000 data points. This diagram was an important tool in helping the project team make sense of the large amounts of data collected during this broad-based survey.

The affinity diagram revealed a coherent story about the range of activities being done in the home and the scope of issues important to the customers. For example, we observed that people in these households wanted to accomplish important and meaningful work for themselves, their families, and their communities. These activities include such tasks as exploring career and job opportunities, keeping better contact with extended family members, and organizing a community effort. All of these life-enrichment activities involve gathering and organizing information to accomplish a specific goal, such as creating a resume after exploring job opportunities, or writing the family's history after contacting extended family members. The work models, with their rich detail, nicely complemented the affinity diagram. From the work models, we gleaned a good sense of how the tasks or activities are accomplished. For example, we learned that the kitchen is the "hub" of activities in the homes we visited, and the kitchen's physical space or the objects within support effective communication between family members. We also learned a great deal about how families maintain and effectively coordinate their hectic schedules.

From this data, the team built a tangible statement about the range of home activities and the integration of those activities. Twenty-seven core home activity areas were identified, so the project team was able to meet one of its key objectives: Determine the 20 most common home tasks and understand how the user accomplishes those tasks. In addition, approximately 300 design ideas were generated during the project. From this pool of knowledge about home activities and collection of design ideas, several new product opportunities were identified. As product opportunities emerged from the data analysis, market research was conducted to pinpoint whether product opportunities identified in the research project could be turned into viable, revenue-generating ventures.

REPORTING THE RESULTS

Communicating the study's results was another deliverable of this project. Findings were reported in separate meetings to Microsoft management, program managers, and the leads of individual product teams. In two months immediately following the study's conclusion, the project team "toured" many designers and developers through the data, pointing out key insights and discussing new products, innovative features, and integration opportunities that could possibly be developed for the home software consumers. We emphasized that the data tells us how we can improve the key tasks or activities these customers want to accomplish. During those two months, the affinity diagram and the most interesting work models were displayed on the walls in the project's team offices as well in the surrounding hallways. This allowed Microsoft personnel to freely browse it. Personnel were encouraged to annotate the affinity diagrams and models with their own comments, thus providing another way to build and communicate a shared understanding of the customer. In addition, detailed reports were written for five of the 27 activity areas, and then published. These reports have been used by Microsoft teams in developing business cases and specifications for some of the identified product opportunities.

With respect to "touring" other people through the data, the project team discovered that it was important to preface each presentation with an introduction that stated that, given the qualitative nature of the data and the study's sample size, we could not generalize from the data to answer a question such as "What are the household activities and their relative frequency in an American home having X, Y, and Z characteristics?" While we encouraged product teams to validate our findings with market-research techniques, we were clear that questions of sample size or statistical inference could not be answered by type of qualitative research contained in the affinity diagrams and work models. On the other hand, we did generalize in terms of the explanatory adequacy of the findings, talking about how the data "made sense"; that is, how consistent it was with our general understanding of how people act in the world and (more specifically) in our United States society. For example, if someone in the home was maintaining a comic-book collection as an activity, the data helps us make sense of that person's activity—what he or she is trying to do, how he or she wants to do it, and what's problematic about doing it. However, the team did not say that every household or even every person maintaining a comic book collection would be like this person.

The project team's presentations have centered around answering the following questions for Microsoft teams, who were using the data to make product design or planning decisions:

1. Of these five households that we have chosen to visit because of X, Y, or Z, what are the activities and their relative frequency?
2. What are the relationships, dependencies, and meaning of the household activities in these homes, and how are they similar and different?
3. What design opportunities can we find in these households? The answers to the third question are particularly valuable, because

they originated from open-ended conversations/dialogues with users in context of their home or workplace. We weren't getting answers to pre-prepared survey questions.

In an effort to disseminate the information more widely to Microsoft employees worldwide, the data contained in the affinity diagram has subsequently been put into a database so that it could be electronically searched and sorted. The work models have also been put online so they can be easily disseminated across the company's network.

IMPACTING PRODUCT DESIGN

The project team has not yet archived the data, as product teams are still reusing the data. We are still presenting the results to Microsoft teams across the company who are interested in data. Some teams are using it to glean a couple of feature ideas for an upcoming product release; some are systematically walking through the data and looking for brand-new product opportunities; some are using it to validate their own, independent research; some are using it to help them create informed focus statements for their own contextual-inquiry or field studies. For example, several product teams have used the data to evaluate the implementation of Wizards and templates typically found in Microsoft products. One technique they use is to compare the current Wizard or template implementation with the work models derived from this study, and evaluate how the current implementation could be enhanced to support an activity coherently.

Regardless of their purpose for using the data, most teams look at the data with a "lens" that is attuned to the merits of their product's current implementation or proposed product plan, as well as informed by the knowledge of their product's target customer. The model being employed by the product teams systematically walking through the data involves some or all of these elements:

- Shifting through the affinity diagram and work models looking for relevant data about the user's work practices and building better understanding about them.
- Recording insights about user requirements, design ideas, product-integration opportunities, product cross-sell or up-sell opportunities, and questions for further research.
- Analyzing the recorded items and prioritizing them in terms of what could be developed for upcoming versions of their product.

- Deriving a focus statement for their own CI projects after learning where more research is needed in order to better understand the customer's tasks or activities.
- Validating findings in the existing research, or from subsequent CI studies with market research.
- Surveying users to determine which proposed features or requirements are most important to them.
- Develop customer task scenarios from the data, which can be used when usability-testing the product.

FUTURE WORK

The project's second phase would include using CI or field-oriented techniques in international home sites to determine if the data collected on home activities and our customer's work practice models are consistent across both domestic and international markets. Also, we'll use market research studies both domestically and internationally to validate the study's findings.

CONCLUSION

The research project was completed in 60 days, as scheduled. The cost of this project in terms of resources was comparable to the cost for conducting two or three focus groups. The project team felt these costs were reasonable given the breadth and depth of information obtained about customers' tasks, and the benefits being realized from data reuse.

Although the project was a success, the research team experienced a few challenges along the way. First, resources to help conduct site visits or participate in data interpretation sessions were not always readily available. Second, it was especially challenging to quickly, yet accurately, analyze the mounds of data we collected during the project. Third, at the end of the study the project team found it was difficult to clearly and succinctly communicate the results to upper management. Although management was satisfied with the depth of the data collected and the product opportunities identified, they wanted to be presented with results in a more concrete, quantifiable form. That was difficult to do given the qualitative nature of the study's data and results.

Microsoft product teams involved in this and other CI projects have "echoed" these reflections. While they indicate that the CI technique is basically sound, they felt there are two inherent, process-related weaknesses with this type of field-oriented, qualitative research study:

1. CI studies feel too time-, labor-, and attention-intensive given that Microsoft product teams typically have very limited resources to do such studies and still ship products on schedule.
2. It is difficult to generate clear deliverables for upper management.

   The Microsoft Usability Group (in collaboration with product teams) is working to address these issues.

First, while it is recognized that field-oriented techniques are not necessarily a "good fit" in applied research environments and in settings that have rapid product-development cycles, the company is currently deploying CI studies that are more narrowly focused. These projects can still help teams build an understanding of their customer while meeting product-delivery goals. Time will tell whether we're trading off a more coherent understanding of the customer and the overall task environment by doing these more-narrowly focused projects.

Second, because CI is typically a technique used to support subsequent user-centered design activities, it may explain why it is difficult to distill the data into a form that can easily be digested by management. While we're currently investigating ways for generating quantifiable data from CI studies, we continue to emphasize that CI best supports the design process. The strength of the CI technique is that it provides a well-defined and structured process for collecting data from users in context and rolling it into product-design specification and product-marketing plans. Microsoft's design teams say that CI and follow-on user-centered design activities provide the following value to them:

- A long-term vision for product development efforts.
- A coherent picture of how products can be better integrated to provide solutions for customers' task or activities.
- An understanding of the customers' needs.
- Detailed descriptions of the users' work activities, which can be used for writing preliminary product specs and usability test case scenarios.
- Strategies for designing software that support, and transform, the users' work practices.
- Long-range, scalable product-design plans and prioritized solutions.
- Confidence that the product's design will support tasks that users want or need to do, becoming a "sanity check" for program managers as they move from planning to spec-writing to coding.

REFERENCES

Agar, M. 1985. *Speaking of Ethnography.* Newbury Park, CA: Sage Publications.

Bernard, R. 1994. *Qualitative Research Methods in Anthropology*, 2nd edition. Newbury Park, CA: Sage Publications.

Beyer, H. and Holtzblatt, K. 1995. "Apprenticing with the Customer." *Communications of the ACM* **38**(5), 45–53.

Holtzblatt, K. and Beyer, H. 1993. "Making customer centered design work for teams." *Communications of the ACM* **36**(10), 93–103.

Kirk, J. and Miller, M. 1986. *Reliability and Validity in Qualitative Research.* Newbury Park, CA: Sage Publications.

Using Contextual Inquiry to Discover Physicians' True Needs

Janette M. Coble, MS
Judy S. Maffitt
Matthew J. Orland, MD
Michael G. Kahn, MD, PhD

Section of Medical Informatics,
Washington University School of Medicine
BJC Health System, St. Louis, Missouri

EXECUTIVE SUMMARY

This chapter describes an effort undertaken to generate the requirements for a physician's clinical workstation. Contextual Inquiry was used to gather detailed information about the physicians' needs. This detailed information was analyzed, and requirements were generated from it. The physicians rated the requirements, resulting in a prioritized set of requirements. This prioritized set is being used as a basis for determining what requirements are initially implemented.

BACKGROUND OF THE STUDY

This effort was undertaken as the requirements-generation task for the Clinical Workstation (CW) of Project Spectrum (Cable et al. 1995). Project Spectrum is a joint technology consortium consisting of Washington University School of Medicine, BJC Health System, IBM, Kodak, and SBC Corp. (formerly known as Southwestern Bell) (Fritz and Kahn 1995). The purpose of Project Spectrum is to provide users with comprehensive, longitudinal clinical information across all 15 hospitals and affiliated ambulatory care settings in the BJC Health System. The User Interface (UI) team was specifically tasked with defining the physician requirements for Phase I of this project, which had been scoped as providing clinicians with the capability to view all readily available, clinically significant test results (e.g., radiology, laboratory, pathology) for their patients from the office, home, or hospital. The target user for Phase I is a clinical physician (not a resident, intern, or nurse) in the field of general medicine or general surgery in either the academic or community environment.

Due to past experiences with introducing information systems for physicians into the BJC Health System, it was believed and emphasized by managers at all levels that the resulting CW must truly meet the needs of the physicians in a highly usable manner. To ensure that this outcome would be the case, we knew we needed to start with (and focus on) the physicians. As we were developing the plan for determining the users' needs, one team member attended CHI '94. After talking to many people and attending various sessions, it was determined that Contextual Inquiry (CI) (Wixon et al. 1990; Wixon and Raven 1994; Holtzblatt and Jones 1990) would be the best approach.

The process of generating requirements using CI within Project Spectrum was implemented by the Project Spectrum user-interface team. The physician on our three-member user interface team did not participate in the CI sessions, because we were concerned that his presence might influence his colleagues' actions. He did, however, participate in generating the requirements from the CI data and in giving the requirements a clinical organization. Another member of the UI team had a user-interface background, but very little knowledge of the physicians and how they perform their day-to-day activities. The third member of the UI team had experience developing information systems for physicians and was more familiar with the physicians' day-to-day activities, but did not have user-interface experience.

PLANNING THE STUDY

We chose CI because we felt that going to the users' actual environment would be the only way to assimilate the actual needs of the physicians. One method that was proposed prior to selecting CI was to get all of the physicians together in a meeting setting and generate requirements using a facilitator. We were concerned about taking this out-of-context approach because people generally can't verbalize their needs when they are not actually performing tasks in their own environment. People are often not thorough, and sometimes not even accurate, as they describe their needs when they are away from their work environment.

We had one example of this problem during our CI sessions. Before the CI session started, a physician explained the purpose and details of each section in his office chart, including the physician's notes section. Later, when he was doing actual work in context, the person performing the CI session noticed that the note he was looking at was written with red ink. She probed and the physician said it told him the previous encounter with this patient was a hospital visit. That fact told him he needed to review the hospital discharge summary and hospital laboratory results before entering the patient's exam room. The physician was surprised that he had not mentioned that need before. It was so ingrained in how he worked that he did not even process that highly relevant detail consciously anymore.

Because we were new to CI, we did not initially modify the process. We conducted the CI sessions and the analysis of the resulting data as closely as possible to what we had learned in a CI training class we attended. However, our training did not take us through the whole process, so we improvised during the data-consolidation phase. We then added a new step after the consolidation process to develop the requirements, because we needed to mix a new method (CI) with a traditional deliverable, a "Requirements Document." Once we generated the requirements, we had the physicians rate each requirement to determine the physicians' priority.

CONDUCTING THE STUDY

The next sections provide an overview of the users who took part in the research and of the research process itself.

The Users

The BJC Health System is made up of approximately 15 hospitals, ranging from small rural hospitals providing primary care services to large tertiary hospitals providing subspecialty care. For Phase I of Project Spectrum, six hospitals were chosen as the initial deployment sites. We formed a team of ten general medicine and general surgery physicians, representing these six hospitals and Washington University School of Medicine. We selected physicians that were open to change and new ideas, who had the willingness to work with us over time, and who fit the profile of our Phase I user. We did not focus on physicians who already had computer experience. We wanted the resulting physician group to be representative of the user population. We ended up with a good mix of physicians who used computers, physicians who had computers but did not use them, and physicians who did not even own computers.

We found our initial candidates for the team of physicians using various methods. We received physician names from chairpersons of departments and committees, from physician practice support groups within the hospitals, and from physicians already involved with Project Spectrum. The physician on our user-interface team made the initial contacts with the candidates. The resulting composition of the team met most of our criteria, although we did end up with a few physicians with subspecialties. We felt that their presence would actually help, because we need to be open to the needs of specialists in the future, and these physicians also perform a significant number of general medicine or general surgery tasks in the course of practicing their subspecialty.

It also turned out that all physicians chosen for the team were male. We felt that at this stage in the project, having a user group consisting of all male physicians would not be a problem. It was more important to control for differences across hospitals than to control for gender differences. Because the team consisted of only male members, references to them in this paper are in terms of the male gender. We have now added new members to the physician team, some of whom are female.

Overview of the Process

The goal for Project Spectrum is for physicians to be able to access their patients' clinical information from their offices, homes, or hospitals, so we wanted to perform the study in these sites. Although we did not visit the physicians' homes, we performed CI sessions in their offices and inpatient (hospital) settings.

Our overall process began with CI sessions in the office, and then inpatient settings. After each session, we analyzed the information. At two points during the process (halfway through the sessions, and after they were complete) we consolidated the information across physicians. We generated the requirements from the final set of consolidated information, and then the physicians rated the requirements independently. We generated the mean rating and standard deviation for each requirement from the physicians' individual ratings, and used that as a basis for prioritizing the requirements for Phase I of Project Spectrum.

For the first half of the CI sessions, our focus was broad. We looked at how the physicians processed any type of information to care for their patients. We wanted to make sure we did not miss any opportunities to support their work by beginning with a focus that was too narrow. Based on the data from these sessions, we narrowed our focus during the second half of the CI sessions to the processing of clinical test results, the original scope given to us as Phase I.

The Contextual Inquiry Sessions

The Contextual Inquiry (CI) sessions involved one member of the user interface team interviewing the physician in his work environment while the physician performed the tasks in our focus. A typical session had three stages:

- The orientation (approximately 10–15 minutes), which included restating the purpose for the session, a reminder of the process for the interview, introductions to people we would meet during the session, and a tour of the facility if applicable (typically done in the office setting). We also had the participant sign a consent form so we could audio tape the sessions and collect artifacts. We stressed that we were going to ask very detailed questions, and that we would want copies of "everything they touched."
- The interview (from one to six hours), which involved the physician performing clinical tasks exactly the way he normally would, except that he would describe what he was doing as he performed the tasks, and we interjected questions to obtain more detailed information. The office-setting interviews took between four to six hours, because it was important to view the physicians before the start of office visits (as they processed clinical information coming in the mail), during their office visits (as they processed clinical information relevant to those patients), and then sometimes after the end of office visits (as they performed additional clinical tasks). The inpatient setting interviews tended to be one to two hours depending on the number of patients the physician currently had in the hospital, and the number of hospitals he had to visit.

- The wrap-up (approximately five minutes), which usually involved a verbal thank-you and a description of the follow-up material that we would provide. We had originally wanted the wrap-up to be closer to 15 minutes and to include a short verbal summary of the session, but it turned out not to be practical because the physician was typically in a hurry to move to the next scheduled event of his day.

We found the orientation to be a necessity for a smooth, productive interview. There was one case in which the interview began without an orientation. The physician started to get annoyed at the detail of the questions being asked. He finally stopped to complain, which gave the person performing the CI session a chance to do a quick orientation. The interview progressed better, although he was still somewhat annoyed. The subsequent interview performed in the hospital with this same physician was completed without any misunderstandings.

We asked the physicians to schedule the CI session on a day that was not too busy, but still within their normal range. We wanted to make sure we could interrupt with questions and yet not delay their patient schedule. This approach turned out to be a good compromise. There were times when a physician got too busy or was dealing with an emergency, so we would simply observe and take notes. When the crisis was over, we would have the physicians walk through the situation that just happened, using our notes to keep the discussion specific. It was also important for us to understand what clinical information the physicians used while they were with a patient in the exam room. The physicians would decide on a case-by-case basis if our presence in the exam room was acceptable. We would not probe while in the exam room, but we would walk through what happened in the exam room after exiting. We would also perform a similar post-examination walk-through on the patients we did not see in the exam room, although we would not have notes on which to base the discussion.

The CI sessions were audio-taped and we took notes. During the first half of CI sessions, the audio tapes were relied upon heavily for filling in missing details in our notes and for providing feedback on our interviewing skills. Toward the end of the CI sessions, we had improved our note-taking skills and did not always use the audio tapes. We also collected artifacts of the clinical information the physicians actually used to care for their patients. We modified ("sanitized") this information by removing all patient- and physician-identifying information.

Because the physicians with which we worked were ongoing participants of Project Spectrum, we wanted to provide continuous feedback indicating the value of their participation. As soon as possible following the session, we sent a short thank-you note to the physician for their participation. After the data from each session was analyzed, we sent the physician a summary of what we learned in their session.

During the last half of the CI sessions, we brought in members of other Project Spectrum teams as observers. The Project Spectrum team members attended a CI session and were asked to participate actively in the analysis of that session. The observers were given a minimal introduction to CI and shown how we analyzed the resulting data before attending a CI session. The purpose of having fellow Project Spectrum team members observe the CI sessions was to give them an opportunity to see the user in his environment performing actual work, without the overhead of more formal training (because we were time-constrained to finish the requirements-generation effort). The observers gained a better understanding of the true context of the user, which helped the observers to understand how various project tasks fit together. The experience also helped the observers understand medical terms and issues they had heard within the project, but with which they were not familiar. Those of us conducting the CI effort felt that the project benefited as a whole, but more training for the observers would have been beneficial. The observers interjected questions during the interview despite the fact they were asked to observe only. These interruptions made the interview more difficult to perform, and made it more difficult to keep the physician on track. The observers asked questions because they were naturally curious and interested in learning more about the user. However, we did not give the observers enough training for them to realize the resulting impact of their questions. The relationship between the user and the person performing the CI session is critical. The physician must be established as the expert, with the person performing the CI session being the apprentice. With a third person in the relationship interjecting questions, the relationship turns into more of an interviewer/interviewee relationship, and the user starts teaching from generalities versus from specific tasks they are performing.

We have given several presentations emphasizing the CI method, and are preparing a class to teach others this technique so that future systems developed at the BJC Health System will also be focused on the user.

ANALYZING AND INTERPRETING THE DATA

Following each CI session, two of us on the user interface team who were performing the CI sessions analyzed the information. The analysis consisted of a walk-through of the CI session while modeling the information obtained. We produced a **sequence model, flow model, context model, detailed observations, user profile,** and **issues list** for each CI session. The person who conducted the CI session began the analysis session by producing a user profile. Then, that person walked through their notes of the session while documenting the observations and pointing out features of artifacts collected during the CI session. The other person documented the sequence and flow models during the walk-through. At the end of the walk-through, the context model was generated, as well as a list of the key issues observed in the CI session. The list of issues was never used, but the list might have been needed if we had been asked to show high-level results to others before the process had produced them. When we had an observer with us during a CI session, they documented the flow diagram during the analysis. Adding two more people to the analysis session would have been useful so that each participant would have a single task during analysis. We feel it would be advantageous to have one person document the flow model, one person document the sequence model, one person document the observations, and the person who performed the CI session walk through their notes.

The **sequence model** (See Figure 13.1) documented the sequences of activities the physicians performed, what triggered the sequences to occur, and the physician's intent at the time the sequences were performed. This model helped to identify common workflows across physicians, and ultimately was used to generate the context-of-use sections for the requirements document. The sequence model was recorded on flip-chart paper. Creating it took two steps: capturing the sequence as we walked through the CI session, and identifying the triggers, intents, and sequences following the walk-through. Following the analysis session, we took some of the intents and sequences and included them in our summary letter back to the physicians.

The **flow model** (See Figure 13.2) documented, in a diagram format on flip-chart paper, the information and items flowing between the physician and other people or places. This model identified information flow bottlenecks, as well as heavy and light information flow areas. Following the analysis session, we transferred the diagram to an electronic format and included a copy in our summary letter back to the physicians.

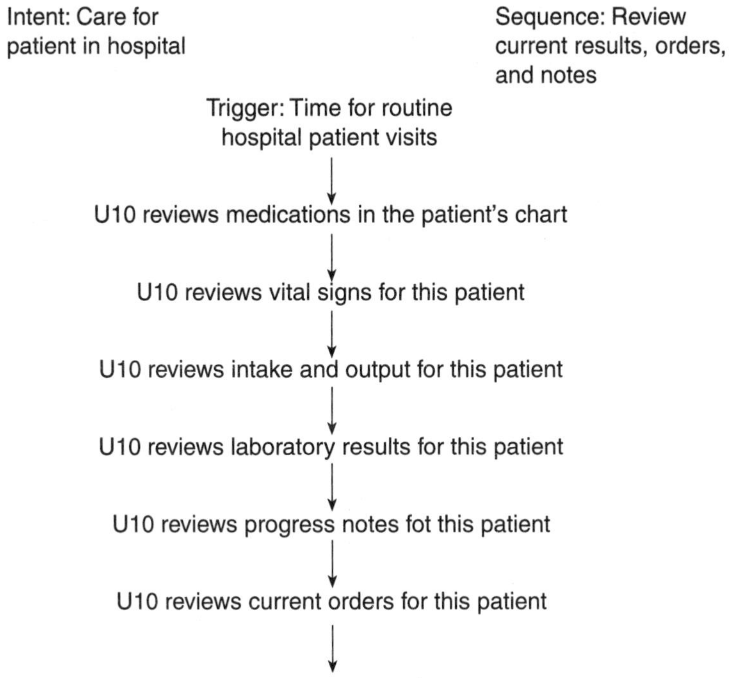

Intent: Care for
patient in hospital

Sequence: Review
current results, orders,
and notes

Trigger: Time for routine
hospital patient visits

↓

U10 reviews medications in the patient's chart

↓

U10 reviews vital signs for this patient

↓

U10 reviews intake and output for this patient

↓

U10 reviews laboratory results for this patient

↓

U10 reviews progress notes fot this patient

↓

U10 reviews current orders for this patient

↓

FIGURE 13.1   Sample from the sequence model.

The **context model** (See Figure 13.3) documented, in diagram format on flip-chart paper, external influences that affected how the physician cared for patients. Some of the issues brought to light here have been documented and given to our management, so that they are aware of them and their possible impact on our project.

The **observations** (See Figure 13.4) were the primary source for the requirements. The observations contained the details of what the physician did, details of the information the physician reviewed, any design ideas the physician mentioned, questions and comments the physician had, and questions we had that needed to be resolved by that physician or by a different physician on a subsequent CI session. These were recorded electronically during the walk-through of the CI session. Following the analysis session, we included some example observations in our summary letter back to the physicians along with a total count of the number of observations generated.

The **user profile** was simply a description of the user's characteristics. It included items such as "U3 is a family practitioner," "U3

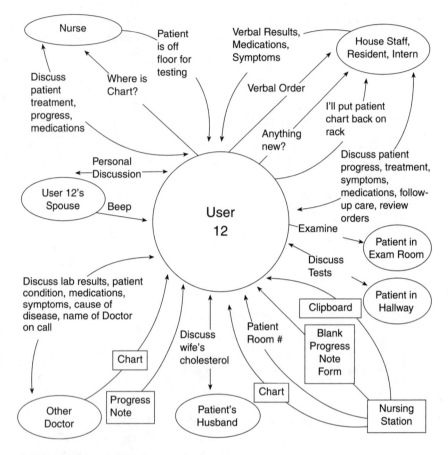

FIGURE 13.2 Sample flow model.

practices at Barnes Hospital and Jewish Hospital," "The number of patients U3 has in the hospital fluctuates between 4 and 13," or "U3 has a subspecialty in pulmonary diseases."

A CI session was performed with each physician in the office setting and the inpatient setting. We noticed after several CI sessions in the office and inpatient settings that we were not getting much, if any, additional information. However, because the physicians were representing different hospitals, we continued with the remaining CI sessions to make sure there were no hidden differences based on hospital influence. We also wanted to ensure that all physicians were equally involved, and that all hospitals were equally represented.

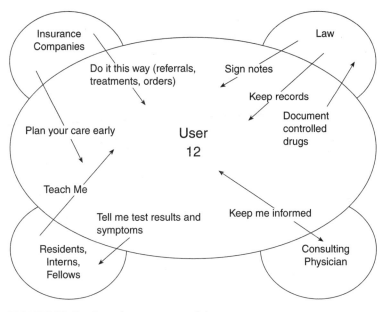

FIGURE 13.3   Sample context model.

The Consolidation of Physician Analysis Data

After analyzing the information from individual CI sessions, we consolidated this information across physicians. We did this task at the halfway mark (after about 10 CI sessions) and again at the completion of the CI sessions. In both consolidation sessions, we created a flow model that consolidated the flow of information and items across physicians, and a context model that consolidated the influences across physicians. We did not consolidate the sequence models due to time constraints. At the time, we did not see an immediate use for the consolidated sequence model. We felt we could get everything we needed out of the individual models. As the project progressed, however, we found several occasions in which the consolidated sequence models would have been extremely useful. We are currently putting our individual models into electronic format, and will then consolidate the models into one.

We took the observations and created an affinity diagram (a logical grouping of the observations in a tree structure) at the halfway point. Creating this diagram was a very helpful process that resulted in the organization of our data on paper and in our minds. The affinity diagram also helped us develop our narrower focus for the second half

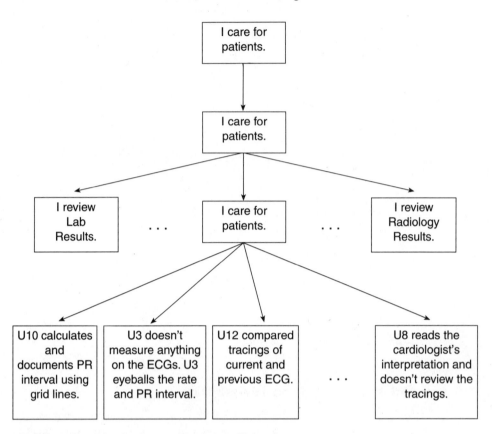

FIGURE 13.4 Sample observations in an affinity diagram.

of the CI sessions. After the CI sessions were complete, we added the observations from the second half of CI sessions into the affinity diagram, expanding it significantly in our area of focus (and not as much outside the focus area). During the time we were building the affinity diagram (and we had the observations posted all over the wall in the conference room), we brought a couple of people in the room to view it. Presenting the affinity diagram to others was not a planned event, but turned out to be a good way to demonstrate what we were doing and the type of information we obtained. The next time we do the CI effort, we will definitely make the affinity diagram more visible to other project members and will probably make this step a bigger public relations event. We found it very enlightening to "walk the wall" of the affinity diagram, and wish others could have also benefitted from it.

Physician Requirements Generation Meeting

After completion of the CI sessions and their analysis, we met with the physicians to give them the opportunity to voice any additional concerns, issues, or requirements. The meetings generated a lot of discussion, but no new requirements within our focus.

The Requirements Generation and Prioritization Process

At this point, we needed to translate the data we had into a "requirements document." The requirements were generated using the affinity diagram of the observations. We walked through the observations generating requirements from each observation. To make sure that the requirements were not unduly influenced by the physician on the UI team, we had the physician generate requirements separately from the other two UI team members. Then, the three UI team members walked through the observations together, generating the final set of requirements. We found that the physician did, at times, have different interpretations of the observations based on his own experiences. We would discuss the context of the observation and come to an agreement within the UI team on which one (or both) of the requirements should be added to the final set of requirements. Part of the way through this requirements-generation process, we decided to note the observation identifier behind the requirement to facilitate referring back to the observations at a later time, as well as to show the weight and impact of that requirement.

We found it more efficient to generate duplicate requirements (to be consolidated later) than to locate a previously generated requirement and add another observation identifier to it. We also found requirements that were only subtly different, but kept them separate in order to get more specific rating information from the physicians. We used the observation reference to clarify these subtle differences in requirements, and to assist us in deciding when to combine requirements and when to keep them separate. Due to the number of requirements we generated, we created an affinity diagram of the requirements. At this stage, we again involved a physician on our user interface team, so that the resulting organization of the requirements would be clinically focused. This clinical organization became the organization of the requirements document.

We took the 542 requirements we generated, added a rating scale to each requirement (See Figure 13.5), and gave this to the physicians to review independently. Their instructions were as follows:

1.9.10   The user must be able to review ECGs.

Necessary			Optional				Unnecessary		
10	9	8	7	6	5	4	3	2	1

1.1.10.1   The user must be able to locate/specify desired ECGs that are needed for comparison.

Necessary			Optional				Unnecessary		
10	9	8	7	6	5	4	3	2	1

1.9.10.9   The user must have the facilities available to calculate rate, PR interval, etc.

Necessary			Optional				Unnecessary		
10	9	8	7	6	5	4	3	2	1

1.9.10.10   The user must be easily able to review the ECG findings and the cardiologist's name without having to review the tracings.

Necessary			Optional				Unnecessary		
10	9	8	7	6	5	4	3	2	1

FIGURE 13.5   Sample requirements with rating scale.

Please circle the number (1–10) that indicates your opinion of how important it is to you as a physician to have this requirement met in the workstation. The meaning of the various ratings (and numbers) is:

Necessary (8–10)   This requirement must be met in the workstation before I'll use it.

Optional (4–7)   I don't have to have this requirement met to use the system, but it would make my life easier.

Unnecessary (1–3)   I can lead a full and happy life without this requirement being met.

Of the 542 requirements, 411 had a mean physician rating greater than or equal to 8. Although the ratings were generally high (as would be expected, because the requirements were generated directly from the physician CI sessions), we were pleased to see some variance in the ratings and meaningful comments scattered throughout the documents the physicians used to rate the requirements (even after page 90 in a 100-page document). It was also interesting to note that only two of the 542 requirements received a perfect ten physician rating. We are currently analyzing the ratings to see if we can make any additional conclusions from them.

The deliverable of our requirements-generation task was a "requirements document." Our dilemma was how to convey all the information we collected about the physician, his needs, and his environment in a traditional "requirements document." What we had, in the form of requirements, were high-level requirements supported by detailed requirements. To support each detailed requirement, we generated context-of-use scenarios for both the office and inpatient settings based on the sequence models and observations. We did this to illustrate the true meaning of the requirements and the context in which the requirements became evident. The context-of-use scenarios are currently being used to exercise the development architecture. See Figure 13.6 for a sample requirement.

Although, the major portion of the requirements document was the requirements, we did include additional information. The requirements document included the following sections:

- Executive summary (2 pages).
- Introduction (6 pages).
- Requirements (95 pages).
- Description of CI process (2 pages).
- Consolidated context model (1 page).
- Consolidated flow model (3 pages).
- List of artifacts collected during the CI session (7 pages).

Although our requirements document did a good job of providing information at a very high level (executive summary level) and at a very detailed level (the requirements themselves), we have found that it is missing a middle level that is appropriate for introducing people external to Project Spectrum to the requirements, and for bringing new people up to speed quickly.

IMPACTING THE DESIGN

We have heavily used two products: the observations and the requirements. After the observations were put into an affinity diagram, they

3.1.9.10 The user must be able to review ECGs. (Mean: 9.00, Standard Deviation: 0.94)

Context of Use

The users' necessity to be able to review ECGs is illustrated in the following contexts in an *office* setting:

- The physician is in his office, sitting at his desk, processing his mail. The mail has been categorized for him (e.g., results vs. junk mail). He accesses the next mail item and it is an ECG. He reviews it by reading the remarks section and the cardiologist's name. The text says it's unchanged, so he doesn't review the signal. He indicates that he's seen it and sends it to his partner for review.
- <additional context of use scenarios omitted>

The users' necessity to be able to review ECGs is illustrated in the following contexts in an *inpatient* setting:

- The physician goes to the nursing station in the hospital at 9:00 a.m. and accesses the new patient's chart. He looks for the medications and vital signs, but nothing is available yet. He reads the current physician orders and the Emergency Department report. He then looks at the ECG reviewing the tracings only (he lives to review his own ECGs). He looks at the physician's note and signs the admission note. He reviews laboratory results. He then enters the patient's room to examine the patient.

Detailed Requirements

3.1.9.10.1   The user must be able to locate/specify desired ECGs that are needed for comparison. (Mean: 9.20, Standard Deviation: 0.87)

<additional requirements omitted>

3.1.9.10.9   The user must have the facilities available to calculate rate, PR interval, etc. (Mean: 7.90, Standard Deviation: 2.30)

3.1.9.0.10   The user must be easily able to review the ECG findings and the cardiologist's name without having to view the tracings (Mean: 7.50, Standard Deviation: 2.42)

FIGURE 13.6   Sample requirements from a requirements document.

were given to other teams within and outside Project Spectrum who needed to look at the raw data to pull out their respective requirements. As the user-interface team generated requirements from the observations, we identified observations that applied to other teams. The other teams reviewed all of the observations and identified which ones they thought applied to them. We then met with the other team leaders and walked through the observations to make sure all appropriate observations were identified and noted. In retrospect, it would have been nice to have the observations in a database suitable for searching and pulling out subsets of the observations as requested.

We had a lot of detailed information and felt we needed to spread the word, so a presentation was given to the entire Project Spectrum technical team to help give all members a better understanding of the users, the users' environment, and the users' requirements. We created two real-life scenarios from the combination of models we generated using CI. We illustrated the scenarios using a slide show of a physician in the appropriate context, and transparencies of actual artifacts collected during the CI session. The presentation illustrated about half of the 542 requirements. The presentation was an effective way to convey the information.

We are performing a detailed scoping of what tasks the physicians will be able to perform with Phase I of the CW. We are using the requirements and the physicians' ratings as the basis for this scoping effort, factoring in data availability, the impact on other teams within Project Spectrum, and the cost and time for development. This scoping effort will be followed by the completion of a prototype and the development of the clinical workstation. In addition, we are taking steps to address each of the key findings discovered during the CI process.

ASSESSING THE COST/BENEFIT

Beginning in August 1994, we estimate that we spent approximately 300 hours executing CI sessions, which includes 80 physician hours in direct participation, 130 staff hours in direct participation, and 90 staff hours in post-session documentation. An additional 1,300 staff hours have been spent in data analysis sessions over a three-month time frame.

In general, management was supportive. The study took longer than we estimated (although we had pulled the initial time estimates out of a hat to begin with), but they gave us the extra time. They were a little apprehensive about using CI when we started, but deferred to our judgment that this was a good approach to determine the physicians' true needs. They are very happy with our effort and feel that we have good results. The work has been used repeatedly in other project activities.

One thing that CI does not provide is timing benchmarks, because the CI performer is probing the physician with questions while the physician performs the tasks. We ended up with requirements that stated that the physicians must be able to do task X at least as quickly as they do now. However, we do not know the current speed. We will be visiting the physicians again to observe their work in context without probing, so we can record how long it currently takes to complete the tasks we plan to support in Phase I. From these observations, we can then establish usability metrics for the CW.

REFLECTIONS

After our CI effort, and the generation and prioritization of the requirements, we extracted the four key findings. The prevalence of two of these findings surprised us and would not have been discovered, we believe, without performing this study in the physician's context (while the physician was performing real work, and while we were probing).

A major benefit of using CI was the resulting relationship with the physicians. We expected this to a degree, but were amazed at the enthusiasm of the physicians regarding Project Spectrum and the process. The physicians feel they are part of Project Spectrum, and believe that the project is being driven by their needs. This is mostly due to the fact that with CI, we spent an extended amount of time with each physician in a one-on-one setting, actively inquiring about their needs, wishes, and problems.

Because this was a new method and only two of us were trained, we began with a two-person effort until we felt strong enough in our skills to bring in others. Having only two people performing the bulk of CI sessions resulted in a longer process (calendar-wise). Having trained members from other teams to help in this process would be of great benefit.

One regret we have is that so few of the Project Spectrum team members have an in-depth understanding of the users and requirements. Next time, we feel the CI team should be enlarged with a cross-disciplinary, properly trained team. In addition, we will make the models (especially the affinity diagram of observations) more visible.

We will also allow more time after the analysis of the CI sessions to document the results and provide the summary feedback to the physicians. We always analyzed a CI session before performing the next one, but sometimes the feedback to the physicians and formalizing the documentation of a session was delayed until a break in the sessions. Also, creating the requirements document took much longer than we had estimated. We felt that it was important to include contexts of use that were truly based on the data, but we underestimated the amount of time this activity would take.

By using CI, we feel we were able to gather accurate and comprehensive information about the physicians' needs for effectively and efficiently caring for their patients. Taking into account not only the requirements we generated using CI, but also the current information flow and contextual influences on the physician, we will be able to provide them with a system that not only meets their clinical information-processing needs, but fits into the context of how they care for patients. This will allow them to adapt from their current process to take advantage of the new technology Project Spectrum will provide. After the physicians prioritized the requirements, we received an unsolicited comment from one of them indicating that they were impressed with the comprehensiveness of the requirements. This was exciting and very gratifying coming from a future user!

ACKNOWLEDGMENTS

Many people were involved in various stages of this effort. The authors would like to acknowledge the following contributors: Keith Ebker, Kevin Fritz, Jim Ross, Charlene Abrams, Bob Balassi, Mike Benesch, Candy Canfield, Tom Heines, Nilesh Jain, and Sherry Steib. Finally, a sincere thanks to the ten physicians who shared their knowledge and time participating in Contextual Inquiry sessions, and for prioritizing the seemingly endless list of requirements.

REFERENCES

Coble, J., Maffitt J., Orland, M, and Kahn, M. 1995. "Contextual Inquiry: Discovering Physicians' True Needs." *Proceedings of the Symposium on Computer Applications in Medical Care '95*. October, 1995.

Fritz, K. and Kahn, M. 1995. "Project Spectrum: An Eighteen Hospital Enterprise-Wide Electronic Medical Record." C. Peter Waegemann (ed). *Proceedings, Toward an Electronic Patient Record*. Volume 2 59–67 Newton, MA: Medical Records Institute.

Wixon D., Holtzblatt K., and Knox S. 1990. "Contextual Design: An Emergent View of System Design." *Proceedings of CHI'90*. New York: ACM. April, 1990.

Wixon, D. and Raven, M. 1994. "Contextual Inquiry: Grounding your Design in User's Work." *CHI'94 Tutorial*.

Holtzblatt, K. and Jones S. 1990. "Contextual Inquiry: Principles and Practice." Technical Report 729. Maynard, MA: Digital Equipment Corporation.

14

Bringing the Users' Work to Us: Usability Roundtables at Lotus Development

Mary Beth Butler
Marie Tahir

Lotus Development

EXECUTIVE SUMMARY

This chapter explains usability roundtables, one method we use to help us better understand our users' work. During usability roundtables, we attempt to recreate a portion of the users' environment by having them bring samples of their work to our offices. Users sit with product team members around a conference table and use these samples (usually data files, sample applications, or hard copy printouts) to explain their work. By explaining the sample data files and printed output that they bring with them, the users can give a product team a good introduction to the major issues they face in their jobs, and how technology helps or hinders them in their work.

Seeing the work that users do ensures that our designs meet their needs. Our initial attempts to visit users in their workplaces were time-consuming and not as productive as we hoped. Usability Roundtables have provided us with an effective alternative for learning more about our users' work.

BACKGROUND

At Lotus Development, a subsidiary of IBM Corporation, we have tried a variety of data-collection techniques in and out of our usability labs. We have developed a repertoire of usability lab techniques, which allows us to effectively test our design ideas. As our experience with lab testing has grown, we have been confronted with the limitations of lab testing. In our lab we are controlling many of the variables, which naturally limits the types of information that we can discover. Recently we have been seeking methods that allow us to capture more realistic information about how our customers use our products in their work.

Usability Testing and User Interface Design in the Desktop Division

Lotus Development produces desktop and communication software for business. The Desktop Division produces Lotus SmartSuite, an integrated collection of business software, including 1-2-3, Word Pro, Freelance Graphics, and Approach. A majority of Lotus' customers are 1-2-3 users, and the roundtable process originated through our efforts to learn more about these users.

Each product team includes product managers and user interface (UI) designers. Product managers define customer requirements for a product and ensure that these are met in the final product. UI designers translate users' needs into specifications for overall screen layout and sequencing of feature operations. Product managers and UI designers work on one product at a time, and are expected to have strong expertise in the product, the users, and the competition.

Usability specialists in the Desktop Division are centralized in one group; each specialist works as a member of a product team to provide usability testing support to one product. Our role is to find creative ways to quickly and cost-effectively test our products, to identify usability issues, and to provide supporting information to answer questions about our customers. We spend most of our time testing products or collecting customer information, and reporting findings and suggestions back to the product team.

Our Attempts at Contextual Inquiry

Our usability group provides a variety of data-collection methods to our internal clients. It is important for us to offer techniques that allow user-interface designers to get quick feedback on their design ideas. We also try to provide testing solutions that are interesting to all parts of the product team (designers, developers, and documentation specialists). Our usability tool box includes the standard array of lab testing techniques, such as thinking aloud, codiscovery, low-fidelity prototyping, and competitive studies, as well as informal testing outside of the lab and customer surveys. This set of techniques has worked well, and we are confident that we have a well-defined process for getting users' reactions to our designs and product ideas in the lab.

After several years of providing lab-based testing, we realized that we were missing techniques for gathering information about our users' work. At CHI conferences, we had heard about the benefits of Contextual Inquiry and other types of field research. At about the same time, the 1-2-3 product team asked us to find ways for them to learn more about how 1-2-3 users worked.

Initially, we attempted to do this by conducting Contextual Inquiry sessions: We sent product-team members out to visit users in their workplaces. Typically, we paired user-interface designers and product managers with usability staff, then tried to match them with appropriate users. For example, we would try to send the product designer who is responsible for the printing feature out to meet a user who said that she printed regularly.

We asked users to let us visit them to watch them work; these sessions were scheduled to last for about two hours. Team members were instructed to watch the users work for at least the first hour of the session, then spend the remaining time interviewing users about their work and their use of 1-2-3. We provided team members with a basic script to follow, including a compilation of questions that the usability specialist had previously collected from the team. Team members were encouraged to use the script as appropriate, but to take the interviews in any direction that seemed productive. Finally, team members were asked to prepare brief reports when they returned from visits.

After several attempts to use this method, it became apparent that these sessions took too much work to set up relative to the amount of information we were able to gather from them. Some of the problems with these visits included:

■ Users were reluctant to let us watch them work. Users found it difficult to justify the time they would spend with us to their managers. Users expressed concern about letting us see confidential financial data that they kept in 1-2-3. Also, users were concerned about disturbing fellow workers, especially if they sat in cubes or other open-plan seating.

- It was very time-consuming to set up these sessions. As noted above, finding users willing to let us watch them work was very difficult. We also had difficulties trying to match schedules of team members interested in a particular feature with users who said that they worked with that feature.
- Team members were too busy to travel to users' locations. Even though all visits were to local users, short trips still proved to be a burden to team members during busy development periods.
- Users rarely did real work at these sessions. Users had difficulty arranging their day so that they had real work to do when we came to visit. They were also reluctant to "bore" us by doing routine work while we sat and watched. Most sessions turned into conversations between the team members and the users, instead of observation sessions.

PLANNING OUR STUDIES

After re-evaluating our process with team members, we developed a process we call *usability roundtables*. The method evolved over time, starting with a suggestion from a designer who wanted to see some examples of how users arranged data in their files. At first, we tried to conduct these sessions in the Usability Lab, but found that the format and the atmosphere were too constraining. We wanted a method in which there could be a free-flowing conversation between users and product designers, product mangers, developers, and other team members. We needed a comfortable place for these conversations. We eventually began to conduct our roundtables in pleasant and sunny conference rooms (where the tables are vaguely round), in which anybody from the team who wanted to could sit around and chat with users who had brought in examples from the work they do every day. The term *usability roundtables* also evolved as a way to communicate that this was a different kind of usability activity, one that included meeting (not testing) users.

Identifying Goals and Users

Before each roundtable, usability staff work with team members to identify product areas for research. We develop a target schedule, and goals for numbers and types of users. Typical goals might be:

- "In the next month, talk to four spreadsheet users who use macros regularly as part of their jobs. See a mix of 1-2-3 and Excel users."

■ "Before the end of the summer, see five examples of applications that are used to produce monthly reports. Some of these applications should be completely using 1-2-3, and some using 1-2-3 and either Freelance or Word Pro."

In order for these sessions to be useful, it is important to specify both the types of users needed, as well as characteristics we want to see in their work. As with usability testing, we find users who we think typify the kinds of people who will be using our product. Most often we attempt to include a mix of users of our products and users of our competitors' products.

Instructions for Users

We ask users to bring in artifacts from their work that show their use of the feature or work pattern in which we are interested. Two types of artifacts are most useful:

■ Sample data or application files, which allow us to understand how users set up their files and how they use our product. (See Figure 14.1.)
■ Hard-copy printouts, which are either sources of data or printed reports from their application. This allows us to see how data gets to the users, and how the users distribute the results of their work. (See Figure 14.2.)

We encourage users to mask or modify their data if they have any concerns about confidentiality; we don't need to see the actual data, we just need reasonable examples of their work. This gives the users more control and addresses the problem of getting users to let us see their work.

Users come to our offices in Cambridge. We find that these sessions are most beneficial if users understand what to expect before they arrive. We tell users that we want to understand how they use our product, and to do that we need to learn about their jobs. We explain that we will ask them to describe their work to a group of us, including some team members who develop the product. We pay users for their time. Sessions usually last 1½ hours. If users have been usability testers previously, we explain the differences between roundtable sessions and usability tests.

We encourage users to bring along a co-worker. This can make the session more comfortable for the participant, but can also provide us with additional information about the application. We encourage users

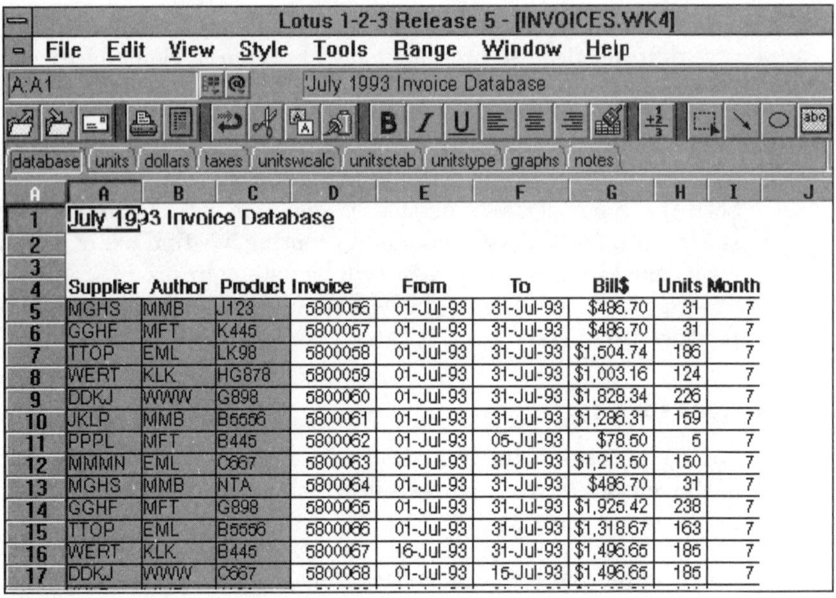

FIGURE 14.1 This is a screen shot showing a typical example of a file that users might bring to a roundtable.

to bring co-workers who use the application, originally developed the application, supply data to the application, or use the output of the application. This gives us a variety of perspectives, and helps us understand how the application fits into the overall flow of the work.

After we have met our initial targets for numbers and types of users, we evaluate the results with the team to determine whether we need to contact additional users, or whether we should move on to new areas of research.

CONDUCTING THE STUDIES

This section describes an outline of a usability roundtable session. For how-to information for moderators and specific examples from roundtables, see Figures 14.1–14.5.

Outline of a Session

Sessions are held in conference rooms. We invite team members (2–8 people) to join the users around a large table. We provide a computer

Expenses (by mo	January	February	March	April	May	June	July	August	September	October	November	D
OPERATING EXPENSES												
Maintenance	$4,000	$4,400	$4,800	$4,800	$5,200	$4,800	$4,000	$3,600	$3,600	$4,400	$5,200	
Rent	$5,000	$5,000	$5,000	$5,000	$5,000	$5,000	$5,000	$5,000	$5,000	$5,000	$5,000	
Advertising	$16,000	$20,000	$24,000	$24,000	$28,000	$24,000	$20,000	$16,000	$16,000	$24,000	$32,000	
Utilities	$6,000	$6,000	$6,000	$6,000	$6,000	$6,000	$6,000	$6,000	$6,000	$6,000	$6,000	
Office Expenses	$3,000	$3,000	$3,000	$3,000	$3,000	$3,000	$3,000	$3,000	$3,000	$3,000	$3,000	
Total Operating Expenses	$34,000	$38,400	$42,800	$42,800	$47,200	$42,800	$38,000	$33,600	$33,600	$42,400	$51,200	
MANUFACTURING EXPENSES												
Equipment	$40,000	$50,000	$40,000	$50,000	$60,000	$60,000	$50,000	$40,000	$40,000	$50,000	$60,000	
Utilities	$8,000	$8,000	$8,000	$8,000	$8,000	$8,000	$8,000	$8,000	$8,000	$8,000	$8,000	
Repairs	$6,000	$6,400	$6,000	$6,400	$6,800	$6,800	$6,400	$6,000	$6,000	$6,400	$6,800	
Packaging	$3,600	$4,000	$3,600	$4,000	$4,400	$4,400	$4,000	$3,600	$3,600	$4,000	$4,400	
Total Manufacturing Expenses	$57,600	$68,400	$57,600	$68,400	$79,200	$79,200	$68,400	$57,600	$57,600	$68,400	$79,200	
PERSONNEL EXPENSES												
Salary	$200,000	$200,000	$200,000	$200,000	$200,000	$200,000	$200,000	$200,000	$200,000	$200,000	$200,000	$
Insurance	$50,000	$50,000	$50,000	$50,000	$50,000	$50,000	$50,000	$50,000	$50,000	$50,000	$50,000	
Worker's Compensation	$6,000	$6,000	$6,400	$6,400	$6,800	$6,800	$6,800	$6,800	$6,400	$6,400	$6,000	
Recruiting	$6,000	$5,600	$5,600	$6,400	$7,000	$7,000	$6,400	$6,000	$6,000	$6,000	$6,000	
Training	$2,000	$2,000	$2,400	$2,400	$2,800	$3,200	$2,400	$2,400	$2,600	$2,400	$2,800	
Total Personnel Expenses	$264,000	$263,600	$264,400	$265,200	$266,600	$267,000	$265,600	$265,200	$265,000	$264,800	$264,800	1
TOTAL EXPENSES	$355,600	$370,400	$364,800	$376,400	$393,000	$389,000	$372,000	$356,400	$356,200	$375,600	$395,200	$

FIGURE 14.2 This is an example of a printed report that users might bring to a roundtable.

with appropriate software, load the users' files on the computer, and let them drive. We provide a 25" viewing monitor so that observers seated around the conference table can easily see what the users are doing.

We follow the same general procedures for each session (See Figure 14.3). Typically a usability person or user interface designer moderates the session. We ask the users to talk about their work, and then walk through the sample applications that they have brought with them. As users talk, we ask them questions that match our areas of interest; we usually create a script of questions in advance. (See Figure 14.4.)

We allow the user's work sample to guide the discussion. Many of our questions are answered naturally as part of the users' explanation of their work. The moderator interjects questions from our preplanned list as appropriate throughout the session. However, we don't put a great emphasis on asking the questions exactly the same way in each session. We will even skip questions if they don't seem relevant to a particular user's work. The goal of the session, really, is to learn about the users' work, and the scripts we create are used to the extent that they advance that goal.

We encourage team members to ask their own questions through-out the session, while the moderator keeps the discussion focused on the users' application and specific instances from their work.

CAPTURING, ANALYZING, AND INTERPRETING THE DATA

The moderator (almost always the usability specialist) takes notes throughout the session. The notes should include the most important questions and answers from the discussion. The notes should coher-ently describe the users' work and explain the artifacts that the users have brought with them. We encourage users to give us copies of their files and printouts when they leave. The moderator prepares a brief report from her notes. (See Figure 14.5.) We store the reports and users' sample files in a Lotus Notes database, which team members and product designers across the company can access.

The level of analysis of the data depends on the goals of the research. If the roundtables were scheduled to answer specific ques-tions about specific features, the usability specialist will analyze the data as appropriate and report summaries back to the team at various points in the study. If the sessions were scheduled to provide the team with general education about users, the usability specialist does not do any further formal analysis. However, the usability specialist usually meets informally with team members to share information and discuss impressions of the information gathered.

Types of Data We Have Collected

We have found usability roundtables successful at collecting the fol-lowing kinds of data:

- Sample files and printouts.
- Typical size and layouts of data files.
- What features are actually used.
- What features are considered essential.
- What features fail and why.
- What features users have constructed for themselves (and what needs these are meeting).
- How applications are built.
- How users learn an application.
- How data flows through an application.
- How often applications are used.
- How applications are used.

BENEFITS OF USABILITY ROUNDTABLES

Usability roundtables allow us to simultaneously achieve two major goals: We collect specific information on the use of particular features and work patterns, and we introduce team members to their users and the work of these users. Usability roundtables also provide the following advantages over other methods we have tried:

■ *Roundtables are efficient.* Users are more enthusiastic about attending these sessions than they are about having us visit them, so it is easier for us to schedule users. Team members do not have to travel, and it is not a big time commitment for them to drop by a roundtable session for an hour. This approach also means that more than two team members can meet with the users. By making the sessions easy to attend and requiring no work on the part of the team members, we lower barriers to attendance.

■ *Artifacts allow us to reconstruct the users' work.* While we can't see the users' office, printer location, dog-eared documentation, etc., users are good at being able to talk about their own work, and respond to questions about whether a work pattern we describe matches their work model.

■ *Team members easily feel more informed about our users.* UI designers and product managers can use these sessions to quickly gather data on specific feature or product use issues. Team members can drop by to see specific examples of how the product is being used and about who is using their product. This supplements the impression that team members get from watching users in a usability lab.

■ *Roundtables provide real-world sample data for usability testing.* The usability specialist can draw on real examples from samples supplied by users to create testing files and scenarios.

■ *We build a rapport with users to lay the groundwork for later visits to these customer sites.* As we have done more roundtables, we have increasingly found ourselves invited back to the users' offices to gather more information. Once users know the team and understand the kind of information that we need, they feel more comfortable with the idea of us coming to watch them work. We find that once we understand some aspects of the users work, we have a better foundation for a more focused site visit.

■ *Roundtables help team members understand what to ask at customer visits.* After team members have attended a roundtable, they have a much clearer idea of what to collect from users. Team members learn from watching the moderator how to focus on the users' work, how to ask follow-up questions, and what kinds of information to collect.

CHALLENGES AND LIMITATIONS OF USABILITY ROUNDTABLES

Usability roundtables do have certain challenges and limitations that make them an incomplete substitute for visits to the field:

- The moderator has a large responsibility to focus the session.
- Users don't always communicate clearly.
- Users don't always choose the best samples.
- Users' work is removed from context.
- Roundtables are not suited for all work situations.

The Moderator's Challenge

The moderator needs to manage the roundtable carefully in order to maximize the benefit of the session. Ideally, the conversation needs to be allowed to drift to interesting tangents; practically speaking, it is hard to anticipate which tangents will be productive. The moderator must manage both the users and the team members during the session.

Users might not understand the directive to "tell us about your work," or they may take that too literally. What we really want to know in a roundtable is how users' work makes use (or fails to make use) of our technology. We rarely need to know all the details about their specialties. However, it is not uncommon for users who are somewhat uncomfortable about the roundtable situation to fall back into talking about their field of expertise, something they understand very well. It can be challenging for moderators to gently steer the users away from providing us too many details about the fine points of their work, but still provide enough information for us to understand the technological issues presented by trying to accomplish that work. Often the moderator needs to tactfully interrupt the users in mid-phrase and redirect them through pointed, but polite, questions.

Team members sometimes will try to solve users' problems rather than just hear them. The moderator has to gently discourage team members from offering solutions to users, even when the users ask for help. Suggestions from product team members tend to intimidate the users, and can quickly change the tenor of the session. We have found that once the team starts solving problems for the users, the bulk of session is spent with team members providing information to the users, and not the users providing information to the team. However, it is extremely frustrating for team members to watch users describing a problem which can easily be fixed, and frustrating when users think we can help them but are withholding information. One solution is to tell team members and the users at the beginning of the session that you will save time for these discussions at the end of the session.

Users Need Good Communication Skills

Successful usability roundtables depend more on the user's communication skills than other methods. Users must feel comfortable talking to a group of people. Users need to be selected not only because they can show us a relevant application, but also for their ability to clearly and concisely explain their work. This is not a question of level of expertise; it is important to bring in less-skilled as well as expert users. It is necessary to screen the users carefully by phone in advance for their communication skills, or draw on users who have demonstrated good communication skills during previous usability testing sessions.

Users Don't Always Choose the Best Samples

In roundtable sessions, we rely on users to choose interesting samples of work to show us. Often users will bring in best-case examples, which are useful, but don't provide us with details about work that is difficult to do. Careful probing by the session moderator can draw users out on problematic aspects of their work. All roundtable sessions should include some in-depth questions about real-life use of the application to try to elicit information from users about problems.

Users' Work is Removed from Context

By asking users to bring in their work, we are removing the work from the context, and hoping the users can reconstruct the important pieces for us. In the work context, there may be additional information that the users no longer notice, or think is irrelevant (perhaps because the work is not done on computer). A trained observer at a user's location can use the context to glean additional information that the users simply do not recognize as important. With experience, team members can learn to pick up hints from users about useful work pieces that deserve some additional discussion. Often, users make offhand comments about work done commonly (or rarely) in which they think we are not interested. With practice, getting users to talk about these points can be quite productive. However, it is possible that these facts might be more easily discovered if the observers were at the users' workplace.

Roundtables Are Not Suited for All Work Situations

Roundtables are not as well suited for work situations where the users' work is heavily determined by the environment, such as a help-desk or data-entry department. Roundtables work well when users are showing us custom applications that they have created, which admittedly narrows our focus.

FUTURE DIRECTIONS

Usability roundtables provide us with another method for better understanding our users, and we plan to continue to use them during future product research. Roundtables can help us to answer many of the same specific and immediate questions about product and feature use as more traditional field techniques.

While usability roundtables give us many of the same benefits of field visits, they are not a complete substitute for them. In fact, usability roundtables often highlight the importance of field visits to our teams. While users can bring us much new information, in almost every roundtable session the users reference data that is back in their workplace, or that would be easier to see in their workplace. In addition, it becomes clear in roundtables that some work just has to be seen in context to be fully understood. As a result, we expect that roundtables will help us demonstrate the importance of field visits to our product teams, so that product teams (as well as users) will want to couple field visits with usability roundtables in our research.

CONDUCTING A STUDY: A CASE STUDY

Because many of the projects for which we have used roundtables are still under development, we will provide an example of a fictional feature, based on the work that we have done with real features.

1-2-3 Release X introduced many innovations to the 1-2-3 for Windows product line, including some new data-analysis tools. These tools were completely new features based on previous research into customer needs. The team did as much research into user requirements as possible prior to releasing these features in the product. However, the team had to make some assumptions about how users would use these tools. Before planning significant additional enhancements to these features for the next release of the product, the team wanted to understand how users were really using the data-analysis tools, so they asked their usability specialist to locate some users.

The usability specialist contacted people who she thought were likely users of this feature. After interviewing the users on the phone about their use of the data analysis tools, the specialist asked some users to bring in their files and show their work to the team. Users were selected because they had a successful (or unsuccessful) application in which they could clearly explain their use of the analysis tools.

Users brought in sample files, data files, and sample printouts. Users were asked to talk about their work. The usability specialist served as moderator, keeping the conversation to the topic of the analysis tools, but allowing the conversation to move to relevant tangents if the team members thought the users had something interesting to share. The moderator interjected the following questions, which the team had identified as particularly important, at various points during the session:

- How large were the data sets that the users worked on?
- Did users always start with a new file, or did they often begin with data sets they had used previously?
- How was the data arranged in the file (on one sheet, on multiple sheets)?
- Were there particular reports that the users wanted to get from the data, but could not currently?

Four sessions were scheduled. Three users brought interesting and relevant samples of work. The fourth user brought a project that he was trying to get started. This session was not particularly useful, as the user did not understand the problem he was trying to solve very well, and wanted to use the session to get technical advice from developers.

The usability specialist who worked on this project prepared the following report, summarizing some of the findings from this research:

Finding	**Implication for Product**
Users who regularly use the data analysis tools produce an average of four alternative designs to make monthly reports and add new data sets to existing information each month. Users complained that it was somewhat difficult to make use of existing data.	UI designer will investigate alternative designs to make it easier for users to reuse data sets.
Users arranged data in their files in a variety of ways, and felt strongly that they required complete flexibility in how data appeared in the file.	UI designer chose not to impose more stringent formatting requirements after hearing this information.
Reporting was adequate, however, two users described one additional report that they had created on their own, which had been somewhat complicated to produce.	UI designer decided the report these users described was fairly specialized, and therefore, it was not necessary to include it in the product. However, the designer did decide to try to enhance the report tools to make generating new reports easier.
One user, in an offhand comment, described a parallel between the data analysis tools and another feature of 1-2-3.	After discussion, the development team decided that they could implement the user's suggestion with relatively little additional work.

To-Do List for Usability Roundtable Moderators

Keep in mind:

- The purpose of roundtables is to learn about the users' work by looking at examples of the users' work.
- You'll get more from sessions where you focus discussion on the examples of work that the users have brought along. Keep bringing the discussion back to specific examples from their work.
- Questions that work well sound like: "Do you use feature/product X in your work? Can you describe the last time you used it for me?
- Questions that work poorly sound like: "Would you ever want to have a feature like X? Could you ever think of a time when you might want to use feature X?"
- Avoid giving the users solutions to problems that they raise or that you see in their work. As soon as the discussion turns to ways that the users can change what they do, they will stop volunteering details about what they actually do. Only provide solutions if the session is otherwise nonproductive, or if you are at the end of the session.

When you bring the users into the room:

- Point out to them where they should sit; tell them what to do with their coat.
- If appropriate, get them to sign a Confidential Disclosure Agreement.
- Help the users load their files on our computer. Familiarize them with the mouse.

Introductions:

- Briefly introduce the users (name and company).
- Briefly introduce the team. Generally, don't bother to introduce each person if there are more than three. Just tell the users "These are members of the development team for project X." You don't have to be overly precise in you introductions; just give the users a basic idea of the kinds of people they are talking to.

FIGURE 14.3 *(cont.)*

Ground rules:

- *Tell everyone*: "We'll take about an hour." (You may want to specifically say the time when the session will stop.)
- *Tell the users*: "We'll have you walk us through your work, and we'll ask you questions as you explain it to us."
- *Tell the team members*: "You can ask questions of the users anytime."

To start off:

- Ask the users to briefly explain what they do.
- Ask the users to start walking through their application.

During the session:

- Try not to let the users get bogged down in details of their work; this might mean interrupting them when they take a breath and asking them a specific question about the file they are showing. Don't be afraid to interrupt the users; they will be happy to get some direction from us about what to talk about.
- If you don't understand what the users are talking about then ask for clarification; generally, you'll find everyone else at the session is getting confused too.
- Again, don't let the session get bogged down in solutions. One good strategy is to tell either the users or the team member that you'll make time for that part of the discussion at the end of the session.
- As moderator, refer to the list of session questions and interject these as appropriate.

Before the users leave:

- Get copies of their files.
- Get hard copies of anything they've brought along.

FIGURE 14.3 Sample of instructions for roundtable moderators.

Sample Questions

Moderators are encouraged to use the following questions as guidelines. All of the following questions are posed to the users.

- Tell us what you do, including:
    - Where do you work?
    - How long have you been there?
    - What do you do?

- Describe the application that you have brought along:
    - Who built it, when was it built (get some history of the development of the application)?
    - What's the purpose of the application?
    - How is the data organized?

- How is the application used:
    - How often is it used (does it get reused)?
    - How large is it?
    - Where does the data come from that goes into it?
    - What do you do with the information produced by the application?

- Does anyone else use the application?
    - Did someone else develop it?
    - Do other people add data to it?
    - Do other people edit it?
    - Do other people get the output of it?

- Tell us about the last time that you used this file:
    - Was that a typical set of events? If not, what was different from typical?
    - If not, tell us about the time before that. Was that typical?

- Do you have any problems using this application?
    - Tell us about the problems?
    - Are there things we could do to our product to help you?

- When you don't know how to do something using this product, what do you do?

FIGURE 14.4 *(cont.)*

- Do you use documentation or online Help? Are you able to find what you needed?
- What forms of documentation do you use?
- Do you use different documentation for different tasks?
- What resources do you recommend to others?

■ Products:
  - What products do you use?
  - What hardware do you use?
  - Are software and hardware standard across your office? Division? Company?

■ Other Projects: If the users mention any other projects, get a description of them. Often these offhand comments are incredibly useful sources of information:
  - Do you do this project regularly?
  - Tell me about that special/unusual/difficult project you just mentioned.
  - Find out the purpose of application, who will build it, origin of data, who will use it, what products will be used to produce it, how often it will be used, and how often will they reuse the application.

■ Print samples and ask:
  - Are these samples typical?
  - If not, how are they different from what you typically do?

■ Daily activities:
  - How do you spend most of your day?
  - What are the first five things you do each day?
  - What are the five things you use your computer for each day?
  - What five important things do you do each day that don't involve your computer?

■ Wish list:
  - What suggestions/wish list do you have for our product (or competitor's product)?
  - If there was one thing that we could do to make your products easier to use, what would it be?

FIGURE 14.4 Sample Questions

Sample Report

This is an example of the type of report that a usability specialist might write following a roundtable. The report and the referenced sample files would all be stored in a Lotus Notes database.

Description of User

Tom is an experienced 1-2-3 user who also uses the rest of Smart-Suite. His job at the time of this session was Chemical Engineer at XXX Corporation. This job primarily involves writing computer simulations (in C) to model chemical processes.

Tom uses 1-2-3 at work to develop his models; he frequently creates spreadsheets that allow him to work out details of the models, so that he has test data to check his models against. He also uses 1-2-3 at work for charting the results of his models. Tom uses 1-2-3 at home as well, to calculate personal financial information. He brought examples of both kinds of files.

Sample applications: PROCESS.WK4 and STEAM.WK4

These files are fairly typical of the kinds of things that Tom does with spreadsheets at his job. In PROCESS.WK4, he imported ASCII data that was output from his model (written in C), then used the data to create charts. In STEAM.WK4, he created formulas in his spreadsheet to test his assumptions before building the model in C.

Some common characteristics of his spreadsheets:

- All used multiple sheets.
- He commonly includes very small charts near his calculations. Often he uses line charts to check his regression calculations (to see how well his data points fit to a line).
- He makes extensive use of range names, often naming single cells. Because the cells contain information on various elements, he names the cells with the element names. This allows him to create formulas that resemble chemical formulas (and are relatively easy to read and decipher).
- He uses very small fonts and zooms the screen so that he can see more of his work on the screen. He used to turn off the edit line to get a little more space, but since he was using very small fonts, he found that he needed the edit line in order to be able to read his formulas (so now he leaves the edit line on all the time).

FIGURE 14.5   *(cont.)*

- He often imports or exports ASCII data. He really likes the improved parsing in 1-2-3 Release 5, and was particularly impressed that data is parsed into separate cells, that number formatting was recognized (e.g., percentages were parsed as percentages), and that dates were formatted correctly.
- He rarely reuses spreadsheets at work. Each project is unique, so he generally starts from scratch with each spreadsheet.
- He often uses Backsolver.
- He occasionally uses 1-2-3 to create schedules or flow charts and said, "This is pretty easy for simple projects."

How User Learns New Software

- He learns using the following techniques, in this order:
  - Starts the product up and sees what happens.
  - Reads manuals (when he's not actually in front of his computer).
  - Uses online Help, if he can't figure it out any other way.

Charting

Tom frequently charts his information to present it to others, as well as to help him check his data (e.g., plotting points to check regression data). He likes that 1-2-3 now allows him to plot as many data points as he wants.

He sometimes prints in color. He'll mainly choose to do this when the chart is complicated and too hard to read if it is only in black and white.

Use of E-Mail, Networks, and Other Ways to Exchange Data

XXX Corporation uses cc:Mail (DOS version). Files are increasingly exchanged as attachments. However, not everyone is on e-mail, and not everyone checks their e-mail frequently, so this isn't always a reliable way of distributing information. (Tom described one case where he e-mailed information to a co-worker of someone in another office and asked them to hand-carry the information to the intended recipient, who doesn't yet have e-mail.)

They rarely put files on the network for common use because there is insufficient disk space in public directories.

Important information is more frequently distributed by fax than by e-mail.

Use of DOS vs. File Manager

Tom often works at the DOS prompt to do file operations. He said that he uses File Manager "when doing 'major surgery' like moving directories."

FIGURE 14.5 Sample of a report from usability specialist.

An Overview
of Ethnography
and System Design

John M. Ford

Alpine Media

Larry E. Wood

Brigham Young University

EXECUTIVE SUMMARY

The purpose of this chapter is to introduce and describe the field of
ethnography to those who would like to use ethnographic methods in
system design. We will begin with a brief description of ethnography
and then progress to an explanation of why this approach is well-
suited to needs analysis for system design. We will then review several
common methods used in requirements analysis, and how their
strengths and weaknesses are related to those of ethnographic methods. Finally, we will trace the development of the use of ethnographic
methods in system design and speculate on the future of this trend.

A BRIEF OVERVIEW OF ETHNOGRAPHY

Ethnography has its roots in the descriptive research conducted by
social anthropologists investigating little-known cultures, and has been

shaped by the common problems faced by this type of researcher (Atkinson and Hammersly 1994; Fielding 1993; Pelto and Pelto 1973). Anthropologists are usually tasked with studying cultures that are quite different from the society in which they have lived. They not only need to note the differences between their experience and the customs of the new culture, but need to understand how the culture "works." They need to understand it from the point of view of people who live in it. Because much of what each person in the target culture does is based on unspoken or *tacit* knowledge (Reber 1989) about how to behave, it is not sufficient for an anthropologist to ask direct questions. In addition, he or she must observe what people do, the tools that they use, and how they talk to each other.

Anthropologists are motivated not to repeat the mistakes of a long history of misunderstanding the cultures that they are studying. Traders, explorers, missionaries, and others who have initiated "first contact" with unfamiliar cultures tended to impose incorrect European interpretations on native customs, resulting in problems ranging from simple misunderstanding to armed conflict (Vidich and Lyman, 1994). Ethnographers attempt to guard against this problem by recognizing that any or all of their initial assumptions may be incorrect. They attempt to make as many as possible of their assumptions explicit, and then systematically examine and question these assumptions during their research activities. Ethnographers believe that this is important, because they will have to discover what is most relevant to study in the target culture while they are in the field. Thus they plan only minimal structure for their research before going into the field. What is most important to know will "emerge" from extended study of the "natives" going about their business in their natural context.

As they learn the language of a new culture (sometimes an actual language, but just as often the specialized jargon of an otherwise "English-speaking" subculture (Moffet 1992)), ethnographers try to understand how the terms are used and how they relate to one another. They attempt to avoid the trap of distorting the meaning of native language by simply "translating" terms into more familiar language (Spradley 1979). Similar care is taken with the documents and physical objects that are used in the target culture. Ethnographers observe how these cultural artifacts are used to accomplish meaningful goals, rather than imposing simple classification systems based on physical properties or on apparent similarities to tools used in their home culture.

The type of research described above typically results in volumes (literally!) of written field notes, boxes of audio and videotapes, collections of "native" artifacts, and all manner of things collected during the research. Ethnographers have developed specialized approaches to documentation of this information that facilitate analysis and identification of patterns in this data (Gladwin 1989; Miles and Huberman 1994). An ethnographer uses these collections and records to guide the direction of the research, engaging in an iterative cycle of observation, recording and collecting, analysis, and renewed observation with a new set of questions. One of the challenges of ethnography is the management of the large quantity of rich, descriptive data produced by such a study (Sanjek 1990).

Ethnographers face some additional challenges in comparison to researchers who use more structured research methods. The time needed to conduct a thorough ethnographic study is greater than that needed for survey or experimental methods. This can make an ethnographic study difficult to justify to research sponsors. The extended and in-depth nature of this type of study necessarily means that fewer individuals are studied than is the case with other methods. This means that conclusions are based on data from fewer individuals and may be seen as less reliable or generalizable to larger populations. Finally, because much of the resulting data is unstructured description rather than tightly defined quantitative measurement, ethnographic research is sometimes suspect because it seems superficially less "scientific" than other approaches. For these reasons, it can be a challenge for ethnographers to defend their results to those not accustomed to this type of research.

There are a number of similarities between the research projects of the anthropologist and the requirements-definition tasks of system designers. They both need to understand an unfamiliar culture of tasks and priorities in a way that both preserves the sense of the new culture and translates it into terms that others can understand and use. Like the anthropologist, the system designer faces the need to understand and document the "language" of prospective system users as it relates to their actual work tasks (see Wood, this volume). They need to speak this language to users as they gather design information, instead of the more technical language of software engineering that many users find incomprehensible and intimidating. System designers need to use information as it is gathered, to change their design ideas and return to their investigation with new questions. Like anthropologists, they must often begin from "ground zero," with not only little knowledge of the user's environment, but with a potentially misleading set of assumptions about what users know and understand about technology.

Of course, unlike anthropologists, system designers must produce something beyond a written report. The final product of a system design effort is a software system that must be accepted by users and integrated into their work environment if it is to be successful. But the need for detailed information from the user's perspective makes ethnographic methods well-suited for system design. As we can see from the previous trend in the evolution of consumer goods, users of computer systems are becoming more demanding of user interfaces. They are less willing to adapt their work habits unnecessarily to accommodate incompatible design. Good system designers must supplement their arsenal of requirements-definition methods with approaches such as ethnography if their products are to be accepted and used by an increasingly critical audience of users.

TRADITIONAL SYSTEM-CENTERED DESIGN

Because of the engineering/technology environment out of which computers and computer systems arose, historically software development has been done from a system-oriented perspective. Very early on, software was written by those who used it. Because of the limitations on input devices (e.g. switch panels and punched-card readers) there was little opportunity for developers or users to be concerned with a "user-friendly" system.

In the late 60s and early 70s when interactive and distributed computing first became available through the use of teletypes and combinations of keyboards and CRT displays, there began to be a greater separation between those who used software and those who developed it. However, computing resources were still very limited (by today's standards) in that CPUs were relatively slow, random access memory was limited, and permanent storage devices were expensive and slow to access (e.g., sequentially accessible magnetic tape drives). It was difficult enough to provide sufficient code to meet the functional needs of software applications. Thus, the additional code and other overhead required to develop a "usable" interface was not considered a viable option in most cases. More importantly, by then there existed a general attitude and expectation among developers and users that there was simply a heavy price to be paid in learning to use any software application.

By the late 70s and early 80s, there was certainly a large base of users of computer applications that was separate from developers, and there was a growing concern among user groups and user advocates that more attention should be devoted to making software easier to learn and use. However, it was the introduction of the personal computer and applications such as electronic spreadsheets that finally provided the momentum for a widespread change in orientation from system-centered to user-, client-, and customer-centered design. A recent article by Hutchings and Knox (Hutchings and Knox 1989) provides an interesting account of efforts (and associated resistance) to change that orientation inside a large development company.

FROM SYSTEM-CENTERED TO CLIENT-CENTERED DESIGN

Prior to the introduction and influence of ethnographic methods, developers who were becoming sympathetic to the plight of users began to attempt to address the concerns of users in various ways. Under a system-oriented approach to development, almost all large-scale software projects include some form of beta-testing phase. Although the goals of beta testing tend to be oriented toward uncovering "bugs" in the features and functions of the software, some valuable information regarding the usability of the software is gained because it results from realistic use of the software by actual users in their natural work environment.

Unfortunately, in spite of well-designed user questionnaires and report forms distributed with beta software, attempts to debrief beta testers, and other heroic measures, the quality of beta test reports is often low. The primary reason for this is that this form of testing places too great of a burden on the beta tester, who must simultaneously play the twin roles of software user and observer of his or her own behavior. Another problem with beta testing is that this data is often obtained too late in the software-development cycle to significantly impact the design of the software system.

Because beta testing sensitized developers more to issues regarding "ease of use," developers began to perform usability tests on software prior to its release in beta versions. There now exist in many companies formal usability laboratories, where carefully controlled studies are performed with users attempting to perform realistic tasks that are measured in terms of time to completion and errors made. These measures are compared to predefined criteria to determine how well the software meets expectations (see Dumas and Redish 1993 for a description of methods of usability testing). Unfortunately, because formal usability tests are conducted so late in the development cycle, major changes must wait until later revisions before they can be implemented (see Page, this volume).

One technique sometimes used to help users report on their work activities is "think aloud" protocol analysis (Ericsson 1984; Jorgenson 1990), which has a history of use in cognitive science research. An system designer requests that a software user "think out loud" while using software or performing other work tasks. The investigator then observes (and often audio or video tapes) the user while he or she works and talks. This approach is often useful for obtaining information about *why* users are performing sequences of actions. A useful extension of this approach is to have the investigator and user review a session audio or videotape together to discuss the users comments. This allows the user to comment further while reviewing a rich set of memory cues and gives the investigator a chance to ask questions without actually interrupting the user at work.

One weakness of this approach is that researchers often find that talking aloud interferes with users' natural work and thought processes. This technique is also focused on the activities of single users, and misses important aspects of cooperative work. Nevertheless, this is a method that has been used in the field and is largely compatible with ethnographic approaches. Some researchers have observed that well-structured protocol analysis studies can reach a point of diminishing returns for new information after review of a small number of participants. This is an encouraging finding for system designers who are interested in field methods, but concerned with the possibly large time commitment needed.

One well-established method for obtaining information from a group of users, particularly information about how they interact, is to conduct a focus group (Morgan 1988). A group of users is gathered together and asked a series of questions by a moderator. They are encouraged to react to one another's comments and describe the way that they work together. One advantage to this approach is that the participants' comments are better memory prompts than the moderator's questions. This is a more "natural" approach, and with it that more information is obtained from each participant in the group than would be obtained if they were interviewed separately. Drawbacks to this approach include the fact that, once again, participants are typically removed from their work environment to participate in the focus group. Another typical problem with focus groups (when applied to work-description tasks such as requirements analysis) is that participants are talking about the task, not performing it. Discussion can be dominated by atypical examples rather than shaped by the usual flow of work.

Conducting focused investigations of users in usability labs is one way to relieve users of the burdens (and limitations) of reporting on their own use of a software package. These labs often present a wide range of data-gathering possibilities, including audio and videotaping equipment, user-action-logging software, and other technology-intensive approaches. A significant weakness of this kind of data gathering, however, is that the participants are removed from their work context. These studies do not allow system designers to observe participants using all of their informal job aids and other tools present in their work environment. This situation also does not recreate the interpersonal aspects of the work environment. For example, the quick phone conversations, office mail, sticky notes, etc. circulated by users of a specialized database system in a small company can be useful clues about important information tracking that the database should be revised to support.

Rapid prototyping (Beevis and St. Denis 1992; Hartson and Smith 1991) is an effort to create an actual context similar to the user's environment. Interestingly, the strengths and weaknesses of prototyping are something of a complement to those of focus groups. Prototyping focuses on creating a simplified model of a proposed system so that users can simulate how they would interact with the finished system. This is often done very early in the development process so that information gathered can be used in redesign. This approach is helpful in examining user performance in actual work tasks using the proposed system. The danger, however, is that user reactions will be influenced more by the form of the prototype (and therefore by the designers' assumptions about the work the prototype is designed to support) than by their natural work context. Prototyping focuses on work rather than on discussion of work, but the work context is based on the designer's viewpoint rather than the user's viewpoint. System designers interested in improving the prototyping process have begun to develop methods in which users have greater involvement and impact on prototype development (Bodker and Gronbaek 1991).

One of the most structured methods available to system designers is to administer some form of user survey or questionnaire. Whether administered by telephone, electronic mail, or in paper form, this is a quite efficient method when the information gatherer knows enough about the topic to ask good questions (Sudman and Bradburn 1986). The time savings from the efficiency of questionnaire administration and data analysis permits questions to be asked of a large number of users. This allows questionnaire designers to be confident that the resulting information is representative of the larger audience of users. And, although users usually do not respond to questionnaires while actually performing work tasks, they often *do* respond from within their physical work context where they can refer to job aids, consult with colleagues, and be generally reminded of the way their work is performed.

Of course, it is often not the case that system designers initially understand what they need to know well enough to ask specific questions. While asking open-ended questions (which do not have a small set of response categories) is a partial solution to this problem, this approach also has its limitations. Like beta testing, this approach places too much responsibility on the user to observe and report his or her own behavior. When writing answers to open-ended questions, questionnaire respondents often take a minimalist approach, writing only what seems needed to provide a brief, narrow answer to the most literal interpretation of the question (Sudman and Bradburn 1974). This reduces question writing to the same problematic task of writing closed-ended questions: knowing enough about the topic in the first place to write a sufficiently focused question. Clearly there is a need for methods that can be used before this much information is available (Bauman and Adair 1992).

The last of existing "methods" we should discuss is informal investigation of user needs and work context. It may seem surprising to consider this a method in the same context as questionnaires and more formal approaches, but we believe that there is an important reason to do so. System designers need to acknowledge that the constraints of time and other resources often pressure them into using less formal methods of gathering information than they would prefer. However, they should understand the tradeoffs involved in not using more structured methods. Another reason that developers are tempted to be less rigorous than they should be is that they sometimes feel "constrained" by formal methods. We understand that there are good reasons to standardize the way questions are asked, the way prototypes or other system descriptions are presented to users, and the way samples of users are selected for interviewing. Alternatively, we also recognize that important information is learned about users and their work environments every time there is an opportunity to observe or talk with them, however informally.

CURRENT ETHNOGRAPHIC APPROACHES TO SYSTEM DESIGN

As system developers began to appreciate the value of information gained from users through the methods described above, the climate became suitable for the introduction and adaptation of ethnographic methods, which were designed to not only learn about others' environments, but to do so from their perspectives. An approach to studying users that makes use of information obtained by observing and talking with them in their natural social and work environments is important in designing artifacts for them. Ethnographic methods are particularly useful for gathering information from users when too little information about them is known to produce a prototype or an effective questionnaire.

In addition to the close match between the basic agendas of anthropologists and system designers, there is a pattern of strengths and weaknesses in existing requirements-gathering methods that is compatible with ethnographic techniques. Some of the structured methods make assumptions about what questions are most appropriate to ask, and are thus well complemented by the open-ended approach of ethnography. Other methods tend toward the same open-ended approach as ethnography. Designers familiar with these methods will be able to make a comfortable transition to ethnographic methods. Ethnographic methods also present a disciplined alternative to informal inquiry. A number of system designers have agreed with this point and have specialized ethnographic methods for use in system design (Schuler and Namioka 1993). We will list and briefly describe a few of those that have become more widely recognized. It is not our intent to be exhaustive nor to describe methods in depth. Other chapters in this volume do this as well as demonstrate the use of these methods in a variety of situations.

Participatory Design

Participatory Design has its origins in Scandinavian Design (Floyd et al. 1989). The basic assumption is that the task of system designers is not to replace workers by automating their tasks, but to provide tools to make workers more efficient in doing their jobs (Schuler and Namioka 1993). Designers are viewed as technology consultants who help users (the task experts) to redesign their work tasks for maximum benefit. The goal is not just to represent users' needs, but to involve users deeply in the design of the broader context of their work and to provide them an active influence in cooperative decision-making regarding the work environment. A general introduction to the use of ethnographic methods in Participatory Design can be found in Namioka (this volume) and (Blomberg et al. 1993).

Contextual Inquiry

Contextual Inquiry is another method that draws heavily on the tenets of ethnographic methods and has grown in popularity during the last several years (Beyer and Holtzblatt 1994; Wixon and Holtzblatt 1990). As the title implies, Contextual Inquiry emphasizes interviewing and observing potential users in their natural work context and making every effort to understand their work as they do. An attempt is made to involve all members of a development team in efforts to gather firsthand "data" from potential users. Those data are then analyzed in a variety of ways to provide a shared understanding of the work to be supported by a potential application. That analysis is then turned into a design that supports and enhances the users' work.

Joint Application Design

Joint Application Design, while not having obvious historical roots in ethnographic methods, grew out of a similar philosophical foundation of user involvement. As discussed by August (1991), Joint Application Design (JAD) was originally developed at IBM in 1977 and arose out of frustration with trying to develop requirements of distributed systems with which users would agree. It is a structured method that involves users in all aspects of the development cycle, including the development of detailed requirements and scope, designing screen and report layouts, and developing system prototypes.

The process begins with a JAD/Planning phase where a small group of individuals (usually from the higher ranks of the organization) identify high-level system requirements, define the system scope, plan the successive JAD/Design activities, and choose additional participants from other levels in the organization groups of and potential users. During JAD/Design activities, the group then carries out the activities mentioned above, being careful to document the results of each stage, so a common understanding can be agreed upon and shared among members of the group and with others outside the group. Proponents claim that the method increases productivity, enhances design quality, promotes cooperation among members of the development team, and lowers development and maintenance costs.

PICTIVE

The PICTIVE method (Plastic Interface for Collaborative Technology Initiatives through Video Exploration) involves users in collaborative design of the system that will impact their work (Muller 1991; Muller, this volume). It assumes that information regarding the work that is to be supported has already been gathered and that an initial shared understanding of the work has been established. Deliberate use is made of low-tech materials (e.g., paper, pencil, markers, plastic "icons," and Post-it notes) that can be easily changed or discarded as necessary. This fosters unconstrained participation by all users and helps to produce an atmosphere that will encourage trial and error, without concern of serious consequences resulting from a mistake. Furthermore, PICTIVE attempts to address one of the difficulties of rapid prototyping by ensuring that all participants (particularly users) have the same access to the prototyping medium. Team members are videotaped during their attempts to collaboratively design potential system interfaces, and the information is used to inform later stages of system development.

FUTURE TRENDS

One interesting possibility is that sophistication in ethnographic methods, like sophistication in user interface design and other aspects of system design, will migrate into the user community. A certain amount of this is inevitable, as designers explain the rationale behind the methods they are using to better understand the user's work context. But how might an increased awareness of how to study their environment affect the requests for enhancement and other communications that are generated by users themselves? Even a casual review of user newsletters, Usenet news groups, and other user-driven channels of communication shows informal use of surveys, focus groups, and other needs-analysis methods. Watch for an increase in descriptive methods in these forums as well, particularly as they increasingly become regarded as more "scientific" in other fields.

Another trend to watch for is an increase in the sophistication of system users as "informants" in the system-design process. As cooperative users become more accustomed to ethnographic methods, they will grow better able to anticipate the kind of information for which system designers are searching. Cooperative and "design-wise" users will volunteer more useful information and become skilled and noticing and recording useful aspects of their own work environment. Anthropologists have noted this trend among their own research participants (Agar 1980) and find it a useful enhancement to their research.

A final trend that will increase the usefulness of ethnographic methods in system design is the increasing availability of software tools that support the organization and analysis of ethnographic data. Of course, word-processing programs are as useful in managing the volumes of descriptive data as spreadsheets are to managing numerical data generated by surveys and rating scales; but more specialized programs are being developed that support the exploration and analysis of text and video data (Davies 1990; Fritz 1990; Weitzman and Miles 1995; Wise 1995). As ethnographic methods are increasingly employed by computer professionals, the technical sophistication and usefulness of these programs can be expected to increase. This trend promises to improve the efficiency of ethnographic methods in system design.

REFERENCES

Agar, M.H. 1980. *The Professional Stranger: An Informal Introduction to Ethnography*. New York, NY: Academic Press.

Atkinson, P. and Hammersley, M. 1994 Ethnography and participant observation. Norman K. Denzin, Yvonna S. Lincoln, Eds. *Handbook of Qualitative Research*. pp. 248–261. Thousand Oaks, CA: Sage Publications.

August, J.H. 1991. *Joint Application Design: The Group Session Approach to System Design*. Englewood Cliffs, N.J.: Yourden Press.

Bauman, L.J. and Adair, E.G. 1992. "The Use of Ethnographic Interviewing to Inform Questionnaire Construction." *Health Education Quarterly,* **19**(1), 9–23.

Beevis, D. and St. Denis, G. 1992. "Rapid prototyping and the human factors engineering process." *Applied Ergonomics,* **23** (3), 155–160.

Beyer, H.R., and Holtzblatt, K. 1994. "Apprenticing with the customer." *Communications of the ACM* **38**(5), 45–52.

Blomberg, J.; Giacomi, J.; Mosher, A. and Swenton-Wall, P. 1993. "Ethnographic field methods and their relation to design." Douglas Schuler, Aki Namioka, Eds. *Participatory Design: Principles and Practices*. Hillsdale, NJ: Lawrence Erlbaum Associates, 123–155.

Bodker, S. and Gronbaek, K. 1991. "Cooperative prototyping: Users and designers in mutual activity." *International Journal of Man Machine Studies*. **34**(3), 453–478.

Davies, J.R. 1990. "A methodology for the design of computerized qualitative research tools." *Interacting with Computers*. **2**(1), 33–58.

Dumas, J.S. and Redish, J.C. 1993. *A Practical Guide to Usability Testing*. Norwood, N.J.: Ablex Publishing Corp.

Ericsson, K.A. 1984. *Protocol Analysis: Verbal Reports as Data*. Cambridge, MA: MIT Press.

Fielding, N. 1993. "Ethnography." Nigel Gilbert, Ed. *Researching social life*. pp. 154–171. Newbury Park, CA: Sage Publications.

Floyd, C., et al. 1989. "Out of Scandinavia: Alternative approaches to software design and system development." *Human Computer Interaction* , 4(4). 253–350.

Fritz, R.B. 1990. *Computer Analysis of Qualitative Data*. National Institute on Drug Abuse Research Monograph Series, **Mono 98,** 59–79.

Gladwin, C.H. 1989. *Ethnographic Decision Tree Modeling*. Newbury Park, CA: Sage Publications.

Hartson, H.R. and Smith, E.C. 1991. "Rapid prototyping in human-computer interface development." *Interacting with Computers,* 3(1). 51–91.

Hutchings, A.F. and Knox, S.T. 1995. "Creating products customers demand." *Communications of the ACM* **38**(5), 72–80.

Jorgensen, A.H. 1990. "Thinking-aloud in user interface design: A method promoting cognitive ergonomics." Special Issue: *Marketing ergonomics: IV and V. Ergonomics,* **33**(4), 501–507.

Miles, M.B. and Huberman, A.M. 1994. *Qualitative Data Analysis: An Expanded Sourcebook*. Newbury Park, CA: Sage Publications.

Moffat, M. 1992. "Ethnographic writing about American culture." *Annual Review of Anthropology. 21*, 205–229.

Morgan, D.L. 1988. *Focus Groups As Qualitative Research*. Sage University Paper series on Qualitative Research Methods. Vol. 16. Newbury Park, CA: Sage Publications.

Muller, M.J. 1991. "PICTIVE—An exploration in participatory design." *Proceedings of the CHI '91*. ACM, 225–231.

Pelto, P.J. and Pelto, G.H. 1973. "Ethnography: The fieldwork enterprise." John J. Honigman (Ed.). *Handbook of Social and Cultural Anthropology*. Chicago, IL: Rand McNally.

Reber, A.S. 1989. "Implicit learning and tacit knowledge." *Journal of Experimental Psychology: General. 118*, 219–235.

Sanjek, R. 1990. *Fieldnotes: The Making of Anthropology*. Ithaca, NY: Cornell University Press.

Schuler, D. and Namioka, A. eds 1993. *Participatory Design: Principles and Practices*. Hillsdale, NJ: Lawrence Erlbaum Associates.

Spradley, J.P. 1979. *The Ethnographic Interview*. New York: Holt, Rinehart and Winston.

Sudman, S. and Bradburn, N.M. 1986. *Asking Questions: A Practical Guide to Questionnaire Design*. San Francisco, CA: Jossey-Bass Publishers.

Sudman, S. & Bradburn, N.M. 1974. *Response Effects in Surveys: A Review And Synthesis*. Chicago, IL: Aldine.

Vidich, A. and Lyman, S. 1994. "Qualitative methods: Their history in sociology and anthropology." Norman K. Denzin, Yvonna S. Lincoln, Eds. *Handbook of Qualitative Research*. pp. 23–59. Thousand Oaks, CA: Sage Publications.

Weitzman, E.A. and Miles, M.B 1995. *Computer Programs for Qualitative Data Analysis: A Software Sourcebook*. Newbury Park, CA: Sage Publications.

Wise, J.A, et al. (In press). Visualizing the non-visual: Spatial analysis and interaction with information from text documents. *IEEE Information Visualization Proceedings*. 1995.

Wixon, D. and Holtzblatt, K. 1990. Contextual design: An emergent view of system design. *Proceedings of CHI '90: Empowering People*. Seattle, WA.: ACM, 329–336.

Introduction to Participatory Design

Aki Helen Namioka
Christopher Rao

INTRODUCTION

This chapter will focus on two aspects of participatory design: the history of participatory design in Scandinavia, and the philosophical underpinnings of participatory design (including why it makes sense in any country that is developing software).

CONCEPTS AND FEATURES OF PARTICIPATORY DESIGN

Participatory design is not a single theory or technique, but rather an approach that is "characterized by concern with a more humane, creative, and effective relationship between those involved in technology's design and its use. . ." (Suchman 1993).

As noted in the introduction to the proceedings from the first participatory design conference (PDC'90), there are fundamental ways in which participatory design differs from traditional design (Czyzewski et al. 1990):

- It rejects the assumption that the goal of computerization is to "automate" the skills of human workers, instead seeing it as an attempt to give workers better tools for doing their jobs.

- It assumes that the users themselves are in the best position to determine how to improve their work and their work life. In doing so, it turns the traditional designer-user relationship on its head, viewing the users as the experts—the ones with the most knowledge about what they do and what they need—and the designers as technical consultants.
- It views users' perceptions of technology as being at least as important to success as fact, and their feelings about technology as at least as important as what they can do with it.
- It views computers and computer-based applications not in isolation, but rather in the context of a workplace—as processes rather than as products.

Their differences from traditional software development offer several corollaries:

Users are experts. In traditional development environments the user is usually not consulted during the design and implementation phases; thus, the first contact a user has with a new software system is during the alpha test phase. Participatory design acknowledges the importance of using the expertise of users and treating them as equal partners on a development team.

Tools should be designed for the context in which they will be used. In traditional development environments, software applications are created in labs that are often not colocated with the user environment. Participatory design realizes that an important step to designing new tools is to know where they will be used and in what context, which makes it difficult to design a tool away from the environment in which it will be used. Colocation of the software developers with the user community is recommended during the design phase and sometimes also in the implementation phase. This facilitates ongoing communication and supports the iterative nature of a participatory design project.

There should be methods for observing or interviewing end-users. To gain an understanding of the environment in which the new or modified application will be placed, there are several techniques used to watch, observe, and interview users in their workplace.

Recreating or play-acting a work situation will facilitate the design phase. A participatory design session often has hands-on learning experience using mock-ups, play acting, and role-playing that focuses on the workplace, not the system. This serves several purposes. First, it is more fun than just drawing ideas on an easel. Second, it provides a context for the new or modified tool. Third, it mediates the expectations of the users by not providing a nonfunctional prototype at the very beginning of the design phase.

Iterative development is essential. The ideal participatory design project has several iterations of a design-feedback loop, where the developers ask the users for their opinion as the implementation evolves. Colocation of the developers and users makes the iteration cycle tighter and more efficient.

HISTORY OF PARTICIPATORY DESIGN

When PDC'90 took place, a participatory design approach had already been in practice in Scandinavia for almost two decades. It started with the work of Kristen Nygaard in Norway in the late 60s and early 70s. Nygaard is best known for helping to develop SIMULA, the first object-oriented programming language.

Trade unions also strongly influenced the creation of the Scandinavian model. It evolved as not only a political issue (that of giving workers democratic control over changes) but also as a design issue for software systems. This fundamentally altered the relationship of researchers with workers—the end-users of the products (Ehn 1989).

Nygaard discussed the origins of the Scandinavian model at PDC'90 (Nygaard 1990) and stated that the development of object-oriented programming and the development of participatory design came from the same roots. SIMULA was developed not as a programming language, but rather as a mechanism to communicate about complex systems in terms that were understandable; i.e. to be able to describe and comprehend these systems.

The Scandinavian combination of strong industrial relations and a highly educated, homogeneous work force contributed to the democratization of the workplace. In the 1970s new labor laws and practices resulted in a codetermination environment that is still embraced today by unions, parliament, and national employers.

When people started using SIMULA to describe systems, they realized that the SIMULA language could prompt change in working conditions, social networks, and even workplace competence. The next logical step was to contact the trade unions to discuss how to build up competence, understanding, and strategies for technology.

In the 1970s–80s Pelle Ehn, at the Center for Working Life (Arbetslivscentrum) in Sweden, led an effort to further develop concepts that were inspired by Nygaard and others. These ideas are illustrated by the DEMOS (Democratic Planning and Control in Working Life—on Computers, Industrial Democracy and Trade Unions) project (Ehn 1989).

DEMOS started in 1975, about the same time that the codetermination laws were being enacted in Sweden. A method called work-oriented action research was applied to four different areas: a repair shop, a newspaper, a metal factory, and a department store. Investigation groups were formed with local unions, where the academic researchers acted as a resource, but the starting point of the investigation was from the workers' perspective. The investigation groups became more knowledgeable about technology, and were able to consider more possibilities. The information learned was disseminated to other workers via an education program through central trade unions. Ehn felt at the end of the DEMOS project that he wanted to participate in a more pro-active approach. This led to the UTOPIA project.

The UTOPIA project (an acronym for Training, Technology, and Products from the Quality of Work Perspective) (Mayer 1986) helped the Swedish Graphics Union to develop a newspaper layout system that worked with the skills of the graphic artists. Other systems that existed tended to de-skill workers, resulting in layouts that were boring and homogeneous. The project made clever use of mock-ups to determine how a computer could translate the job that the graphic artists were already doing and make it electronic. The system also allowed artists to do things that were difficult to do without a computer, e.g. reverse a picture, change the contrast or lighting, etc. Ehn calls his design ideals "work-oriented design of computer artifacts."

In Scandinavia the "work-oriented" approach has evolved as a cooperative effort between researchers/developers, trade unions, and workers—where trade unions have continued the tradition of educating the employees and negotiating on behalf of their right to participate. From their experience, computer systems need to be viewed as tools that enhance and support worker skills. In contrast, many applications seek to displace, de-skill, and fragment workers. This leads to a drop in quality and inhibits creativity.

An example of this is illustrated by the Scandinavian Airline (SAS) repair shop in Stockholm (Mayer 1986). SAS introduced an expert system to determine what repairs were needed on airplane parts that came in. Quality control declined, and an SAS manager suggested that it was due to workers trusting the system to the point that they didn't question the decisions that were made by the computer. When management changed in the company, the expert system was replaced. The new system allows repair technicians to evaluate a problem themselves, and gives them control over operations and scheduling, using a computer only to present various repair options. Called a "system for experts, not an expert system," this solution has reduced bureaucracy and increased quality.

PARTICIPATORY DESIGN TECHNIQUES

There are several different strategies to incorporate the concepts of participatory design. Of the many possible approaches to participatory design, this section will highlight four approaches that were discussed in Schuler & Namioka (1993). These strategies are not mutually exclusive, and can be considered part of a tool suite for practicing participatory design.

Ethnographic Field Methods (Blomberg et al. 1993)

Building on the ". . . growing recognition that an understanding of users' current work practices would be useful in the design of new technologies," anthropologic ethnography is increasingly being linked to the design process.

Ethnographers, who seek understanding, often do intensive field work in observing, informal interviews, and participation in the ongoing events of a community. Designers, by contrast, have traditionally focused their attention on testing and design evaluation relating more to the needs and abilities of users than to understanding the behavior their technologies hope to support. Although designers sometimes try to better understand the users themselves, their methodologies have been limited. Ethnography offers a useful new methodology, that of accessing the everyday practices of people in social groups.

This approach also relates to the new field called CSCW, computer support for cooperative work, which evolved in the 80s out of the understanding that, while technology often focuses on individual tasks, most human activities involve cooperation with others.

While there is no universal standard dictating ethnographic techniques, the approach focuses more on trying to interpret and give meaning to activities than to simply describing them. Toward this end, four main principles may be applied:

Natural Settings. Ethnography is based on first-hand experience of activities, and is thus done in a field setting, not a laboratory or experimental setting.

Holism. Behavior is understood in a larger social context, an everyday context, and not removed piecemeal out of that context.

Descriptive. People are described nonjudgmentally, as they really behave, not how they ought to behave. For example, a description states that "Several people handle a document before it is completed. All involved discover problems and are asked to account for changes to the document." A prescriptive view of the same activity states " They're still manually processing 'routine' documents. Passing hard copy from person to person is such an inefficient way to update documents. An electronic mail system linked to an intelligent database could really improve their process."

Members' point-of-view. Behaviors are seen from the view of a group's members, and how they make sense of the world around them. Descriptions are made in terms that are meaningful to the group members, not simply the researchers.

To follow these methods requires the researcher to follow an improvisational more than a strictly scientific approach, making adjustments to research strategy as more is learned. For example, the researcher may alternate between a strictly observational role and a highly participatory role, depending on the what is appropriate to the setting. The interviews may also be more open-ended, allowing the interviewee to shape the content and character of the interview. The list of people to be interviewed may also change as the project evolves.

This ethnographic approach is highly relevant to the design process for several reasons: First, designers often know little about the work settings they design for; this leads to an artifact serving the needs of the designer more than that of the end user. Second, because many applications have unknown uses, such an approach may help to identify possible users. Third, traditional operability testing does not focus on the context of using a technology. Fourth, users are often unable to discuss a radical new technology without first envisioning it. Such a process will give users a context to envision this, and thus take part in a useful dialogue with designers. Finally, this method allows for more focus on task integration, not simply the single-task focus so common in new applications.

Customer surveys, operability assessments, focus groups, and field trips have traditionally been used to gain user input, with some success. These methods, however, tend to focus on the technology rather then the work, and (with the exception of field trips) are outside the place of the users' work. Ultimately, they offer little room for true collaboration with users over an evolving design, looking to users instead for verbalizations of design inadequacies given at an isolated test.

Ethnography offers a context where mutual understanding between designers and users can evolve alongside the evolving technology. This offers an opportunity to improve existing products and find niches for new products. Taking advantage of this opportunity, however, requires designers to reconceptualize their role, developing skills in interviewing, observation, analysis, and interpretation. Development teams must also shift focus to allow for higher user participation, if such opportunities are to be realized. Such conceptual leaps are often not easily made, and the front-end costs are significant. The rewards in long-term quality improvements, however, are even more significant.

Cooperative Design (Bodker et al. 1993)

Participatory design can be implemented, in part, through group exercises such as future workshops, organizational games, mock-up designs, and cooperative prototyping.

The future workshop is split into three phases: the Critique, the Fantasy, and the Implementation. Run by two facilitators with no more than 20 participants, speaking time is allotted equally to all participants to ensure equal participation. Management is often asked to not participate, to ensure that the workers feel more free to speak their minds. The Critique phase is a structured brainstorming, to find different angles on common workplace problems. Statements generated in this phase are listed under various headings, then inverted into positive themes; this sets the stage for the Fantasy phase. In this phase, the emphasis is on creative ideas, no matter how far-fetched. These ideas are then boiled down to fantasy themes, and some of these themes are chosen for elaboration in smaller groups to prepare for the Implementation phase. Here, each group presents its "utopian outline," outlining what actions might be started immediately after the workshop. The goal of the entire workshop is not necessarily to achieve consensus, but rather to arrive at a common understanding.

Insights from the Future Workshop are used by researchers to come up with an appropriate Organizational Game to play out at a 2-1/2-day seminar. The organizational game aims to play out various ways of organizing work, and confront the problems that each creates. Using situation cards and mock-ups of technology not yet invented, the game is created along the lines of a theatrical play, where participants not only react to situations written by the researchers, but eventually create and solve their own situations. Like the Future Workshop, the game travels from the present situation to an imagined future, and then seeks to find tasks to create that future. The game finishes with an action plan that focuses on what can be done immediately at the office, and what requires external resources, such as new technology.

During the Game, inexpensive mock-ups using paper and cardboard are used to encourage new visions and options for use. All participants are encouraged to feel competent to change how the mock-up works, and to focus on design that appeals to them. Participants are also encouraged to imagine technology that is not yet feasible, such as a 100″ screen at 1,000 pixels per inch. Such mock-ups also have obvious limitations: Design changes on cardboard menus can be time-consuming, they lack the realism of a prototype, and finally, they are not grounded in technical feasibility. They do, however, offer details of how a future technology might work with the cooperation of users and designers.

Such details lead to a new kind of prototyping called *cooperative prototyping*, in which both users and designers actively participate. Users try the prototype in a real or imagined work situation, and the results are analyzed together with the designers. If there was a breakdown, both parties analyze whether it was a training problem, a design problem, or some other problem. If it was a design problem, an effort is made to rapidly improve the design. Each prototyping session will be different, of course, and many questions must be answered in advance, including how stable the prototype should be, to what extent modifications should be done in-session, how a session should be evaluated, etc. The advantages of such prototyping are not only in the finished technical product, but also in training future users even before the application is finished.

A greater problem for such prototyping are the contractual or social relationships between parties in this process. For example, an existing contract may spell out specific requirements for an application at a fixed price. Also, management may have different interests in the product it purchases than the end users, the workers; hence the design process takes on a political scope. The end users thus need a forum where they can express their own interests to the designers.

Finally, cooperative design means a shift among system developers from project manager to project facilitator. While traditional design relies on control by "system developers and management through discrete procedures, and marked by clear-cut milestones and exit criteria," it may create only an illusion that a project is on target. In fact, it may scarcely suit the needs of the end user at all, necessitating "an almost unending epilogue of modifications" after an application is supposed to be finished. The tools outlined in cooperative design may mean less front-end control and somewhat more front-end work for designers, but promise greater certainty that the end product will efficiently serve the needs of its users.

Reciprocal Evolution (Allen 1993)

Reciprocal evolution embodies the idea that use is design. Just as the dominant use of computers as word processors was unforeseen by the original computer manufactures, so uses of other current technology will influence the production of future technologies.

Reciprocal evolution may be broken down into three activities: study of work practices with technology, design of technologies, and furthering basic research.

The study of work practices looks at how individuals and workgroups change their activities based on what resources they have available, how they use technologies in different ways than the designers intended, and how work practices and relationships change as technologies change. Studying work practices also helps set expectations of how a particular technology will succeed or fail. The technology then becomes not just a solution to work problems, but a probe to offer directions for further research. The basic research itself draws on many disciplines, including cross-cultural cognitive psychology, cognitive anthropology, anthropological linguistics, technology design, and ethnography.

Together, this process looks for naturally occurring situations using technology, and studies a current practice before a new tool is added to understand work practice evolution. It looks for relevant variables that shape interaction with technology, and so avoids preset variables and rigid hypothesis-testing.

While reciprocal evolution has more in common with participatory design than with traditional design, it seeks out general patterns of technology use, whereas participatory design might be focused on use at a few particular sites. It shares with participatory design the view of users as co-innovators in adapting a tool to workplace tasks, and looks beyond the design implications to insights into marketing, strategy, customer support, and service.

Reciprocal evolution may help catalyze a conversation between corporate support services and users to learn how users have modified a product to their work. With corporate commitment, this bridge between customer support and design can lead to a modular approach to product development that capitalizes on insight from real users to rapidly proto-type improved products. For long-term competitiveness, reciprocal evolution helps shift the focus from a finished product to an ongoing cycle of design, listening to emerging needs and desires to meet the demand in both existing and new markets.

Contextual Inquiry (Holtzblatt & Jones 1993)

Contextual Inquiry offers a way to gain truly helpful information about the work of users within project-resource constraints in order to design systems that support similar work in varying business contexts and cultures.

To start such a process is to reassess what is meant by usability. Usability is an optimum match between the work intentions, concepts and workflow of the user, and the work expectations of the designer. By focusing on just the designer's expectations, a company simply develops a new technology, then seeks a market for it. Instead, it should understand the users' work to find its target market. The product should adapt easily to work, and empower users to expand their work concepts. Usability is thus not an attribute of the system, but of the users' interaction with the system. What the system provides ought to match how the users want to do their work—the way they think, talk about, and structure their work.

From this goal flows three principles that guide the contextual inquiry process: context, partnership, and focus.

Context. Process descriptions tend to be idealized models, but rarely describe actual workflow. Designing a system based on such abstractions will generally fail. Contextual Inquiry helps people to be concrete about their work by talking to them while they are actually working. For example, a user will have vague likes and dislikes of an application when asked about it, but the same user will be much more specific if asked while she is using the application.

Partnership. "Partnership creates the opening for participatory design." Users' experience of work and systems is invisible to a designer who stands outside the work process, merely watching behavior and taking notes. A dialogue is necessary, and this dialogue requires a partnership. To do this, the designer must first acknowledge that the user is the expert. This makes it comfortable for the designer to ask questions, not merely act as a problem-solver. It also entails sharing control during the inquiry, and following the issues that the user—the expert—deems important. Doing this helps create a shared meaning between the two.

Focus. Sharing control of the process does not mean abandoning focus, but rather expanding the focus. Focus is dynamic, changing with the perspectives of each party. To expand the focus, the designer asks about what he or she doesn't know, and double-checks what he or she thinks he or she understands. The designer probes behind the solutions offered by the user and shares his or her interpretations and design ideas with the user. Finally, "design is always a matter of seeing the possibilities within constraints," (Holtzblatt and Jones 1993) and finding a shared focus can help create more robust possibilities in the final design.

Interviews are usually done in teams, and so members of a team can help the team to find its focus before an interview and work together to analyze the results. Rather than seeing results only in terms of the technology, the team may interpret results within a proven framework focusing on:

- Work structure or work flow.
- Problems accomplishing the work.
- Problems in system use.
- Disruptions caused by the system.
- Workarounds that are used to avoid disruption from the system.
- Transparency of the system.
- Aspects of the work process and system use that support work.

This framework allows the team to record understandings of these results in the following way:

- A description of users' work.
- The flow or structure of the work.
- A description of problems in their work.
- A description of problems with the computer tools.
- Design ideas that emerge from our understanding of their work.
- Questions for subsequent interviews.

Post-it notes may then be used to link related concepts in a fluid way to improve design. Contextual Inquiry is also used in conjunction with other participatory design techniques such as Future Workshops and paper prototyping, and can be used during each development phase of a product. To begin, the focus revolves around four basic questions:

- What is the user's work?
- What tools are currently used?
- What works well and why?
- What are the problems that the designer can address with his or her technology?

These questions help specify the system requirements for the project. Later, paper prototyping might be used to define a system work model, and users might be invited to participate in design meetings. During the design and coding of the application, Contextual Inquiry can be used to codesign the system work model and user interface. Users might also be invited to take test drives at this point. During field testing and after product shipping, Contextual Inquiry can be used to improve both learnability and usability within the work context.

Contextual Inquiry can thus be used throughout the development cycle, from defining the product early on, to specifying the user interface later on. While the degree of true collaboration may differ from case to case, it provides an opportunity for users to participate in design, and for designers to create better products as a result.

Why Use Participatory Design In The United States?

Since the 1980s, Participatory Design has been a growing presence in the United States. The first Participatory Design Conference in 1990 (PDC'90) was conceived and planned by the CPSR (Computer Professionals for Social Responsibility) Workplace Project with assistance from the CPSR Seattle chapter. The location in Seattle was designed to coincide with the SIGCHI (Special Interest Group for Computer Human Interface)-sponsored Computer Human Interaction (CHI'90) conference.

CPSR is a national nonprofit organization of computer professionals who are concerned with the social impact of computing and technology. It is based in Palo Alto and currently has 21 chapters around the country. Since its establishment in 1983, it has gained an international reputation in the areas of reliability and risk, civil liberties, privacy, and computers in the workplace.

The CPSR Workplace Project started as a group of members of the Palo Alto chapter who were interested in "preventing abuses of computing technology and in developing positive strategies for integrating new technologies into the workplace" (Namioka & Schuler 1990).

The purpose of the conference was to promote Participatory Design in the United States. Till then, to the extent it was used at all in the US, it had been applied mostly to custom software systems and not to commercial off-the-shelf (COTS) applications. The conference wanted to explore the applicability of Participatory Design in the United States by bringing together researchers, system designers, and users through a series of talks and workshops. The speakers ranged from Kristen Nygaard, who launched a movement of cooperation between trade unions and system designers in the late 60s through the early 70s, to Ellen Bravo from 9to5, the National Association of Working Women.

The conference was such a success that it continues as a biennial event; it was last held in 1994 in Chapel Hill, North Carolina.

The growing movement toward Participatory Design in the United States does not enjoy the grounding in strong trade unions and labor laws that the Scandinavian countries enjoy. Pragmatism rooted in a long tradition of democracy, however, is proving to be a driving force of its own (Greenbaum 1993). These pragmatic reasons include strategic market advantage, reduced training and maintenance time for the introduction of new software systems in the workplace, and reduced development and maintenance time in updating and creating new systems.

Ellen Bravo has an excellent story that illustrates what happens when the users of a system are not consulted in the design. A law office installed some new carpeting and decided that they didn't want the casters from the secretaries' chairs to mar the new rug. The solution they choose (without consulting the secretaries) was to nail the chairs to the floor. The next day the secretaries arrived at work and they couldn't move, making it almost impossible for them to do their jobs (Bravo 1993).

More than 60% of the work force now use computers in the workplace. Occupational hazards that were almost unheard of 20 years ago (or were peculiar to clerical workers) are becoming general work force issues, e.g. carpal tunnel syndrome, eyestrain, focusing problems among workers in their 20s and 30s, and stress-related conditions.

Can the increase in office automation and the use of computers affect the stress level in the workplace? Many hours are lost every year because new technology is introduced that doesn't make any sense to the end user. We are creating tools that are making the job harder— not easier. An example is the timekeeping system that was introduced into Aki Namioka's workplace within the last year. Until last year Aki filled in her time cards by hand. It was a fairly simple process—it consisted of filling in the hours and the budget numbers for the projects worked on. The card was turned in at the end of each day. The new automated system was introduced with the mandate that employees had to use it, or they would not get paid. To record her hours now Aki must:

1. Start a terminal emulator that allows her to connect to the mainframe that is running the system.
2. Type in "prd2"—a seemingly meaningly character string.
3. Type in <user id> <tab>.
4. Type in <password> <return>.
5. Type in "etsp" (Don't forget the space.) A menu appears.
6. Type "s" next to the desired menu item to get an electronic form to fill out.
7. Fill out the form and type <return>.
8. Hope that the form is accepted by the computer and that the system doesn't freeze up. If the system freezes up, the user must hit a reset button that is hidden within a series of pull-down menus.
9. Select the F24 key.
10. Select the F10 key.
11. Quit the terminal emulator program.

The interface is menu driven, character-based (no graphical user interface), with no helpful prompts, and with no indications of how to find online help. There was an uproar at Aki's workplace when the system was put in place. Even employees with advanced degrees in Computer Science were confused.

This is an example of what happens when technology is introduced without worker participation. If participatory design had been used, a much more intuitive user interface could have been developed and the amount of time that confused employees spent trying to figure out the system would have been reduced considerably.

The good news is that, despite such recurring examples of bad application design, there is evidence that participatory design ideas are starting to take hold in mainstream software development—rapid application development (RAD), for example.

As with participatory design, RAD is an approach to software development, not a single tool, methodology, or technique. It focuses on the rapid and flexible assembly of new software applications. Software vendors are marketing tools and techniques that support a RAD development environment, including automatic code generators, analysis and design tools, plug-together components, etc. With the promise of reduced development and maintenance cost, RAD has become an industry buzzword.

In the 1995 article "RAD Realities: Beyond the Hype to How RAD Really Works" Ellen Gottesdiener notes that RAD is associated with iterative prototyping and the use of techniques like joint application development (JAD). JAD requires intimate customer involvement and commitment. JAD sessions are conducted like "focus groups" where customers and developers work together in defining the scope, functionality, and time frame of the project. These sessions also establish a partnership between the developers and the customers and a sense of "buy-in" to the design. In the book *Joint Application Development* by Wood and Silver (1995), participatory design is explicitly cited as a related methodology, the major benefit being the focus on the workplace, not the application.

Other related fields are also converging towards ideals similar to those seen in Participatory Design. In strategic marketing, recent trends in industry point toward more "customer in." In recent training classes for employees at Aki's place of employment, the increasing focus has been on providing customer satisfaction. It is emphasized that all activities should be viewed from the customer's perspective, and that it is the company's job to conform to their needs and specification. Among the guiding principles discussed, there are several that echo the underlying concepts of participatory design: "[The] customer's use of a product is the critical design criterion," and "Customer input and complaints are like gold, to be sought out, and carefully mined to increase customer satisfaction." The company realizes that, to stay competitive these principles have to be embraced by the entire company.

Though the development of participatory design in the U.S. is motivated somewhat differently than in the more socialistic European countries—one by the pragmatic needs in the marketplace, the other by a worker democratization movement—worker empowerment is also a rising industry trend in the U.S. (sometimes called socio-tech). The changing face of the work force is forcing companies to accommodate diversity. This is resulting in a flattening of the traditional hierarchy, flexible scheduling, open communication, telecommuting, and shifting the focus of manager to facilitator, not dictator. These cultural changes go hand-in-hand with the software-development paradigm shift that participatory design represents, and present a positive note on what the future workplace might be like in the U.S.

CONCLUSION

Though the social and political aspects of industrial relations are different in the U.S. than in Scandinavia, the concepts and philosophy behind participatory design are just as relevant here. Quality products, job satisfaction, and responsiveness to the market are necessary for any company to maintain long-term competitiveness. All of these can be achieved, in part, by using methods and techniques that support a participatory design outlook when introducing new technology into the workplace.

REFERENCES

Allen, C. 1993. "Reciprocal Evolution as a Strategy for Integrating Basic Research, Design, and Studies of Work Practice." D. Schuler & A. Namioka (Eds.). *Participatory Design: Principles and Practices*. Hillsdale, N.J.: Lawrence Erlbaum Associates.

Blomberg, J., et al. 1993. "Ethnographic Field Methods and Their Relation to Design." D. Schuler and A. Namioka (Eds.). *Participatory Design: Principles and Practices*. Hillsdale, N.J.: Lawrence Erlbaum Associates.

Bodker, S., K. Gronbaek, and M. Kyng. 1993. "Cooperative Design: Techniques and Experiences From the Scandinavian Scene." D. Schuler and A. Namioka (Eds.). *Participatory Design: Principles and Practices*. Hillsdale, N.J.: Lawrence Erlbaum Associates.

Bravo, E. 1993. "The Hazards of Leaving Out the Users." D. Schuler and A. Namioka (Eds.). *Participatory Design: Principles and Practices*. Hillsdale, N.J.: Lawrence Erlbaum Associates.

Czyzewski, P., J. Johnson, and E. Roberts. 1990. "Introduction." A. Namioka and D. Schuler (Eds.). *Proceedings from the Conference on Participatory Design*. Palo Alto, California: Computer Professionals for Social Responsibility.

Ehn, P. 1989. *Work-Oriented Design of Computer Artifacts*. Hillsdale, N.J: Lawrence Erlbaum Associates.

Greenbaum, J. 1993. "A Design of One's Own: Towards Participatory Design in the United States." D. Schuler and A. Namioka (Eds.). *Participatory Design: Principles and Practices*. Hillsdale, N.J.: Lawrence Erlbaum Associates.

Gottesdiener, E. 1995. "RAD Realities: Beyond the Type to How RAD Really Works." *Application Development Trends*. August 1995, 28–38.

Holtzblatt, K. and S. Jones. 1993. "Contextual Inquiry: A Participatory Technique for System Design." D. Schuler and A. Namioka (Eds.). *Participatory Design: Principles and Practices*. Hillsdale, N.J.: Lawrence Erlbaum Associates.

Mayer, J. 1986. *Computers in Context*. San Francisco, California: California Newsreel.

Namioka, A. and D. Schuler (Eds.) 1990. *Proceedings from the Conference on Participatory Design*. Palo Alto, California: Computer Professionals for Social Responsibility.

Nygaard, K. 1990. "The Origins of the Scandinavian School, Why and How?" *Participatory Design Conference 1990 Transcript*. Palo Alto, California: Computer Professionals for Social Responsibility.

Suchman, L. 1993. D. Schuler and A. Namioka (Eds.). *Participatory Design: Principles and Practices*. Hillsdale, N.J.: Lawrence Erlbaum Associates.

Wood, J. and D. Silver. 1995. *Joint Application Development*, New York, N.Y.: John Wiley & Sons, Inc.

Contextual Design: Principles and Practice

Karen Holtzblatt
Hugh Beyer

InContext Enterprises, Inc.

INTRODUCTION

Contextual techniques aim to ground the design process in a solid base of customer data. As an industry, we are still learning how to accommodate to the demands of customer-centered design. A new approach to product design and development requires readjustment from everyone. The pioneers in this area are working out new relationships between the design team and their customers,[1] between designers and developers, between development and marketing, and between development and management. The case studies in this book give examples of handling some of the primary issues.

In this chapter we will describe our experience over the past nine years coaching many different development teams in collecting and using customer data in their projects. Through this process we developed Contextual Design, a structured, step-by-step roadmap to guide a team from initial project set-up and field interviews through design and the transition to implementation. This continual use of the process has forced us to address many of the common issues of collecting, interpreting, and using customer data.

As we describe Contextual Design we reveal the underlying motivations of each part of the process. We show how each part is intended to solve organizational or interpersonal problems, or to support the process of design. This allows us to identify design principles guiding the adaptation of a customer-centered process to the needs of a particular organizational situation. The other chapters of this book describe specific experiences using field research techniques, and provide a rich mine of ideas and descriptions of how these ideas worked in practice. We offer this discussion of Contextual Design as a framework for the whole design process, tying together different techniques into an orderly sequence, and showing some of the issues customer-centered design must address.

BACKGROUND OF CONTEXTUAL DESIGN

Contextual Design had its roots in a challenge from John Whiteside to his usability team at Digital Equipment Corporation: To develop new techniques that would lead to fundamental changes in products, rather than minor iterations. The usability testing techniques he was using on Digital's products at the time collected feedback on an existing product or prototype, and as is always the case with this kind of testing, tended to produce iterations on the existing theme rather than creating new approaches to the problem.

Karen Holtzblatt responded to this challenge with the recognition that radical corrections to a design can only come from a better understanding of how customers work. The resulting process, which came to be called Contextual Inquiry, drew on several disciplines. Ethnography provided the fundamental method of understanding work practice by living in a culture; psychology supplied techniques to shorten the time needed to study long processes, and an understanding of how to manage the interpersonal dynamics of an interview. The need to see design implications within the constraints of quickly delivering real products dictated the style of interaction in the interview. Holtzblatt worked out these ideas in collaboration with Sandra Jones and through iteration with design teams at Digital. Putting the first field research approach in practice, a new problem emerged: Suddenly engineers had access to huge amounts of data about their customers. This created a need to organize, interpret, share, and represent the data in an external form. As a member of Lou Cohen's quality group, Holtzblatt borrowed the concepts of a cross-functional team and adapted affinity diagrams, one of the "seven new Quality tools" from Japan (Brassard 1989) to collect, organize, and present the major design issues from a set of interviews.

Contextual Inquiry was first named and formalized publicly in a tutorial at the conference on Computer/Human Interaction (CHI) developed by Holtzblatt, Jones, and Steve Knox, with substantial support from John Bennet and Dennis Wixon. Their assistance, and that of the rest of the usability and quality groups, is gratefully acknowledged.

Further work revealed that teams found it difficult to know what specifically to build based on the hierarchical set of issues presented by an affinity. Hugh Beyer, familiar with the use of graphical formalisms from his software engineering background, began to look for more formal representations of the thought steps implicit in representing customer work and system structure. Together, we developed work models as a more natural and coherent representation of customers' work, and introduced work model consolidation to see common patterns across all customers. As we worked with teams, we discovered that they kept getting stuck in user interface (UI) detail when we wanted to talk about the underlying structure of the system. We had no way to discuss this structure except by drawing UIs. Software engineering methods offered different ways of representing a system, but none of them showed system structure as it supports the user (Keller 1992, Seaton 1992), so we developed the User Environment formalism. We were already using paper mockups with Contextual Inquiry to develop the UI, and discovered they were as effective to test structure (Kyng 1988, Ehn 1991; see Muller 1991 for related work). Finally, we found that engineers needed assistance with the transition to implementation. We had already included work objects in the User Environment formalism, so we were able to build on it to make definition of the system object model easy.

This evolution led to the structure of Contextual Design as it is now: Contextual Inquiry to gather field data from customers; interpretation sessions with work modeling in a cross-functional team to understand the data from single interviews; affinity diagrams and work model consolidation to see the scope of issues and the common patterns of work across all customers; redesign to invent how to improve work practice; User Environment design to specify how the system should be structured from the user's point of view and drive object modeling; and paper mockups to test and extend the structure and user interface with users. At each point, we were driven to extend the method by the needs of our teams attempting to ship products. Very little in Contextual Design is totally new. We have adopted and adapted processes developed by others and have formalized practices that existed informally, putting them together into a smooth flow of work to solve the problems of defining systems.

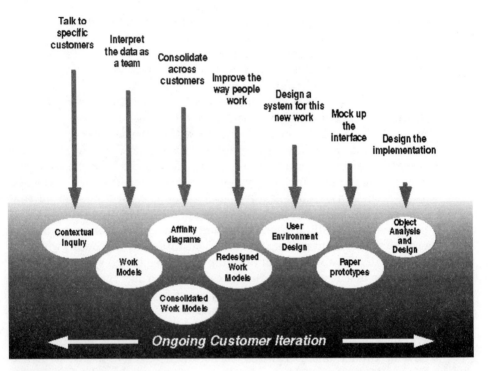

FIGURE 17.1 Contextual Design.

The base structure of Contextual Design has stabilized over past three years. However, in the spirit of continuous improvement, not only do we continue to evolve it but every team we work with evolves it as well. Having learned to study work practice, teams apply their knowledge to their own situation, and create new processes and techniques to handle their unique situations. Because it has been taught on its own, Contextual Inquiry is widespread and is being used and evolved independently. We thank all the teams who have worked with us and who, through their questions and commitment, have allowed us to synthesize a coherent approach.

CREATING THE PROJECT

The first challenge of any customer-centered design project is to define the project so that it is focused on the right problem, includes the right people, and has a clear process to follow. Coming to a complete understanding of the customer, defining a system which solves real work problems, and handling the host organization are all simplified if these tasks are done well.

Defining the problem. We find that projects usually start with too narrow a statement of their job. Either they focus on a single tool or task, they assume they will just add some features to what they already have, or they want to exploit a particular technology; but a tool supports some aspect of work, and that work is a small part of the users' whole job. Unless the design team understands the whole job and sees the task the tool or technology supports in the context of its use, they cannot support the job well. They cannot ensure that the tool they create will fit with other tools, systems, or manual processes without causing breakdowns in the work when users have to move into or out of the tool.

Designing well means designing systematically: Seeing the whole work practice of the user, and designing a coherent response that hangs together as a new work practice. This doesn't mean the system has to be huge—only a small part of the new work practice might be automated. However, it does mean that the new system design takes the whole work practice of the user into account. Systemic design not only supports the work better, it leads to innovation. As long as spreadsheets thought they were tools for calculation, they could only supply more math function; once they realized that their numbers had to be presented and used, they started to make formatting and presentation functions available. The first spreadsheets to do this supported more of the work, supported it better, and differentiated themselves from the rest.

We develop this broader focus by working backwards from a team's original problem statement to identify the whole of the users' work practice or job that is affected. Then we ask who else in the customer organization is affected or cares about this job. This is the wider context the team needs to understand to design well. It defines what the team needs to care about and who they should interview to understand the work.

Defining project membership. We borrow from Total Quality Management (TQM) (Demming 1982; Ishikawa 1985) and define a cross-functional team to design the system. The goal in TQM is to ensure that the product which is designed can be manufactured, tested, marketed, and delivered. Taking these considerations into account during the design of a new manufactured product means that many potential problems that would have to be overcome by these other functions are solved before they ever occur. The involvement of the other functions in the design eases the transition to production—each team member ensures the design accounts for their issues, and can start gearing up even before the last details of the design are finalized.

In the same way, a cross-functional software design team gives responsibility to those who have a stake in the design. The biggest roadblock to rapid development of software systems isn't technical—it's coming to a decision on what to build and sticking to that decision. Any time a small group defines a system which others have to live with, they put themselves in the position of having to convince the others that their decisions are right. This is true whether the designers of a commercial system are trying to convince everyone else involved in getting a product out that this is the right thing, or whether the designers of a custom system are trying to convince their clients that they want to use the new system.

Instead of trying to convince them that the design is sound, we put marketing, usability, UI design, test, and customers (for custom systems) on the team with software designers. Each member of the team collects and interprets data and influences the design to account for the issues with which they are familiar. Interacting with the team in face-to-face meetings, they teach other team members their own perspective. The design becomes more marketable, usable, aesthetically and ergonomically pleasing, robust, and useful. Each member of the team can recognize the implications of the design on their own organization, and can prepare their organization accordingly. The result is fewer problems in the design, and more buy-in to the new design.

In our experience, nondesigners do not see the design implications of customer data as readily as those who have been involved in software design, so at least half the team should be designers. And most importantly, all members of the team must have credibility and respect in their own organizations. Everyone must trust that the solutions they come up with are reasonable.

A team size of more than 8–12 people is too difficult to manage, so the team must communicate progress and results to the rest of the organization. Any team needs to capture their work as they go, both to support communication to others and to track their work for themselves and for new team members later. Contextual Design includes points in the process where others can learn what progress has been made and can contribute to the design.

Defining the process. To gain the benefits of cross-functional perspectives, the team needs a clear process that allows them to do real design together: gathering detailed customer data effectively, supporting design conversations and making them concrete, and supporting team design. Without a clear process, the team spends its time working out the process instead of working out the design.

This is difficult—doing actual design together as a team is rare in our industry. It is much more usual to divide a problem up into small parts, give the small parts to individuals to solve, and have them bring their solutions back to the group for review and approval. Any real design is worked out through informal conversations in the hall and in offices. A project leader or architect might attempt to keep all parts of the system coherent by being the conduit between the different project members. Where difficult decisions must be made, one person might be appointed to dictate the answer. There is no sharing of perspectives, and little collaboration among the whole team to guarantee that the system will hang together.

A clear process gives the whole team rules to live by. It provides a well-defined framework for design activities, with principles to guide how to tailor them to each situation. It makes the role of each team member within that framework clear. Each design activity has its own clear task, and a defined way to resolve disputes. It is clear where the data that drives each design activity comes from, and what results are expected from it.

Contextual Design is such a process.

UNDERSTANDING THE CUSTOMER

The first concern for design is to bring valid, useful data about how people work into the engineering process. Any system controls how people work on a day-to-day basis. Making a system fit well with the work people do requires understanding work at the level of daily action. However, finding out about work at this level of detail is hard. Not only are developers building for customers doing work in which the developers are not expert, but customers themselves have difficulty saying what they do. People are adaptable and resourceful creatures—they invent a thousand work-arounds and quick fixes to problems, and then forget that they invented the work-around. The detail of everyday work becomes second nature and invisible. Customers do not reflect on their work, and cannot describe it in a way useful to designers. An organization might have a defined process, but continuous modification in practice means that the defined process no longer reflects what is really going on. Contextual Inquiry is our approach to getting data on the actual work practice.

Contextual Inquiry

Contextual Inquiry gathers design data by sending individual designers to watch people do their own jobs, interspersing observation, discussion, and reconstruction of past events (Holtzblatt and Jones 1993). A contextual interview, the most typical way of applying principles of Contextual Inquiry to define the data gathering situation, usually lasts two to three hours. Each aspect of Contextual Inquiry addresses some problem in gathering data.

It's important to watch ongoing work, because it is only while people are actually working that they have access to the details of what they do. Customers commonly say they do a task one way and then, during the interview, do something different. It is common for them to say they spend most of their time on one task, when in fact other tasks consume more time. A person's summary of the experience of months in a statement of what they do is simply not a reliable basis for design. We have found that the only way to ensure that a design team does not solve the wrong problem in the wrong way is to watch the real work as it happens.

Contextual Inquiry uses apprenticeship as a model for the relationship between customer and designer (Beyer 1995). Using this model puts the designer in the customer's world and gives both people a natural guide for how to behave. Once there, designer and customer can jointly build a shared understanding of how the customer works based on the specific actions of that day's work. The apprenticeship model suggests how to run the interview. It precludes taking a list of questions—the apprentice does not know what is important to ask about. It suggests that a one-on-one interview is best—the apprentice needs to build their own understanding, and having several apprentices do this at once adds confusion. The basic inquiry process is described by Holtzblatt and Jones (1993), though it has since been somewhat extended.

The apprenticeship model leads to turning control of the interview over to the customer, while at the same time allowing discussion of the work as it unfolds. It is critical to discuss observations and interpretations with the customer during the interview. Designers will go back to the team and make specific design suggestions based on what they learned; however, the most important knowledge is not the specific actions the customer took, but the motive for those actions. If the new system can support the motives more directly, it will improve the customer's work. The only way for the designer to be sure that they understand the motivation correctly is to share their understanding with the customer. Interrupted in the moment of doing the work, the customer can say what is really going on. Without this shared interpretation, the team's design will be based on an interpretation that the designer made up.

Retrospective accounts (detailed reconstructions of past events) uncover more about the work than can be observed in two to three hours. A retrospective account leads the customer through an event in order, using the artifacts constructed in doing the work to help tell the story in detail. When a work process extends across weeks, months, or years, designers can learn about the whole process by retrospective accounts, and by interviewing different customers at different points in the process and performing different roles with respect to the task.

Some decisions of how to put Contextual Inquiry into practice are driven by pragmatic considerations of software development organizations. First, we assume that design teams are building products and systems, not conducting research. It is more important to deliver a useful system quickly than to understand everything possible about how people work. Second, we assume that the system will support more people than a team can reasonably interview given limited time. These considerations influence how Contextual Inquiry is used.

We train and send out designers rather than specialists in work practice, because it is the designers who have to understand the customer in order to design. If only specialists conduct interviews—whether they be psychologists, sociologists, or usability professionals—they have to teach the designers what they learned so well that the designers believe it and act out of it automatically. We find that the data gets in the designer's head better if designers and specialists conduct interviews and interpret them together, rather than if specialists conduct all the interviews.

We usually do not recommend videotaping interviews, because the overhead of setting up and running the cameras and reviewing the videotape later is usually not worth the additional level of detail. We use videotape when the problem requires studying work at such a detailed level that there is no other way to capture it; otherwise, audiotape and notes are good enough. Even when we do use videotape, we have the interviewer review the videotape with the customer so they can build a shared interpretation of the customer's work together.

Customer interviews are conducted to discover the common underlying structure of work and the range of variation across all potential users of the system. The best way to collect this base structure and variation is to interview a wide variety of disparate people, rather than studying fewer people in greater depth. Common aspects of work will recur when new people are interviewed, and the team will see more variation. Even if there are aspects of a customer's work that the interviewer did not understand, it's often better to clarify them by going on to the next customer rather than returning to the same one.

This way of collecting customer information is new, and most organizations do not have the procedures in place to make scheduling these interviews easy. The groups that have the easiest time are those who already create events with individual customers, such as for usability tests or focus groups. There can be internal resistance, too— the sales force or marketing department can be suspicious of letting engineers talk directly to customers. But the reactions to the visits are nearly always enthusiastic. Customers feel like they are being listened to for the first time, and the sales force and marketing department soon recognize the benefits. When the customers are internal, they feel like they have control over the new system. Teams developing custom software often do more interviews than are strictly necessary, just to allow everyone to participate.

The Interpretation Session

As an interviewing process, Contextual Inquiry successfully uncovers data about customers' work in detail. But it's not enough for individual developers to talk to individual customers. Each person on the cross-functional team needs to learn about every customer. Each person will see something different in every interview, and needs to feed their unique point of view into the design. And each person needs to learn what the other team members see, so they can take on each other's perspective.

Interpretation sessions provide a forum in which everyone can learn about an interview, all relevant data can be captured immediately, and in which everyone has a job to do so that no one's attention wanders. The interviewer acts as informant, recounting the entire story of the interview in order, leaving nothing out. Everyone makes observations, asks questions, and shares insights and ideas for the system design; one team member (acting as recorder) types these points online as independent notes. Simultaneously, other team members draw work models as they hear them in the story. Because we run an interpretation session with four to six people, everyone has a job to keep them involved. When the session is done, all the data has been captured in the form in which it will be used. The captured points and work models will be used by the team to build their consolidated representation of the customer, and are also the medium of communication to anyone who was not present. They make communication to the larger team and to the customer community possible.

We find interpretation sessions to be more effective than reports or individual reviews of the interview for leading the team to meaningful insights. We have to be realistic about what to expect of people. With the best will in the world, people cannot communicate effectively through lengthy written reports—and any complete account of a customer visit will be lengthy. If the interviewer shortens the report by summarizing key findings, no other perspective can be brought to bear on the data—less will be learned from the interview, and there will be less sharing of perspectives across the team. The interpretation sessions produce more insight from each interview, and makes a team of the participants by giving them shared work to do.

Work Modeling

Before people can communicate knowledge, they need a language. The words of the language must represent the concepts of the knowledge domain—the more specialized the domain, the more specialized the language. The diagramming formalisms of software engineering are graphical languages that use symbols to embody those concepts necessary to understand and communicate different aspects of the software problem (J. Martin 1992). Because a formalism is so limited, it structures thought. It encourages the use of its symbols, and therefore of the concepts those symbols represent.

Work models are diagrams that make work practice concrete. They provide symbols for representing the different aspects of work practice. Created during the interpretation session, they capture the work of specific customers as it is revealed. They record work practice as it was discovered, and support communication about it to others. They manage the complexity of work by defining five different perspectives on the work and providing a coherent model to represent each perspective. They uncover and represent the structure of work of individual users, making it possible to consolidate models across all users to see common structure. These consolidated models form the basis of design. Unlike a list of findings, requirements, or wishes, work models show how all aspects of work relate to each other.

Though we often create new work models to handle specific situations, we find five types of work models to be useful to nearly every problem. We will present each model and discuss the design conversation it supports after consolidation.

Context models. (Figure 17.2) Context models show how organizational culture, policies, and procedures restrict and create expectations about how people work and what they produce. Context work models represent standards, procedures, policies, directives, expectations, feelings, perceptions, and other emotional and cultural influences on how people are willing to work. They show which influences originate from outside the organization, and which are internal to the organization. The context model drives design by showing what changes in culture customers are willing to accept. Where a design enables customers to handle an influence on their work, or enables them to get control of it, it is likely to be accepted. Where a design con-

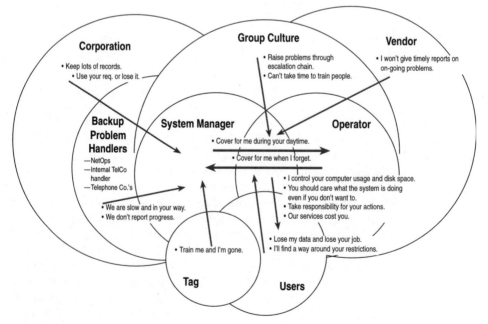

FIGURE 17.2 Context model.

flicts with an influence, customers will work around it or will not use the system. Designing with this knowledge lets the team choose how to make the system fit into the work. Developers of internal systems have the additional choice of working with the client to impose new influences on the work (such as cost-consciousness) that are desirable, but not currently present.

Physical models. (Figure 17.3) Physical models represent the physical environment as it impacts the work. They show how work is split across sites, buildings, and rooms, and how these spaces relate to each other. They show the organization of work places—the tools, artifacts, and work areas, and their relationships to each other. They show movement between spaces and forms of communication in doing the work, and they show hardware and software where it is used.

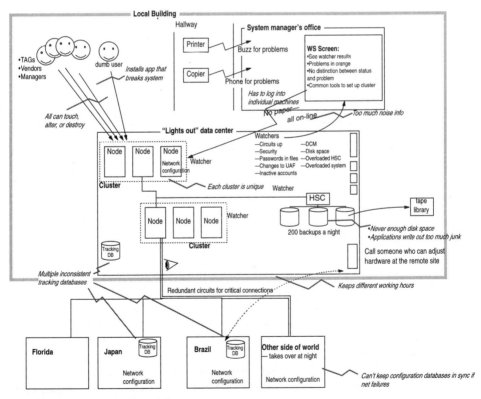

FIGURE 17.3 Physical model.

To the extent that they can, people structure their environment to support the work; then they work around any problems put in their way by limitations in the physical layout, location, hardware configuration, or technology. Physical work models support design both by revealing the constraints imposed by the physical environment, and by revealing the work strategies made manifest in the way the environment is structured and used. The physical model reveals what kind of communication is required, whether the system must support movement, and what platforms the system must support. They reveal the natural organization of work, which might be mimicked or supported in the system.

Flow models. (Figure 17.4) Flow models represent people's responsibilities, communication, and coordination, independent of time. They show what people do, who communicates with each other, what they communicate to each other, and how they communicate. When we consolidate, the flow model shows how the work breaks down into roles, sets of responsibilities, and associated tasks for accomplishing part of the work. Whereas job responsibilities are idiosyncratic to the organization, roles tend to be very consistent from one organization to the next. The flow model shows how people combine roles in performing their jobs.

Flow models drive system design by showing who the users of the system are. Each role represents a coherent set of responsibilities for the system to support. By presenting a wide view of the work, the flow model identifies peripheral roles that might be more directly supported in the future. It identifies roles that are unnecessary to get the actual work done, and which could be eliminated (which usually means removing or automating the tedious parts of a person's job, not the entire job). The flow model determines the communication paths and artifacts the system should support or replace.

Sequence models. (Figure 17.5) Sequence models show the sequence of actions to accomplish a specific task in time. A sequence model can be focused on the coordination of activities across individuals, on the thought steps and strategies of a single individual in doing one activity, or on the steps taken by a person in using a tool to accomplish an activity. They are similar to flow charting and task analysis (Carter 1991). They show the intent, or motive, for the activity and for sets of steps, and they show the trigger (the event that caused the sequence to be initiated).

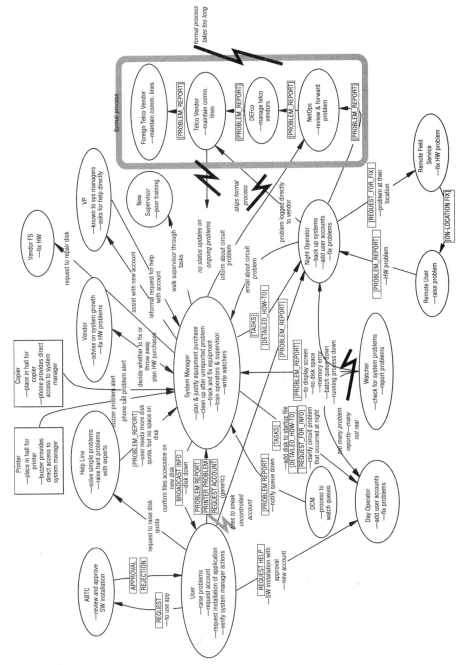

FIGURE 17.4 Flow model.

U1: Move user to larger disk

Intent: Give user more disk quota

Trigger: User requests higher disk quota
↓
Requests more quota of customer support
↓
Customer support discovers there's no more room on the user's disk
↓
Customer support calls U1
↓

**Intent: Relocate user to a disk with more free
space without losing any user data**
U1 looks for a scratch disk
↓
Initializes and mount scratch disk
↓
Creates user directory
↓
Moves user's files to the new disk
↓
Uses DIR to check that files are there
↓
Call user to confirm the user agrees all files are there
↓
User checks and confirms
↓
Delete user files from the old disk
↓
Send mail to system manager to add new disk to regular start-up
↓
System manager adds new disk
↓
Done

FIGURE 17.5 Sequence model.

. Sequences are a detailed map of the work a system must support, improve, or replace. They tie specific steps to the intent of those steps, allowing the design team to see where replacing a step is possible and where the step supports some critical intent. Sequence models reveal strategies to support, ensure that work practice continues to work in the new system, and drive test cases for system design, usability, and system test.

Artifact models. (Figure 17.6) Artifact models reveal the detailed structure of artifacts created and used to support the work. They show the structure, usage, and intent of the artifact. Through their parts and arrangements of parts, they reveal how customers break up the work conceptually and how they use the presentation of the artifact to support its use.

Artifact models guide the creation of new system artifacts. They reveal what is used and what is not used in existing artifacts provided to customers. They indicate what new artifacts might be created in the

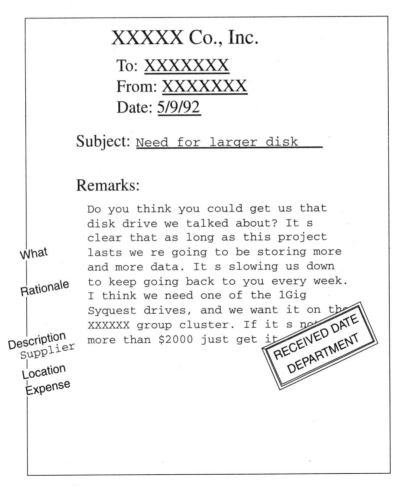

FIGURE 17.6 Artifact model.

informal annotations and additions customers have made, and they indicate the appropriate structure for new artifacts by showing the conceptual structure customers put on the work.

Work models provide a concise way to represent the work of individuals and their organizations. Because each model is tailored to a specific perspective, they guide the team in thinking about the aspect of work they focus on. They provide the concepts necessary to understand how work is structured, and lead the team to see common aspects of work across their customers. They focus the team on the elements of work practice they must support and account for in the system.[2]

CONSOLIDATION ACROSS USERS

It is easy to be overwhelmed by the huge amounts of data gathered by contextual techniques. With such a wealth of detail, it is hard to see the common issues and themes across all customers that a new system could address directly. Affinity diagrams and consolidated work models provide a coherent, manageable representation of the market or customer base for a new system.

Affinity Diagrams

During interpretation sessions, key points, insights, questions, and design ideas are written as separate notes. Each interview usually generates 50–100 such notes, in addition to the work models. Fifteen to twenty interviews (typical for most projects) generate 1000–2000 notes in all. Affinity diagrams provide a technique for organizing and structuring this vast quantity of detail. Affinity diagrams were originally designed to handle 200–500 notes, but we find the process scales up well with more people (we try to get one person for every 100 notes). An affinity is built by putting up notes one at a time (clustering those that go together) that have an "affinity" for each other. The clusters are named, and then they are grouped into higher-level structures. Rather than impose a structure from the beginning, an affinity allows structure to bubble up from the detail. We encourage this by banning familiar categories such as "usability" and "quality," and by giving the groups names that express the user's intent: For example, "Let me browse to learn the structure of the system." In the groupings, the affinity reveals new insights (derived from the data collected from all customers), and lays them out on the wall in a coherent structure.

When done, the whole team walks the affinity to read what each part is about, and brainstorms design ideas for that part. (Anyone else in the organization who wants to influence the design can do this too.) Because the affinity organizes whole sets of issues into larger themes, it naturally pushes ideas that respond to whole themes rather than single features. Each person writes their ideas on Post-its and attaches them directly to the affinity itself. Later, when the team picks up these ideas to develop, they will be directly tied to the customer data that sparked them. People also identify holes (places where the data is weak) in the same way. Identifying holes helps the team plan what data to collect next.

An affinity shows the scope of the issues to address within the defined focus of the team. It captures and structures the team's insight into the customers' work. The cluster names represent these insights and tie them back to individual customer's data through the notes in each cluster. Because the structure is derived from data instead of predefined categories, it drives the creation of new insight into the problem.

Work Model Consolidation

The affinity organizes and structures customer issues, but it is not a good representation of customer work practice. Its hierarchical, textual organization does not show how the work hangs together coherently. Individual work models do show the work practice of individual customers, but do not reveal common strategies and structures across the market. Designing a system to support the work practice of multiple people depends on understanding the common strategies across customers. Otherwise, the overwhelming tendency is to design for the specific customers interviewed and to create isolated fixes for single problems.

Work model consolidation provides a single synthetic representation of work. Consolidation brings together common aspects of all models of the same type, showing common structure but also capturing key variants. Consolidation is applied to each kind of model individually, resulting in a consolidated flow model, a consolidated context model, a consolidated physical model for sites and work places, and consolidated models for each task represented in the sequences and for each type of artifact.

Work model consolidation reveals structure that is pervasive and consistent across customers. Focusing on the exact job title or the specific steps taken in a tool obscures the consistent structure across users; work models focus on the division of responsibilities into roles, the intent driving work steps, and the strategies to achieve them. By revealing the fundamental structure, work models make it possible to see how that structure recurs in different ways across users.

A description of flow model consolidation will serve to illustrate the method. First, team members pair up and look at each actual model in parallel. For each bubble representing an individual, they identify the key roles that person plays. A role is a collection of responsibilities that go together naturally. (When someone says, "I wear two hats, programmer and analyst" they are describing two of their roles.) They name and list the roles and their responsibilities. When roles have been identified for all individuals on all models, they bring together similar roles from each of the models and name the role. They write a single list of responsibilities, removing duplications but otherwise retaining them all. Then they transfer the lines of communication from the actual models to the consolidated model. When done, the model shows the fundamental division of work into roles and communication between roles across the entire market or organization. A system designed to the work described in the consolidated flow model will be useful to everyone, no matter what idiosyncratic assignment of roles to individuals an organization may adopt.

Consolidating other models is conceptually similar. The first step is to look at the parts of each actual model and identify the intents of each part; then the parts with similar intents from the different models are collected. After that, the parts are laid out on the consolidated model in proper relationship to each other.

We frequently encounter skepticism about whether work across a market is so similar structurally that this kind of consolidation is possible; but in any work domain, we find there are only a few different strategies people use to get their work done. Most teams stop seeing new variants after incorporating 10–15 different individual models into their consolidated model. Consolidated work models are a powerful tool for any design team. If the system is for sale to a market, they describe the market at the level of how people work. They define who the customers are, what they do, and what they care about. They show who is affected by the system, who needs to buy into it, and who represents potential markets for related products. If the system is for a single organization, the models show how that organization works, who it depends on, and who its customers are. They show all the inefficiencies in their work and all the opportunities for process redesign. When the team redesigns the work, the models show the impact of their changes and help them anticipate how the new system might break

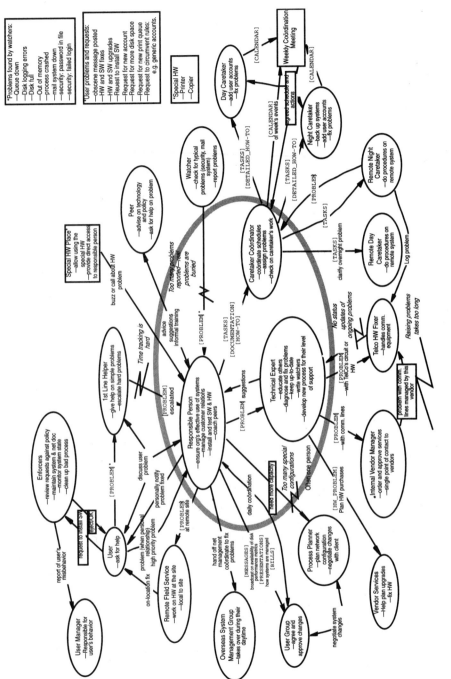

FIGURE 17.7 Consolidated flow model.

the work. A complete set of consolidated models gives a team a solid base for design, identifying issues and opportunities for the system and ensuring that it does not disrupt work.

The Design Room

With an affinity and a set of consolidated work models, a team really needs a design room. These represent the team's knowledge of the customer on the wall; they don't want to have to unroll all the models and affinity to be able to think. Given the opportunity, the team will continually return to this data throughout the design process. It is common in our meetings for a team member to gesture or walk over to a part of their affinity to support a point they are making. It is hard to achieve this kind of fidelity to the customer when the data about the customer is tucked away, out of sight.

Having the data spread out on the wall is very different from having it online. Online representations are important too, for permanence and to share with remote sites, but a video screen cannot present the breadth of data that a wall can. By its very size, the screen reduces the scope of data that can be considered together in relation to a design. It works against systemic design—broad responses to a whole work problem—and toward single features.

Most of our teams start out complaining that it's impossible to get a dedicated room in their organization. However, it's hardly unreasonable to expect that, if a group of people have real work to do together, they should have a space in which to do it. This means a place where they can work together for days at a time, and where they can leave their work lying around. In the end, somehow, all our teams do manage to create themselves a room. Several have become so attached to working together that when the time comes to code their systems, they bring in their computers and code in the room. There they can reference their customer data, redesigned models, User Environment design, and implementation models.

The design room is an excellent mechanism for communicating progress and insights to the rest of the organization. When designed to communicate, the room is a living record of the design process. A team member or manager who wants to catch up can browse the walls on their own, or another team member can use the walls to tell them what has happened. Teams commonly invite other interested or affected groups to walk the affinity and consolidated models, writing comments and ideas on Post-its and sticking them up. The guests get the benefit of learning the data, the team gets the benefit of their ideas, and everyone feels like they can be part of the conversation. One manager told us he prefers to use the room to find out how the team is doing—he found it more immediate and more real than a status report or presentation.

SYSTEMIC DESIGN

Working with specific customers gives the team an understanding of the work of those customers. The next challenge is to design a response which transforms work in new and useful ways. This is a new design conversation. Up to now the team has focused on work as it *is*; now they will design the work as it *will be*, when the new system is in place. This conversation is inherent in design. Every system changes the work of its users. We prefer to think about and design the effect the system will have explicitly, ensuring that innovations are driven by real customer problems and that they fit into the customers' work context.

We use an explicit visioning step to brainstorm alternative ways to redesign work and systems to support the new work practice. First the team walks the consolidated models and affinity to identify the key issues, roles, and aspects of work to address. They brainstorm alternatives as a group, elaborating each one for five to fifteen minutes. They compare the alternatives using a modified Pugh matrix process (Pugh 1991) to identify the good and bad points of each alternative, and finally merge the best parts of all the alternatives, fixing the problems and building on the good parts. The resulting vision is a signpost for the team, identifying what they are trying to do with their system.

The vision is just a sketch. It contains no details at all—we intentionally focus on the big picture before working out the details of the parts. The next step is to bring the vision down to earth, to say exactly what we will do to implement the vision.

The vision is brought back to reality through redesigned scripts. When the team analyzed a customer's work in terms of work models, they broke it up into five different views of work; a script reunites all these different perspectives to show the new work practice coherently. A script shows the *role* performing the work step, the *work step* itself, the changes in the *physical environment* required for this step, and the *concepts* or artifacts used in this step. The scripts are driven by redesign of all the consolidated models in light of the vision. So if the vision prescribes how to support a particular role, the team goes to the consolidated flow model, updates the role's responsibilities in light of the vision, and writes the script to ensure that the role can do its tasks. The other consolidated models support redesign similarly.

Role	Step	Changes to physical environment and technology	Concepts
User	User presses "Help" button on their telephone.	Telephones with special buttons tied to particular functions.	Phone is the way to talk to someone; it is integrated into getting help on a problem.
First Level Help	Phone rings from user and sees user name and context, on his screen. Context includes system and location	Telephone tied into system: button dials number and prompts system.	Problem screen: user name, system, location; current screen. Provides an area to enter comments for self and anyone who looks at this problem.
	First level help adds any additional information they collect and actions taken. Decides he can't solve the problem and presses his "HELP" button.	Speaker phones in every office.	
	Problem logged in system.	Central database of calls.	Simple stopwatch visible for entire time problem is worked on: shows problem name, elapsed time on this problem, "Pause/Resume" and "Done" buttons.
	Problem routed to the right responsible person for this user.	Database of experts and what kinds of problems they can solve.	
Responsible Person (RP)	Trigger: Phone rings. When answered, shows problem context and anything first level help captured. Problem context overlays anything now on screen. (Issue—what if RP not there?)		Same problem context as above.
	System starts logging time spent on this problem. Displays time spent on screen so RP can stop it when he switches to another task.		Same time log as above.

FIGURE 17.8 Redesigned script.

Each script corresponds to the consolidated sequences from which it is built. Consolidated sequences define how the key tasks of central roles are performed. They show the key processes and strategies, together with the intents driving each step. Each consolidated sequence drives a redesigned script that shows how that task will be done in the new system. Each step in the consolidated sequence must be accounted for in the redesign; either the step must be supported, the intent of the step must be met in a new way, or the step is obviated because changes to a higher-level intent made this step unnecessary. Multiple scripts taken together drive the system design.

This work redesign step makes the invention of new work practice an explicit, recognized part of system design. Using the consolidated models and affinity as a base promotes systemic thinking, because they present the whole work problem coherently. Visioning promotes divergent thinking—inventing and considering unusual and innovative solutions to the problem, rather than proceeding along traditional lines. The Pugh evaluation process gives the team a way to consider the alternatives as collections of possible ideas, looking for the best aspects of each, rather than choosing a "winner" from a set of designs. And the redesigned scripts tie everything back to reality. Each of these principles—systemic design, divergent thinking, egoless evaluation, and fidelity to the data—is critical to good design, but never more than in this step where the system itself is defined.

Separating Conversations

Going from consolidation to redesign is a switch between conversations. The team stopped talking about the work as it is done now, and started talking about work as it would be done in the future with the application of technology. The next step in design is another switch in conversations, from redesigned work to the structure of the system that will enable that work. Just as we supported the switch from consolidation to redesign by providing clear physical artifacts that support each conversation and keep them separate, so we will support the switch to system design by providing a new artifact, the User Environment model, to keep that conversation separate.

Design meetings are difficult, contentious, and lack clarity when the team unknowingly mixes conversations. Here's a case study: Joe argues that the mail system should allow people to read and answer other people's mail as their agent. Sue claims that would be a security hole. Joe says no, we could implement a password. Sue points out that we cannot implement anything as secure as the operating system.

In this short interchange, conversations have become completely confused—Joe was making a point about the work, but expressed it by proposing a system feature. Sue reacted to the design idea without recognizing the work conversation at all. Joe responded by fixing the design, at which point Sue went into an implementation conversation. They never even discussed whether the original work redesign idea—allowing people to act as agents for others—was reasonable. Any process that hopes to make face-to-face team design possible must provide a mechanism to untangle conversations.

Using models to separate conversations and make them concrete goes a long way towards clearing up this confusion. Each time a separate conversation is needed, a separate model supports that conversation. The work as it is *now* is a set of consolidated work models on one part of the wall. The work as *redesigned* is a set of scripts, on a different part of the wall. The *system design* will be on yet another part of the wall. Each model defines a place for the appropriate design conversation, and provides a physical prop that focuses the team on the issues for that conversation. Separating conversations is one element among many in providing an effective process for teams to design together. See Holtzblatt's article (Holtzblatt 1994) for a more complete discussion of making team design work.

User Environment Design

The User Environment model defines how the system is structured to support the work of its users appropriately. It defines the places in the system to support the user's activities, the functions each place provides, the work objects manipulated in each place, and the flow between places to support the flow of work tasks. Just as a floor plan lays out a house, revealing its structure and the relationship of its parts, the User Environment lays out a system design. A floor plan allows the architect to see all the parts of a house and how they relate to each other. A User Environment design allows the team to see all the parts of a system and how they relate. It shows the system as a whole.

The User Environment model is a language for communicating and recording system structure independently of the UI or implementation. Building a User Environment model focuses the team on the appropriate level of detail. It puts off low-level decisions about look and layout until after the fundamental decisions about structure are made. It focuses the team on the structure of the system as experienced by the user, rather than the structure of the implementation. It defines the requirements on the implementation, provides initial objects for the system data model, and defines the structure of the user interface.

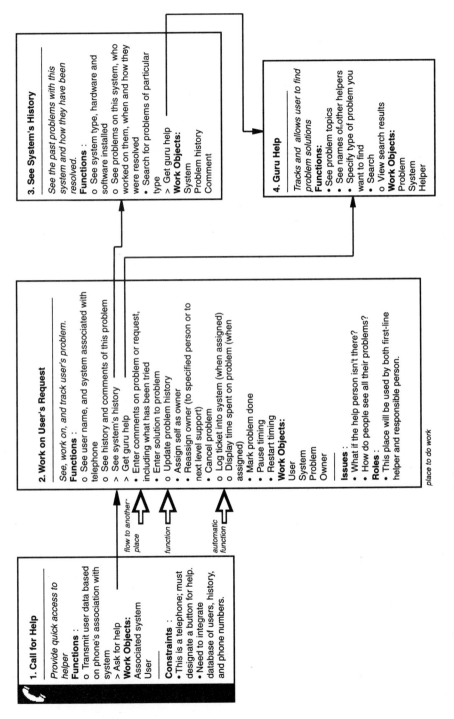

FIGURE 17.9 Mail user environment design.

Redesigned scripts drive the development of the User Environment design. The team walks each script extracting implications for the system design. They define places in the system to support each work activity, and define system function, work objects, and flow between places. As each redesigned script is fed into the User Environment design, a system structure emerges that supports all the work described in the different scripts. Because it is represented in a single model, the team can ensure that the system structure is coherent and consistent.

The User Environment design supports team discussions about whether the system supports work well—whether it provides the right function and the right organization of function for a smooth flow of work. It allows the team to check the system against the work described in consolidated and redesigned models: whether the system provides adequate support for a role, whether it provides for a particular communication path, whether it inhibits an influence from the context model, and whether it accounts for the constraints of the physical model. Actual and consolidated sequences can be run through the User Environment to ensure that it supports the real work of individual users.

The User Environment model is an ideal method of planning and communication with other design teams. In one company, two teams with overlapping responsibilities had been arguing about who should ship what. They used their User Environment models to describe their own plans, see and resolve the overlapping designs, and reassign parts of the new, coherent design to each team amicably. In another, a team used the User Environment to define the system they wanted and evaluate off-the-shelf software to see which met their needs best. Others have used the User Environment to define whole families of applications and how they should work together. By making the issues of structuring systems for the users explicit, the User Environment model makes all these conversations easier.

Iteration with Paper Mockups

Once a team has a base User Environment design, development proceeds through rapid iterations with the user. The team moves quickly to test the partial design with paper prototypes. The first goal in prototyping is to test the User Environment design—to see whether the basic structure and function are useful—and to collect detailed data in the area of work the prototype supports. Structure can be tested through simple mockups with almost no UI detail, for example by mapping places in the system to windows and functions to menu items. The team takes the prototypes to the users' workplace and asks them to pretend it is a system and to work with it. Users do not give us their opinion—they simulate doing one of their own tasks using the prototype, so they can react as they would to a real product. Interviewers observe and probe in the same way as a contextual interview. They do not have to tell their users what level of detail to respond to—the roughness of the prototype does that.

Initially the prototypes are very rough, and interviewers encourage users to explore, trying to accomplish a task of their own. When they ask if the system does something, interviewers design on the spot: "Yes. How would you expect it to work? Show me." The user sees that the design is incomplete and open to change, and is drawn into the design conversation. (This requires members of the design team to run the interview, to respond appropriately and to design with the user.) The team soon discovers whether the initial structuring of the work in the User Environment design makes sense. As the User Environment design stabilizes, the focus of the interview shifts to the user interface. The team builds more careful prototypes, and in customer interviews asks users to live with the limitations of the system as designed. Finally, it becomes useful to build and test running prototypes that can evolve into the real system.

Iterating with customers early, before the design is complete, is an effective way to keep the design on track. Any design proceeds best if the large structure is defined before detailed design, because changes in the overall structure will force changes to the detail. This is hard—most engineers would rather get all the details right before testing anything. Quick iteration with the user checks the structure before much time has been wasted designing detail that might change. Because some parts of the system will be tested before others, they will be fully designed and more stable, which is also an advantage—it allows development to proceed in stages, taking a chunk of the system at a time.

Frequent iteration keeps the team focused on the customers and their problems, not on each other. The longer the team works on the design without feedback, the more committed they will be to that design, and the more they will resist discovering that it is wrong. Interestingly, iteration with customers also keeps the team creative—when our teams get bogged down, it's usually because they've lost contact with the customer (Beyer 1994). When they mock up the ideas they developed from data and take them out, suddenly they get moving again. We keep prototypes in paper until the level of UI design is so detailed that paper cannot test it. Building prototypes on the computer before this is not only extra work, it's actually counter-productive. Not only do the team members get overinvested in their design, but users invariably respond to details of the look and the layout. If we present a hand-drawn prototype on paper, they respond to the structure and function in the system.

As a design process, Contextual Design is based on a few overriding principles: that customer data is the only sound basis for design; that the cognitive process of design is enabled by supporting systemic thinking and providing concrete models that create clean design conversations; and that the design process must support face-to-face team design and coexist with the host organization. We have used these principles repeatedly throughout Contextual Design to create a process that is effective at designing systems, and that supports the people who must live in it.

CUSTOMER-CENTERED DESIGN IN THE ORGANIZATION

In this chapter, we've presented a summary of how Contextual Design is structured and why it is structured as it is; but any process needs to be adapted and adjusted to meet the needs of a particular project, and Contextual Design is no exception. In fact, it's been called a backbone for organizing the use of a whole range of techniques for customer-centered design. Depending on project goals and context, team membership and application of techniques would change. For example, Contextual Design is not necessarily participatory in the full sense of the term. It does not require that customers be a part of design in the way that Participatory Design specifies. However, Contextual Design can be used to support a Participatory Design project:

1. Define a team consisting of designers and customers, including users of the proposed system.
2. Use Contextual Inquiry to gather information about the work domain. Interview all classes of customers. All members of the team (including customers) conduct interviews. Interview the customers on the team at work if their work needs to be understood.
3. Consolidate work models and build an affinity. Bring in additional customers to help, especially on the affinity. Hold sessions for people in the department to walk the models and comment on them. Use the comments as a focus for future interviews.
4. Brainstorm and redesign with additional customers not on the design team. Envision process changes as well as system behavior. Run several envisioning sessions with different sets of cus-

tomers. Use the modified Pugh matrix to merge alternatives and build a single vision.
5. Build a User Environment design and mock it up. Test it with customers throughout the organization.

We have followed variants of this outline on several projects with great success. The customers are involved throughout the process, and become enthusiastic supporters of the project. One IT manager even told us how unusual she found it to have her clients eager to have her work with them, instead of viewing her organization as an obstacle.

Anyone introducing any sort of customer-centered design should be aware that success will lead to organizational change. CACM 1995. Organizations are not currently structured to facilitate customer-centered design or to take best advantage of it. As the approach becomes more widespread, the mismatch between the new and old ways of doing business will cause complaints. These complaints reflect real problems, but will tend to go away as the new approach becomes institutionalized and tailored to the culture.

- *Setting up customer visits is hard.* Most organizations have procedures to make field testing easy. Interviews are a far smaller logistical problem, but currently the full burden of arranging them falls on the design team. We need channels supporting this new relationship with the customer, particularly in those organizations developing commercial products.

  The new approach to design implies a new relationship between marketing, engineering, and the other organizations that help ship products. People are not yet comfortable with their new roles. Marketing is responsible for bringing their focus on the business to the team, but is not unilaterally deciding on what to build. Engineering brings technology expertise to the room, but they are not unilaterally deciding what to build either.

- *Teams using the new approaches still have to interact with other teams and managers. who are used to the old ways.* When teams are expected to produce working documents as part of design, they still need to create those documents expected by the organization, whether or not they duplicate the team's internal design documents. Our teams have used the User Environment to generate requirements documents, specs, and UI designs in the form expected by their organizations. Over time, statements of "user needs," "requirements," "specifications," and other milestone deliverables may start to conform to the structure the team had to create anyway, as part of design. The overhead of documenting and reporting would then lessen, replaced by processes that record real work as it happens.

■ *After customer-centered design becomes common, but before it becomes institutionalized, bringing new people up to speed is a problem.* Training needs to be created for new people and for teams who want to start using the new approach. If they are not trained, teams will tend to call whatever they are doing with the customer "Contextual Inquiry" or "customer-centered design," even if it follows none of the principles.

Customer-centered design is a new approach to designing software, and the processes are still evolving. The specific techniques used at any point are always open to modification and adaptation, just has we have borrowed from many places to create Contextual Design. The definition of the new process will be driven by principles of how to support design well; it will also be driven by the restrictions and requirements of the host organization. All the writers in this book are practicing the fine art of balancing these two sets of requirements. On the one hand, we cannot push the organization so hard that the process falls apart; on the other, we cannot limit what we do so much that the process is not useful. The happy medium is always unclear and constantly shifts as we seek the best process for each situation. We wish the reader well in striking the right balance in their own organizations.

NOTES

1. Throughout this paper, "user" refers to those who actually interact with a computer system. We use "customer" as a more general term to indicate those who are affected by a system, whether they use it themselves or not. This includes users, managers of users, buyers, those who use a system's results, and those who provide input to a system.
2. For other discussions of representing work, see the September 1995 issue of *Communications of the ACM* (CACM 1995).

REFERENCES

"Requirements Gathering, The Human Factor." *Communications of the ACM*, May, 1995. vol **38**, No 5. This is a special issue devoted to the organizational changes resulting from new customer-centered design practice.

"Representations of Work." *Communications of the ACM.* **38**(9). This is a special issue discussing different approaches towards representing customer work.

Beyer, H. 1994. "Calling Down the Lightning." *IEEE Software.* September 1994, Vol 11 No 5. p. 106.

Beyer, H. and Holtzblatt, K. 1995. "Apprenticing with the Customer." *Communications of the ACM* **38**(5), 45–52.

Brassard, M. 1989. *Memory Jogger Plus.* Methuen, MA: GOAL/QPC.

Carter, J., Jr. 1991. "Combining Task Analysis with Software Engineering for Designing Interactive Systems." John Karat (Ed.), *Taking Software Design Seriously.* NY: Academic Press, p. 209.

Deming, W.E. 1982. *Out of the Crisis.* Cambridge, MA: Massachusetts Institute of Technology, Center for Advanced Engineering Study.

Ehn, P. and M. Kyng. 1991. "Cardboard Computers: Mocking-it-up or Hands-on the Future." J. Greenbaum and M. Kyng (Eds.): *Design at Work.* Hillsdale, NJ: Lawrence Earlbaum Associates, p. 169.

Keller, M. and Shumate, K. 1992. *Software Specification and Design.* New York: John Wiley & Sons, Inc.

Kyng, M. "Designing for a Dollar a Day." *Proceedings of CSCW'88: Conference of Computer-Supported Cooperative Work* (pp. 178–188). New York: Association for Computing Machinery.

Holtzblatt, K. and Jones, S. 1993. "Contextual Inquiry: A Participatory Technique for System Design." Aki Namioka and Doug Schuler (Eds.), *Participatory Design: Principles and Practice.* Hillsdale, N.J.: Lawrence Earlbaum Associates.

Holtzblatt, K. 1994. "If We're a Team, Why Don't We Act Like One?". *Interactions.* July 1994, Vol. 1 No. 3, p. 17.

Ishikawa, K. 1985. *What is Total Quality Control?.* Englewood Cliffs, NJ: Prentice-Hall.

Martin, J. and Odell, J. 1992. *Object-Oriented Analysis and Design.* Englewood Cliffs, NJ: Prentice-Hall.

Muller, M. 1991. "PICTIVE—An exploration in participatory design." *Human Factors in Computing Systems* Proceedings of the CHI'91. ACM, 225–231.

Pugh, S. 1991. *Total Design.* Reading, MA: Addison-Wesley Publishing.

Seaton, P. and Stewart, T. 1992. "Evolving Task Oriented Systems." *Human Factors in Computing Systems. Proceedings of the CHI'92.* Monterey, California: ACM.

Index

Page references followed by lowercase *f* indicate illustrations, while references followed by lowercase *t* indicate material in tables.